SPIRITUS CREATOR

SPIRITUS CREATOR

REGIN PRENTER

Translated by John M. Jensen

Muhlenberg Press   **Philadelphia**

Translated from Spiritus Creator
Studier i Luthers Theologi av
Regin Prenter, Samlerens Forlag,
København, 1946

Printed in U.S.A.   *UB721*

PREFACE

This volume is a translation of the book published in Danish in 1944. An almost unchanged second edition appeared in 1946. In the translation of the text there are only very slight differences from the Danish original. But in the footnotes containing the references to Luther's works and the discussion of other authors the translation differs very much from the original. The number of footnotes has been brought down from 750 to 160. This means that the discussion of modern Luther research of German and Scandinavian origin has been practically left out. Besides that the quotations from Luther's writings have been replaced by references, and the total number of references (quotations) has been reduced to the minimum. Thus, in Part I the number of references to Luther has been reduced from about 860 to about 350.

This radical reduction of references to the sources has been done in order to make the book more readable to nonscholars. But of course the scholar will miss a good many of the references which the Danish original contains. And perhaps even other readers sometimes will feel surprised at the language used in the text or the remoteness of the problems discussed, not being able to see that the text is referring to a definite passage in some of Luther's writings. It is my hope that the loss in academic accuracy which this reduction of source references inevitably brings with it may be counterbalanced by gains in clarity and readability.

Above all I thank my translator, the Rev. John Jensen, who has had an extremely difficult job in trying to render my academic Danish into current and understandable English.

Århus University, December 18, 1952   REGIN PRENTER

CONTENTS

INTRODUCTION

The concept of the Holy Spirit completely dominates Luther's theology. In every decisive matter, whether it be the study of Luther's doctrine of justification, of his doctrine of the sacraments, of his ethics, or of any other fundamental teaching, we are forced to take into consideration this concept of the Holy Spirit.

In modern times, however, Luther's views about the Holy Spirit have seldom been considered worth a thorough study and a clear and coherent presentation. It has generally been held that Luther's ideas about the Spirit and his work were traditional, and that they in the main agreed with those of medieval theology, except of course for the modifications introduced by the doctrine of justification and the new view of the Word and the sacraments. That later Lutheran orthodoxy generally represented such a modification of traditional thinking only served to support this idea about Luther's teaching.

The only comprehensive study of the subject in modern times is Rudolf Otto's almost obsolete work, *Die Anschauung vom Heiligen Geiste bei Luther.*[1] This book presents Luther's ideas about the Holy Spirit as based on traditional thinking. Otto therefore also reaches the rather disappointing conclusion that the concept of the Holy Spirit has no organic place in Luther's evangelical understanding of Christianity. The functions of the Spirit are here assumed to be those of the Word and of faith; and all concepts about the Holy Spirit as a transcendent cause of the new life seem completely superfluous, since everything may be explained as the result of purely immanent factors such as the Word and faith.

Rudolf Otto's thesis cannot be the final word on Luther's under-

---

[1] Göttingen, 1898.

standing of the Spirit and his work. Yet Lutheran theologians have never come to any final conclusion with respect to Otto's theories, nor have they produced any later and more thorough analysis of the subject which might correct Rudolf Otto's presentation. When Luther's views on the Holy Spirit have been under consideration, it has generally been assumed that this field was well known and that it was clear at the outset what meaning Luther gave the traditional expressions. It was not deemed necessary to make any closer examination to determine whether his theories were really as traditional as first assumed. Or if it was surmised that Luther might have other than the traditional views about the Holy Spirit, the scholars confined themselves to scattered remarks about the subject.

This fact alone is sufficient reason for a renewed study and a systematic presentation of Luther's views about the Holy Spirit. Thus a cardinal but previously neglected part of Luther's theology will be treated anew.

The presentation must necessarily be descriptive. It is of the greatest importance to clarify what Luther himself thought rather than to evaluate and debate his view. This does not mean, however, that we intend to approach the problem from a purely historical point of view. We shall not attempt to substantiate the greater or lesser dependence of Luther upon others or to trace the development of his theology during his life. We shall not, as a rule, ask *whence* Luther's thoughts came or *how* they developed, even though these historical questions may be ever so important. We shall ask only *what* he thought.

On the other hand, we shall not be satisfied by simply making a list of Luther's ideas about this subject. Our chief concern will be to trace the continuity in the series of ideas so that if possible a complete perspective may be gained. Often, therefore, we must ask not only *what* Luther thought, but also *why* he so thought. In this respect our work is systematic rather than historical. It is inevitable that in such a process both historical and dogmatic questions become involved, and we cannot nor do we intend to renounce our right to compare Luther with his predecessors and

successors and with our own theology. Such historical and dogmatic digressions have no independent purpose, however, but
merely serve the chief purpose of the work—clarifying what Luther
himself thought, and why. When this has been made clear the aim
of the present study will have been accomplished.

By setting for our inquiry this narrow, purely phenomenological, systematic, and logical aim, we believe we are best serving both
church history and systematic theology since a correct understanding of Luther is necessary to both these fields.

The previous historical research on Luther has often been retarded because the continuity in Luther's thinking was not appre-
ciated. All too often students have found "contradictions" or have
pointed out "development" or "retrogression" where a deeper
systematic understanding would have revealed that apparent contradictions were actually part of a deeper and real unity. Statements have also been made of Luther's dependence upon or relation to other theological trends, where a systematic knowledge
would have revealed that often similarities in terminology cover
qualitatively different concepts. Without the aid of systematic
Luther research, the student of church history is in constant danger
of insisting on dependence on or development from phenomena
that are not present at all. Systematic research of Luther's theology
therefore always has indirect significance for the church historian.

The dogmatic thinking of our own age cannot avoid an encounter with Luther. Since the church schism in the sixteenth
century, evangelical theology has been destined to center on
Luther. This is especially true of the Lutheran churches. The
theological conflicts of our own age have been decisively influenced
by their relation to Luther. However, regardless of what conclusion
previous ages have drawn about Luther, no age is absolved from
thinking its own thoughts about him. This does not mean that
every Luther renascence is necessarily fruitful theologically. Sometimes the interest in Luther may result in fruitless repetition of his
thoughts. And, what is worse, it may happen that Luther is thereby
made the property of current popular Christian and political
thinking. Evangelical theology cannot therefore accept every

Luther renascence as a happy event. Evangelical theology must never forget that the Holy Scripture is the authoritative standard and not Luther. Lutheran renascence periods have often discarded this fundamental principle, if not in theory then in practice. But the Holy Scripture can at no time be read independently of the voice of the fathers. And among the fathers Luther will always occupy a front seat in the Evangelical church. It is therefore important that the voice of Luther be clear in the chorus of the fathers. It is all the more important since the great interest in Luther caused by the renascence has not always favored a real penetration of his thought. The enthusiasm for making Luther of value to the present age is not always without danger for the correct understanding of Luther. We therefore believe that a "disinterested" and purely phenomenological, systematic study of Luther is of great significance for dogmatic work. It will guarantee that in the inevitable encounter with Luther we shall hear Luther's voice and not just our own echo.

That, however, does not mean that the presentation will aim at "scientific objectivity" in the sense of impersonal indifference. No scientific research, least of all theological, can or will eliminate subjectivity. A student of Luther who succeeds in presenting an absolutely disinterested view of Luther's theology can have understood very little of his subject. Boredom is neither here nor anywhere else an evidence of deep scientific ability. Yet all scientific work demands the self-denial of permitting the matter to present itself as it really is and then allowing it to speak for itself. But this scientific self-denial does not exclude personal interest; it only demands respect for the object. Nowhere is this respect for the object so significant as in theology. That is because the object in theology in itself demands respect. If this demand for respect of the object is to be fulfilled in settling the theological issue with our heritage from the Reformation, then a Luther research which devotes itself exclusively to the phenomenological, systematic point of view is indispensable. Such a Luther inquiry may not be one of the main subjects of theology, for it will never be more than a preliminary work. But as a preliminary work and as an aid it has a mission to perform which must be performed, and which can be performed in no other way.

About our method of procedure a few remarks should be made. Since we do not attempt to present Luther's ideas in their origin, it may seem reasonable not to make a division of our subject from the point of view of time. We could confine ourselves to the research of the so-called "Luther of the Reformation" or the "mature Luther" and arrange the material according to purely systematic lines. There are, however, special reasons why we do not want to use this method exclusively.

In the first place, the writings of Luther are so extensive that to quote him indiscriminately without any reference to time may produce a rather casual impression. Several systematic studies of Luther prove that. By a planless use of all the works of the Weimar edition it is possible to get very much, perhaps too much, out of Luther. Some method seems necessary in dividing the source material. A division of the material from the point of view of time seems the most natural and workable.

Secondly, the use of the sources without regard for the period to which they belong generally causes the student to minimize the young Luther, because the sources of this period are not so extensive or substantial in proportion to their value. And a systematic presentation of Luther's thought which does not integrate the thoughts of the young Luther will present an unfinished and unbalanced picture. The appreciation of this fact is the lasting result of the work of the school of Holl.

Thirdly, even though it is entirely legitimate to disregard the historicogenetic in a systematic work which has a purely phenomenological aim, we must not ignore the danger which is found in oversystematizing and in unjustified harmonizing of thoughts that might possibly belong to completely different stages of development. If the historian, because of a lack of systematic ability, is in danger of discovering contradictions where there are no contradictions, then the systematic theologian, on the other hand, is in danger of eliminating all contradictions by overharmonizing. This danger may in some measure also be avoided by some division of the source material according to time.

Considering these three reasons over against the purely systematic method, one is tempted to choose the completely different method of procedure which the recent systematic study of Luther has been successfully employing as a reaction to the planless use of the Weimar edition's many volumes. That method may be designated as the systematic-exegetical. It is characterized by limiting the source material to but a few writings or even a few parts of these writings, which then are given a very detailed analysis. That such a method has very great advantages compared to the older one, and that it is especially well suited for the presentation of limited systematic themes within the theology of Luther, is proven by such a work as Rudolf Hermann's *Luthers These "Gerecht und Sünder zugleich,"*[2] in which Luther's whole conception of Christianity is developed through a very limited theme with only a limited number of source proofs. This method, however, also has its weaknesses. The author must be very familiar with the other writings of Luther if his work is not to become too arbitrary. There is also the danger that certain select texts are isolated and given more importance than they are entitled to in relation to the total work of Luther. Furthermore this method is applicable only in the study of subjects to which Luther has already given such a systematic presentation that the selection of the texts can be done without arbitrariness. Where this is not the case, as with the present subject, this method cannot be used successfully.

No single method of those employed so far in the study of Luther, neither the purely historicogenetic which traces the sources chronologically from year to year, nor the purely systematic which collects its proofs indiscriminately without regard to the time of writing, nor the systematic-exegetical which works with minute exegesis of a few selected texts, seems to be entirely satisfactory when a systematic-phenomenological presentation of a special subject of Luther's theology is under consideration. The advantage of the historicogenetic method is a sharpened sense for the detail and

---

2 Gütersloh, 1930.

color of the subject. But this advantage is as a rule heavily paid for by a lack of comprehensiveness and systematic clarity. The purely systematic method has its strength in its comprehensive documentation and the great perspective of its presentation. The systematic-exegetical method to some extent eliminates the weaknesses characterizing the other methods, but has too narrow a horizon.

The only possible way out of this problem seems to be a compromise between the various methods, by which the advantages of each can be utilized and the weaknesses avoided. In this work it is our purpose to make such a compromise. Since we are dealing with a systematic subject it is natural that we employ the systematic method. That means that we ignore the historicogenetic viewpoint and that we consider all Luther's thoughts no matter from what period of his development they are.

However, we shall not quote indiscriminately the insurmountable number of sources. We are making a rough chronological division of the sources into two main periods, and we shall treat each as a chronological entity. As a division point between the periods we are using the return from the Wartburg to Wittenberg. Our work is therefore presented in two main parts—an introductory and basic period in which we use only the sources of the first period, and a concluding part in which the sources of the last period will be analyzed.

Our reason for adopting this method is not that we believe that there is a decided point of division between the views of Luther before and after 1522. There is a tendency, especially strong in the Swedish study of Luther, to differentiate between a "pre-Reformation" and a "Reformation" Luther (in which the pre-Reformation Luther is looked for not only in the earliest lectures of Luther's youth but even in the main works of the Reformation such as *Von den guten Werken*). In opposition to this tendency we find it more correct to underscore with Ernst Wolf, *Es gehört mit zu den methodologischen Erkenntnissen der neueren Lutherforschung, dass man dem Versuch, scheinbare oder wirkliche Widersprüche in den Aussagen Luthers "entwicklungsgeschichtlich" aufzulösen, mit wachsender Ablehnung zu begegnen hat, und an Stelle der hier*

*beliebten Scheidung des "jungen" und des "alten" das Wieder-
finden des "jungen" im "alten" sich durchsetzt.*[3] From the moment
that Luther has completely clarified the basic evangelical concept
of the Reformation, he retains this concept without any essential
change until his death. This decisive moment, according to the
majority of Luther scholars, comes during Luther's lectures on the
Psalms in 1513-15. That does not mean, however, that there is no
development of his view. The struggle caused by the indulgences is
one example of a very definite development in a number of points
in Luther's attitude to traditional teaching and to canon law. But
the development is within the new evangelical view of life and not
away from it. It is a development, therefore, which does not signify
any modification of the basic view, but is rather a progressive and
final struggle with the traditional views based on the unchanged
fundamental conclusion.

That we use only sources from the first period in the first part
of our work is no indication that Luther's view of the Holy Spirit
underwent any change after 1522. We have decided to use the
sources before Luther's return to Wittenberg as a basis for the
fundamental part of this work for an entirely different reason. In
the first place, Luther's production in this period contains a rich-
ness, vitality and depth which are never surpassed later, and which
always compel us to study this period when we want to get a comprehensive picture of Luther's view of Christianity. The exegetical
works of this period are to a great extent prepared by Luther himself. They treat the biblical writings out of which Luther in a
special sense has drawn his new evangelical understanding, such
as the Psalms and the most important Pauline letters. The lectures
on the Epistle to the Romans are among the most important, and
no comprehensive presentation of Luther's thought dares to ignore
them even though in certain respects they mark a transition from
the old to the new view. We find the basic thoughts of Luther in a
broad and powerful presentation in the sermons and in the postils
which Luther himself has prepared for publication. In the chief
writings of the Reformation, in dissertations, and in sermons,

---

[3] *Die Christusverkündigung bei Luther.*

Luther is trying to settle the issue with the scholastic tradition. No other period can present such a wealth of fresh and original sources covering almost all phases of Luther's evangelical view of salvation. The original writings of the older Luther are often polemical, which greatly narrows their horizon, while the exegetical and homiletical writings of this period often come to us second or third hand. There are therefore compelling reasons for using the writings of the early period as our basis. Because of our theme there is also a special reason why we should use this material. During the time after 1522, Luther's new attitude toward the enthusiasts takes definite form. It is well known that in Luther's struggle with the enthusiasts his view of the Holy Spirit was a determining factor. If we want to understand Luther's view of the Holy Spirit it is methodically most correct to draw the main presentation from sources before the struggle with the enthusiasts. A presentation based on the polemic would easily be influenced by the problems of the enthusiasts, or rather by Luther's attitude to the definite problem in this struggle. Such a presentation would be likely to be more narrow than Luther's view of the Holy Spirit really is. Furthermore, the method which we have decided to use makes it possible to substantiate whether Luther in his struggle with the enthusiasts actually modified his message about the Spirit, or if it is rather his message about the Spirit that produced the struggle with the enthusiasts. This fairly important question we should not be able to answer so easily if in presenting Luther's fundamental view we used sources from the period when the polemics against the enthusiasts constantly held the front page.

On the other hand, our reason for not limiting our examination entirely to the first period is that the special emphasis, the testimony of Luther about the Holy Spirit in the struggle with the enthusiasts, should not be dispensed with in any presentation of this subject. But the older Luther's more polemical message about the Spirit should be seen in its natural connection with a total view which was established long before the struggle started. Only in this way does it become clear that Luther's testimony about the Spirit is not a reactionary phenomenon brought about by a crisis but that it belongs organically to his total evangelical view.

By thus dividing the sources into those before the struggle with the enthusiasts and those after, we have attempted to ward off the worst objections to the systematic method—in this case the objection to the use of statements formed in a polemical situation as basis for the presentation of a total view instead of understanding the polemical statements on the basis of this total view.

With respect to the use of the sources from each of these two groups, only a few remarks are needed. It is now taken for granted that sources from the hand of Luther are preferred wherever possible, and that in the inevitable use of sources copied and published by others in the case of the older Luther the most direct, usually those by Rörer, should be preferred. With respect to this last rule it is entirely possible that in the future there will not be so much emphasis on the untrustworthiness of the Melanchthonian publishers, although their copious paraphrasing does not, to be sure, give an exact impression of what Luther said. Those publishers were of course Melanchthonians, but they were much closer to Luther on many points than the German Luther research of the twentieth century. I take for granted that a reaction against this often exaggerated skepticism toward the publishers of Luther is forthcoming in future Luther research. However, we proceed here according to the usual custom and quote, where it is possible, the handwritings even when they are not connected and clear and the printed passages would have given a more readable text.

A few remarks are in order about some of Luther's greatest and most interesting works: *Dictata super Psalterium,* 1513-15, and the Commentary on Genesis, 1535-45. These two weighty and interesting works have been used to a very small degree in this study. In the Commentary on the Psalms the conflict between the new and progressing evangelical understanding and the traditional doctrinal forms is yet so strong and the terminology therefore so obscure that it is not so well suited as material in a systematic presentation of Luther. In this connection it should also be stated that the Weimar edition text does not permit a sufficiently clear distinction between Luther's own thoughts and the *collecta* from other authors that he has added. On the Commentary on Genesis there are now two special studies, Erich Seeberg's little and Peter Meinhold's big book about this work,[4] which permit us to distinguish with greater certainty than before between what comes from Luther's own hand and what has been added by the editors. However, these studies have not as yet said the last word in the problem. Therefore, as long as we are not completely certain as to what in this great work is of Luther, it is natural that we use it only where it produces parallels to Lutheran thoughts that are well documented.

In regard to the selection of material within the last period's abundance of texts, we shall aim at some kind of balance between the purely systematic and the systematic-exegetical methods. A complete utilization of all the existing sources would be practically impossible as well as without any real purpose. Instead of trying to cover all of Luther's works we seek to concentrate our source references from the most important works. This will often cause us to dwell at length on single passages so that we will be very close to the systematic-exegetical method. On the other hand we shall try to give the points in question a broader documentation by frequent reference to sources from the different periods in the life of Luther. The references to parallel texts do not aim at completeness. It is their aim to show that the thoughts contained therein are not isolated in the thinking of Luther.

We have not made any division of the sources into groups or types of sources. In using the texts we first quote the original writings of Luther, which are cited with their date in parentheses, and then the second hand sources, which are given with the authority and date in parentheses. These sources are mostly notes from sermons and lectures. Where a thesis is cited, the date and the occasion are given in parentheses. In that manner there will be three groups of sources in the references. We have not used letters and table talks.

---

[4] Erich Seeberg, *Studien zu Luthers Genesisvorlesung;* and Peter Meinhold, *Die Genesisvorlesung Luthers und ihre Herausgeber.*

Finally just a few words about the procedure of the study. We shall start the first part by investigating Luther's views on the work of the Holy Spirit. In accordance with the dogmatic tradition the young Luther interprets the work of the Spirit as the infusion of the true love to God into the heart. We shall see how Luther gives this formula a new content, which indicates that his thoughts about the Spirit have broken away from the Augustinian and scholastic *caritas* idealism and are instead put into a biblical realism of revelation. Then we turn to Luther's view of the organs of the Holy Spirit, the Word and the sacraments, under which the understanding based on the realism of revelation is deepened. We conclude the first fundamental part of this study with an account of Luther's thoughts about the person of the Holy Spirit, by which his attitude to the traditional doctrine of the Trinity is clarified, and the complete view of Luther on the Spirit and his work is summarized and characterized.

In the second main part we begin by showing the continuity in Luther's understanding of the Spirit. The ideas from the first part are further developed, and the full conception previously produced is confirmed through the sources of the second period. Then we treat Luther's testimony of the Holy Spirit in its contradistinction to that of the enthusiasts, and we show how Luther's antispiritualistic view is not a reactionary phenomenon but springs organically from his conception of the Holy Spirit. The result of the second part of the study is a substantiation of the unchanged and realistic conception which supports all of Luther's discourse about the Spirit, the opposition of this conception to every toning down of this realism in scholasticism, orthodoxy, pietism, and modern Protestantism, and the relationship of this conception to genuine biblical realism of revelation.

Part One

LUTHER'S TESTIMONY ABOUT THE SPIRIT BEFORE HIS CONTROVERSY WITH THE ENTHUSIASTS

Chapter I

THE WORK OF THE HOLY SPIRIT

The Work of the Holy Spirit as "Infusion of Love" in the Evangelical Sense

In Luther's lectures on the Epistle to the Romans during 1515-16, we read in the notes on Romans 2:15: "From this I believe that the sentence 'let the law be written in their heart' says the same thing as 'Love is infused into the heart through the Holy Spirit.' It is in the same sense both the law of Christ and the fulfillment of the law of Moses."[1]

This is the young Luther's fundamental formula for the understanding of the work of the Holy Spirit. It is in complete accordance with the traditional way of expression, especially in the Augustinian sense. When the young Luther speaks of the work of the Holy Spirit he very often uses Augustinian terminology and he often quotes Augustine directly. The work of the Holy Spirit is to infuse into the heart the true love of God so that obedience to the command of the law is brought about not by fear of punishment but because of a free and happy love to God.

Has this carried us beyond a purely Augustinian way of thinking?

It has often been stated that in Luther's lectures as a young man his doctrine of justification bears a definitely Augustinian

---

[1] *W. A.*, LVI, 203, 8. [*Vnde puto, Quod 'legem scribi in cordibus' sit 'ipsam charitatem diffundi in cordibus per spiritum sanctum', quae proprie est lex Christi et plenitudo legis Mosi. . . .*]

3

mark, and that it can best be characterized by the idea of a progressive and healing *Gerechtmachung* (process of justification) through the Holy Spirit's infusing of the true love to God. Is that not the true explanation of the problem? Does this bring out any new statement about the work of the Holy Spirit, different from the traditional Augustinian thinking?

In answering this question it is not sufficient to note an apparent agreement in terminology. We must study the connection in which the apparently identical formulas are found in Augustine (and in scholasticism) and in Luther. Then we find that a new content has been put into the forms which Luther has taken over from Augustine.

We begin by asking what sort of *caritas* it is that according to Luther is infused into the heart by the Holy Spirit.

In answering this question we are led right into the heart of Luther's *theologia crucis,* and it becomes apparent that behind the similarity in the vocabulary of Luther and Augustine there is a deep and decisive difference.

Augustine says that love to God is similar to the *amor sui* (love of self) rightly understood. Luther may state it in almost the same way: "For to love means to hate oneself, to condemn oneself, and to wish ill to oneself according to the words of Christ: 'He that hateth his life in this world shall keep it unto life eternal.' Whoever loves himself in this way loves himself truly, for his love of self is not of himself but of God, i.e. according to the will of God which hates and condemns and wishes evil to all sin, i.e. to us all."[2]

Consequently Luther can also speak about a *vere seipsum diligere* but with an important difference from Augustine. The rightly understood "love of self" is not here a sublimation of the

---

[2] *W. A.,* LVI, 392, 20 (1515-16). [*Est enim diligere seipsum odisse, damnare, malum optare secundum illud Christi: 'Qui odit animam suam in hoc mundo, in vitam eternam custodit eam' . . . Qui sic seipsum diligit, vere seipsum diligit. Quia non in se ipso, sed in Deo diligit, i.e. qualiter est in voluntate Dei, qui odit, damnat, malum optat omnibus peccatoribus, i.e. omnibus nobis.*]

See also Anders Nygren, *Den kristna kärlekstanken genom tiderna,* pp. 342-60. For full publication data of books mentioned in footnotes see Bibliography.

idealistic inner urge of man but is qualitatively different from it. The paradoxical "love of self" about which Luther speaks hates, condemns, and wishes the self every possible evil because it agrees with the judgment of God which hates, condemns, and wishes evil upon all sinners, upon everyone, because all are sinners. The rightly understood "love of self" which can become love to God is for Luther identical with an unconditional hatred of oneself, a hatred which agrees with and accepts the judgment of God upon all sinners and therefore also upon oneself.[3]

Thus is brought out the radical development of the motif that appears with constant variations in the lectures on the Psalms and the Epistle to the Romans about *accusatio* as *justificatio dei*. In its identity with love to God this *odium sui* is not man's own work, but the gift of the Holy Spirit.

The understanding of *caritas* as identical with the radically conceived *odium sui* already indicates an important modification of the idea of the Spirit's work as *infusio caritatis*. Here it is very important to note that this *odium sui* must not be understood as the "higher" spiritual nature's hatred of the "lower" sensual nature. To be sure Luther often uses the antithesis *caro-spiritus* (corresponding to *vetus homo* and *novus homo*) to express the tension in the self which is contained in the designations *odium sui* and *accusatio sui*. Luther's thoughts might therefore be said to mean that it is a man's *spiritus* which hates his *caro* and through this hatred loves God. But at the same time it must be remembered that the contrast *caro-spiritus* is not anthropological, so that *spiritus* means the most noble part of man, the source of his idealistic striving for God and the spiritual realities, and *caro* the sensual nature, by which man attaches himself to all the base, the outward and corruptible. No, this contrast is a theological one: *spiritus* is the whole of man, if it is dominated by the Spirit of God; and *caro* is the whole of man, if it lacks the Spirit of God. On this basis *odium sui* includes not only the "baser" part of man, but the *totus*

---

[3] This thought is expressed in *Contra scholasticam theologiam*, thesis ninety-six, of 1517. Adolf Hamel in his book *Der junge Luther und Augustin* finds this a "complete contradiction" to Augustine's basic assumption.

homo, including his spiritual life to the extent that this is not directly one with the Spirit of God. This is the radical conception of sin that the new understanding of salvation gave to Luther, which leads to the view of *caro* as *totus homo.* No part of man that is away from God is not saturated with selfishness, *concupiscentia.*

In the lecture on Romans Luther presents a table of the virtues which the carnal wisdom can "enjoy" rather than "use" and which it by so doing makes its idols.[4] This table begins with *externa bona* and *corporis bona.* But then it goes on to *animae bona, scientiae et artes, sapientia corporalis (humana sapientia intellectualis),* under which also belongs *the acknowledgment of the Holy Scripture.* After that come the virtues of the religious life itself: *gratia affectualis in justitia, devotione, donis spiritus sancti etc. in meditationibus,* until the series closes with *Deus affirmative in proprietatibus divinis,* God himself to the extent to which he can be comprehended through the positive statements of theology. *All* these things, among which some are very "spiritual," the carnal man draws into himself in order to make idols of them.

With this view of the antithesis *caro-spiritus* it is clear that the ideas *odium sui* and *condemnatio sui* must become so radical that the self which is judged and hated also includes the ideal striving of man, his *amor boni,* yes even the good works which are a fruit of grace, just as soon as they are viewed as man's own righteousness. This presents a psychological problem: what kind of self is it that is the subject of *odium sui* and *condemnatio sui,* when the self which is the object is really man's *totus homo?* The problem is more than a specious one, it is the fundamental problem of the theology of the knowledge and consciousness of sin, which gave the young Luther the most unspeakable agonies. When the self in its self-condemnation will put itself and its own pride to death, does it gain anything other than that the pride and egocentricity move from the real self, the object of mortification, into the subject of the act of mortification? And does this not give us the most refined form of pride: the publican's pride of humility and self-accusation? This was a real problem for Luther, for it was the

---

4 *W. A.,* LVI, 343, 16.

whole problem of monastic piety. The only solution to the problem is that the subject of the act of self-condemnation is not the natural self of man, but God himself, who in the act of self-condemnation makes himself the master in man. *Odium sui* or *condemnatio sui* is in reality no human act, but a suffering *(passio)* under the effective judgment of God. This is Luther's solution to the problem of the knowledge of sin. The Holy Spirit himself is the subject of the self-condemnatory act. We have seen how Luther described *odium sui* as a unity with God in his judgment of sin and the sinner. This unity is not effected by man's lifting himself in such a way that he can view the judgment of God, but by the presence of the judging God himself as a power in man, a power which has the effect that man accepts the judgment as his own judgment. It is this presence of God that is the Holy Spirit.[5]

It is noteworthy that Luther in order to describe this direct presence of God still expresses it as the infusion of love into the heart. But that the substance covered by this expression is a different one is proved by the fact that love is no longer the sublimated *amor boni,* the natural idealistic striving of man elevated to the highest point by the help of the grace of God, but love is one with God's love to the sinner, the love that always carries the judgment with it. Therefore Luther is able to designate the paradoxical love with which the sinner hates himself the truly understood "love of self." God loves the sinner with just such a paradoxical love, which hates and judges the sinner in his sin in order to hold on to him. Therefore Luther also says of the paradoxical "love of self" (consisting of *odium sui*) that it is in God. "He loves not of himself but of God, i.e. according to the will of God which hates and condemns and wishes evil to all sin, i.e. to us all." (See page 4 above.)

In Augustine's thinking the idealistic striving of man, his *amor boni,* in the form of the rightly understood "love of self" comes to dominate the view of man's love to God and therefore also God's love to man. Luther's thought, on the other hand, is that the in-

---

[5] *W. A.,* LVI, 229, 24 ff.; 231, 8 ff.; 233, 5 ff.; 234, 23 ff.; 228, 18 ff.; 247, 11 ff.; 325, 27 ff.; 68, 25 ff. (1515-16). LVII, Lecture on the Epistle to the Hebrews, 109, 15 ff.; 186, 13 ff. (1517-18).

comprehensible love of God, which includes judgment upon sin and the sinner, completely dominates man's love to God and therefore also man's love of his neighbor and himself. Thus Luther's expression "love of self," which he uses, though not in a very literal sense, no longer has anything to do with an *appetitus summi boni,* but it means that the individual sees himself with the eyes of God, to "be in the will of God."

With this understanding of love the work of the Holy Spirit must also be differently understood. The Spirit can no longer be understood as a transcendent cause of a sublimated idealism, but it must be understood as a direct presence of God, a sphere of life wherein the will of man can be and remain *odium sui.* How Luther conceives of the direct presence of the Spirit as a new sphere of life, in which something so impossible as *odium sui* can be the most natural of all, we shall be able to learn only when we follow Luther a few steps further in his new understanding of the meaning of *caritas.*

So far we have seen only that the love which the Holy Spirit fuses into the heart is identical with an *odium sui* and a *condemnatio sui,* of which God in the presence of the Spirit is the subject. Therefore it is often possible to describe the content of this love as conformity to the will of God, which means that the will of man becomes one with the will of God, so that it wills, feels and acts as God wills, feels, and acts. Such a conformity between the will of man and the will of God, however, does not take place at the initiative of man but only because of God. It is not man who conforms his will to the will of God, but God who forms the will of man according to His. The most pregnant expression of the view of Luther is his description of the will of man which conforms to the will of God as a spontaneous and happy will. These characteristics are not those of the will that is the result of human striving. Such a will is always forced.[6]

The radicalism with which Luther carried through his thought about *odium sui* and *condemnatio sui* made his teaching about the love of God differ from Augustine's definite conception of *amor*

---

6 *W. A.,* LVI, 366, 14.

Dei as *amor summi boni* which proceeds from the anthropologically founded *caro-spiritus* dualism. But is Luther's view of *odium sui* and conformity to the will of God not more closely related to mysticism? Is not that which Luther produces simply a radically absorbed Augustinian view about the infused love penetrated by the *theologia crucis* of mysticism? Was it not the mystics who spoke so radically about *odium sui* and *condemnatio sui*?

The purely historic question regarding the time and extent of the influence of mysticism on Luther will not be discussed here. It is clear that Luther not only has appropriated some of the terminology of mysticism but also that he actually has been influenced by several of the spokesmen of mysticism. His writings show how deeply he studied the mystics such as Tauler during the years his own *theologia crucis* was being formed, and also that at times he accepted the view of the mystics.[7] However, we must not draw too comprehensive conclusions on the basis of the similarity in choice of words. That Luther's writing about the *odium sui* and *condemnatio sui* is not of exactly the same type as that of the mystics is seen by the development the *conformitas*-idea receives from Luther in comparison to the thoughts about the work of the Holy Spirit.

The idea of conformity in the form in which we have met it in the lectures on Romans and Hebrews is developed in a theocentric manner. He speaks about a conformity between the will of God and the will of man. This theocentric interpretation of the idea of conformity, however, cannot be separated from a corresponding Christocentric interpretation since the will of God, to which our will becomes conformed, is revealed only in Christ and can conform our will to itself only by Christ. The clear expression for this is found in the lectures on Hebrews: *Hoc enim canonicum est, quoties fiunt, que Deo placent, eadem non placere nobis. Sunt enim contrarie voluntates. Ideo fieri voluntatem Dei aliud nihil est quam nostram destrui ac sic magis ac magis conformari divine.*

---

[7] Erich Seeberg, *Luthers Theologie*, pp. 31-61, and *Grundzüge der Theologie Luthers*, pp. 26-33. J. v. Walter, *Mystik und Rechtfertigung beim jungen Luther.* E. Vogelsang, *Luther und die Mystik*, pp. 32-54. W. v. Loewenich, pp. 197-227. P. Bühler, pp. 155-166.

Et hoc est 'crucifigi veterem hominem cum Christo.'[8] The same thought dominates the lectures on Romans, and it is also basic in the *theologia crucis* of the lectures on the Psalms. In the lectures on the Psalms the Christocentric proof of the concept of conformity is emphasized very strongly, because Luther there carries through the exegetical principle that what the Psalms say about persecution, suffering and death must be interpreted "literally" about the cross of Christ and the humiliation, but "tropologically" about the cross of the believer and his humiliation in Christ. The idea of conformity in its Christocentric development is therefore a guiding principle in the interpretation of the lectures on the Psalms.[9]

But this Christocentric idea of conformity[10] is not, as in mysticism, to be interpreted from the point of view of a medieval piety of imitation. Conformity with Christ is not accomplished by imitation of his humble humanity. It is not a result of ascetic technique. It is not at all the work of man's free will. It has no marks of the law at all. It is God who does his work in us, not we who imitate Christ. God by his Spirit makes us conform to Christ, so that we like him can become God's work and in this passive sense conform to his will. Conformity with the will of God is the work of the Spirit, not the result of the struggling of the will.[11]

The mystic can of course also talk about the work of the Holy Spirit and its indwelling in man. But the presupposition for the coming of the Holy Spirit is that man must first have turned to God with all his strength. The abnegation is man's own work which corresponds to and is often identified by the mystics with *facere quod in se est* of scholasticism. When the mystics talk about the Holy Spirit it is entirely on the basis of imitation.

In how radical a sense conformity to Christ must be understood as solely the work of the Holy Spirit is seen in the special way in

---

8 *W. A.*, LVII, Heb., 91, 20.

9 E. Vogelsang, *Die Anfänge von Luthers Christologie nach der ersten Psalmenvorlesung,* pp. 26-30 and 88-104.

10 See also *W. A.*, II, 138, 35 ff. (1519); II, 147, 15 ff. (1519); V, 72, 38 ff.; 128, 37 ff.; 166, 12 ff. (1519-21).

11 E. Vogelsang, *Der angefochtene Christus,* pp. 53-56. W. v. Loewenich, pp. 165-166. R. Bring, *Förhållandet mellan tro och gärningar inom luthersk theologi,* pp. 54-63. E. Wolf, *Die Christusverkündigung bei Luther,* pp. 180-83.

which Luther expresses this thought in his lectures on the Psalms. Just as Christ is conceived by the Holy Spirit, so every believer is justified and regenerated not by the work of man, but by the grace of God alone and the work of the Spirit. It is the tropological exegesis which is used in such a way that the literal incarnation of Christ is interpreted as his *mystica incarnatio* by which he is spiritually born in the believer. Everything related about the first coming of Christ in the flesh may also be said about his spiritual coming. This tropological exegesis, however, is the key to the whole exegesis of the lectures on the Psalms. The idea of conformity, as we saw, became a rule of interpretation. Now we also hear that the conformity with Christ, which is expressed in this tropological exposition, can be effected only through conception by the Holy Spirit, that is, by the birth of Christ in us *spiritualiter*. It could hardly be more emphatically expressed that *conformitas Christi* is not the result of an *imitatio Christi,* but of an act of God in man through the Holy Spirit.

This decisive difference between the idea of conformity of Luther and that of mysticism is indicated in the different attitude which the thought of *resignatio ad infernum* assumes. They who have the wisdom of the Spirit love the will of God and rejoice in being conformed to it. When they know that it is the will of God that the last day shall come with all its horror and wrath, then they are not afraid, but they rejoice and hope that it may soon come to pass. That which others fear is their great joy.[12] The one who is conformed to the will of God does not fear the last day with its wrath but rejoices because then the will of God will be fulfilled. If only the will of God comes to pass he will yield himself to it even though it means he must go to hell and eternal death.

Here the thought of conformity is carried to its final conclusion, but this also definitely shows us the difference from mysticism. *Resignatio ad infernum* is for mysticism a spiritual exercise. It is an imagined hell that the mystic by his own willpower transports himself to in his mortification. Luther, on the other hand, speaks about the real hell and connects the idea of *resignatio ad infernum*

---

[12] *W. A.,* LVI, 364, 35; also X, 1; II, 111, 11 f.

with the joy about the last day. *Resignatio* is a preparation for the grace and the coming of the Spirit for the mystic; it is the culmination of the *Entwerdung*, which is man's *facere quod in se est*. For Luther *resignatio* is the culmination of the conformity with Christ which is the work of the Holy Spirit alone. Therefore *resignatio ad infernum* does not become the proof of the fact that man is now fit soon to receive grace and the Spirit, but of the fact that man already *has* grace and the Spirit. Only in *conformitas Christi*, which is wholly the work of the Spirit, is it possible for a man seriously (and not just as a spiritual exercise) to desire to go to hell at the command of God. Therefore it is possible for Luther to declare that it is impossible for such a man to go to hell. For the man who in all things wants to do what God wants is one with God. This we are able to see in Christ. *Resignatio ad infernum* is for Luther not a product of the imagination but first and foremost a historic reality in the descent of Christ into hell. Already in the lectures on the Psalms Luther interprets the descent of Christ to hades in this way. And when according to the tropological principle of exegesis, which contains the idea of conformity, the descent of Christ into hell is made to apply to the believer, then *resignatio ad infernum* is one with our fellowship with Christ in the Holy Spirit. *Si ergo triduo in inferno fueris: signum est, quod tecum Christus et tu cum Christo sis!*[13]

With this account of the idea of conformity as the content of man's love to God we have departed still further from the Augustinian *caritas* idea. The thought about *odium sui* as a necessary complement to true love of God received its real confirmation by being put into the ideas of conformity. The thought of man's love to God, *caritas*, is here completely taken out of the connection with the natural, idealistic struggle of man, in which it was placed by the Augustinian speculation of *caritas*, and it is made a miracle of which God alone can be the subject.

But we still lack one step in order to be able to see the full consequence of this change in the thought of man's love to God. We have seen that the idea of conformity reaches its climax in the

---

13 *W. A.*, III, 433, 3 (1513-15). Also III, 431, 40-434, 6; 452, 29.

thought about *resignatio ad infernum*. And we have seen that this conformity is not brought about on the initiative of man or by the work of man. It is the work of the Spirit. But it is not yet clear to us how it can be the work of the Spirit to lead man into the torment of death and hell. We must go still deeper into the idea of conformity in order to see that.

When God begins his work in men, those who are dominated by the spirit of bondage again unto fear (Rom. 8:15) will say: God acts as a tyrant, he is not a father but an opponent. And it is true that God is our opponent. But these people do not know that we must agree with this opponent for then he becomes kind and fatherly—otherwise he never will. The relation to God does not mean that he agrees with us and changes himself according to our desires so that we may become his friends and sons. No, God is our opponent in the sense that to our dismay he lets everything happen contrary to our wishes and desires in spite of our prayers. When God begins to do his will, he exposes everything in man, what he has of both inward and outward glory, makes him completely perplexed and leads him into the darkness of inner conflict, where it is impossible either to know or to love God. In this darkness he finally takes away from him even the word of comfort which in the time of inner conflict can assure him that God only for a season has forsaken him. The words of Christ can be used about this darkness: that except the Lord had shortened the days no flesh would have been saved.[14]

Thus it is to be made to conform to the will of God in the crucified Christ; thus it is to be under the *operatio* of God. This is a *theologia crucis* which also is a theology of inner conflict.

In biographical studies of Luther his own inner conflicts have often been made the object of thorough research. But his teaching and his theology of inner conflict have rarely been utilized in the systematic study of Luther. In recent years, however, especially in studies of Luther's Christology, it has become more apparent that what Luther has to say about inner conflict is not merely of biographical interest or of interest in the care of souls but is

---

14 *W. A.*, LVII, Heb., 186, 16.

closely connected with the very heart of his whole conception of Christianity.[15] *Wenn ich noch eine Weile leben sollt, wollt ich ein Buch von Anfechtungen schreiben, ohn welche kann kein Mensch weder die Schrift verstehen noch Gottesfurcht und Liebe erkennen, ja, er kann nicht wissen, was Geist ist.*[16] In this passage, which Vogelsang uses as the theme of his book about the Christ of inner conflict in Luther, it is also stated that inner conflict is of special significance in the understanding of what spirit is. It is in the inner conflict and only there that the Spirit's work is understood.

For Luther inner conflict is not a psychologically abnormal state, a disease of the mind which the pastor should try to remove if possible, but it is a means in the hand of God to reveal man's true state when he is away from God, man's state under the wrath of God. Inner conflict is a common condition, for the Christian it is even inevitable: *ein itzlicher, der do angefangen hatt goth zcw dinen, muss sich darein geben, das er viell anfechtung und anstocss leiden muess. Es wirt kein christen mensch auff erden an anfechtung sein: Goth füret uns zcw der anfechtung.*[17]

When Luther speaks in this manner he is thinking of great, spiritual, inner conflicts. In these inner conflicts the sinner experiences the wrath of God in his conscience, so that God as the gracious one and Christ as the revelation of the grace of God completely hides himself, while death and hell and all creation assail man. *Gottes Ewigkeit, Heiligkeit und Allmacht ist es, die den Menschen in seinem gesammten Dasein und Sosein, in seinem Leben und Wirken, in seinem sittlichen Wollen und Urteilen, in seinem frommen Glauben und Hoffen in jedem Augenblick unendlich bedroht.*[18]

There is hardly another writing in which Luther so persistently describes the pangs of inner conflict as in *Operationes in Psalmos*,

---

[15] E. Vogelsang, *Die Anfänge von Luthers Christologie,* and *Der angefochtene Christus bei Luther.* Lennart Pinomaa, pp. 153-82. Ernst Wolf, *Staupitz und Luther,* p. 207 ff. Hans M. Müller, pp. 61 ff. and pp. 100 ff. Also Paul Bühler.
[16] *W. A., Tischreden,* IV, number 4777.
[17] *W. A.,* IX, 508, 11 (Poliander's codex, 1519 ff.).
[18] E. Vogelsang, *Der angefochtene Christus,* p. 18.

1519-21. Here there is a psychology of inner conflict to which there is no comparison.

The cause of inner conflict is *guilt*. Unpardonable guilt lays hold of the conscience in inner conflict so that man knows he is under the eternal and irrevocable condemnation of God, stricken from the book of life forever.[19] No one and nothing can help in this case. All good works and all merit disappear. No man is able to help. Agreeing with the angry God, the whole creation is against me. All others are righteous and I alone am guilty. The merciful God himself turns his face from me. It is futile to call upon him, for he does not hear me. Then man stands alone face to face with the angry and irreconcilable God, without any mediator. For even Christ has at the command of God turned himself away from me. Then the never-ceasing wrath of the eternal God is experienced.

This torturing experience of the wrath of God in a guilty conscience becomes one with the anguish of death and hell. There is in reality no difference between death and hell and the reality of the wrath of God in one's conscience. Hell is the terror of death itself which always accompanies it, the experience of the eternal and inevitable punishment. If not before death then in death we shall experience this struggle with Satan, yes, with God himself and the whole creation. There is no possibility of escape in this struggle. Man has been forced into a narrow pass from which there is no way out at all.

In this pass terrible temptations beset the troubled soul. Ultimately the result is blasphemy, the desire that God were someone else, or that he did not exist. The most dangerous of all conflicts is lurking there—that caused by the idea of predestination.

But when the believer suffers these inner conflicts he is to know that they are also part of his training in loving God and hating himself, a training by which he is made to conform to the will of God in Christ and by which he comes under the operation of God. For Christ has also suffered the pangs of hell, yes, even the temptation of blasphemy. The inner conflicts, therefore, are the work

---

[19] See also *W. A.*, V, 166, 30 (1519-21); 203, 5; 208, 24; 385, 10.

of God, although as long as this is hidden from the anxious soul it is Satan who dominates in the conflict and who tries to separate the sinner from God. But God pursues his own aim in the conflict. God is not really *(vere)* angry, and he does not desire that man's sin should be unpardonable. But through the cross of inner conflict God wants to teach us to hope only in his pure mercy. Like every other cross and all other work of wrath in the believer, the inner conflicts are God's *opus alienum*, which prepares the way for his *opus proprium*. He takes all peace away from the conscience in order to give it peace. This is the order of the salvation of God. He puts to death before he makes alive. Our will cannot be made to conform to the will of God unless it is first put to death.[20] Therefore it becomes even more pronounced here than before that the love to God which yields itself to his will is not an active yearning and is not like the Augustinian *caritas* a continuation of our *appetitus boni,* but a process of suffering and endurance as God establishes his work. When the work of God is the cross, pleasing God becomes the same as enduring the marvelous work of God in his saints. As the mystics put it faith, hope, and love to God mean walking into darkness, being driven and led by the Word of God, persistent suffering, a narrow and strait way, a steady and increasing impotence. But it is a way on which the sinner is gladly led, because it is God's way, which Christ has dedicated and hallowed by traveling it first himself. In the storm of inner conflict we must learn to know that God, who as our protector forsakes us, as our helper permits us to suffer, and as our Saviour judges us.

It is on this gloomy background of inner conflict that Luther proclaims the work of the Holy Spirit in his exegesis of the eighth chapter of Romans. To endure the work of God in us during the infernal darkness of inner conflict is humanly impossible. Time and again it is emphasized that it is impossible to stand in the darkness of inner conflict. God the Holy Spirit alone can help us by interceding for us with groanings which cannot be uttered. This word from Romans 8, about the work of the Holy Spirit as

---

20 See also *W. A.,* V, 63, 33; I, 540, 8 ff., 22 ff. (1518); VI, 248, 1 ff. (1520).

our comforter and intercessor, is in Luther inextricably united with the experience of the infernal darkness of inner conflict. In Luther's descriptions of inner conflict, Romans 8:26 is the basic testimony about the work of the Holy Spirit as the source of the true love to God. When the sinner groans for God with sighs that cannot be uttered in spite of the darkness of trial, in the midst of the excruciating experience of the wrath of God and the terror of hell, and out through his rebellious blasphemy against God, then this greatest love to God, which groans for God in the midst of the hatred of death and hell to God, is not possible for man. It is not man himself who calls upon his last resources in a final religious effort, it is not man's inward soul that appears, but it is God himself who, as the subject of this greatest act of love, is truly present in us, it is the Holy Spirit himself who, as our helper and comforter, groans in us and for us.

Now for the first time we understand what it means that the Holy Spirit is the subject for *odium sui* and the realization of the true conformity with Christ. And for the first time we understand what Luther means by *totus homo.*

If we are to understand the real content of the young Luther's message about the Holy Spirit it is necessary to compare the message about the Holy Spirit as *interpellator* and *consolator* in the darkness of inner conflict with the traditional forms about the Holy Spirit as a source of *gratia infusa* and of the new life and the happy and spontaneous will, which through pure love to God fulfills the law. All these Augustinian expressions Luther retains and constantly uses throughout his life. But their content must be understood on the basis of the testimony about the Spirit that grew out of his experience with inner conflict. The infused love is that love which in the inner conflicts is hardened to *odium sui.* The new life begins by the crucifying of the old man when he through inner conflicts is made to conform with the Christ of humiliation. The happy will is that will which in the unutterable groanings from the hell of inner conflict is made to conform with the will of God. The Augustinian formulas are retained. They are the form in which Luther constantly presents his testimony about

17

the Holy Spirit. But the content of this form becomes quite different from the Augustinian. The new content harmonized with the message about the Spirit which Luther heard in Romans 8:26, and it corresponds with his experience in the darkness of inner conflict, completely in the grip of death, hell, and the wrath of God, where there was nothing left but the unutterable groaning which did not originate in himself but which was the groaning of the Spirit in him and for him.

On the basis of this testimony and this experience the content of all the Augustinian forms must be understood. This is proved by the fact that the reference to Romans 8:26 is constantly repeated when Luther discusses the work of the Spirit in detail. This Scripture passage is Luther's center of understanding by which all his thoughts about the Spirit are orientated.[21]

However, the new content in the old forms transforms and eventually destroys them. With this center of understanding, the "infused grace" of which Luther constantly speaks can no longer be understood as a *caritas* which supplements and sublimates the indwelling idealistic urge in man, his *amor boni,* but as the actual fusion of God's *opus alienum* and his *opus proprium,* his dying and creating work of redemption. Luther therefore speaks of the infusion in such a way that the death of the old man is God's gift as much as the new life. By the characteristics that *caritas* has received through the idea of conformity the basic Augustinian structure has been dissolved. Grace considered from the point of view of the idea of conformity means the fusion of God's deadly *opus alienum* and his life-giving *opus proprium.* Thus the idea of justification by grace considered as a new nature mediated through the sacrament has become impossible in principle.

As a summary of this first impression of the young Luther's claim about the Holy Spirit we may conclude: Luther no longer

---

21 *W. A.,* LVII, Heb., 186, 21 ff. (1517-18); I, 558, 35 ff. (1518); also I, 532, 31 and 565, 23. V, 385, 17 ff.; 79, 14 ff.; 170, 28 ff.; 203, 25 ff.; 208, 20 ff.; 581, 10 ff., 21 ff.; 607, 30 ff. (1519-21). IX, 330, 20 ff.; 346, 2 ff.; 467, 1 ff.; 610, 14 ff.; 465, 4 ff.; 466, 1 ff. (Poliander's codex, 1519-21). II, 114, 23 ff. (1519). VIII, 61, 5 ff. (1521). X, 1, I, 372, 14 ff.; X, 1, II, 92, 28 ff. (1522). VII, 363, 22 ff. (1521). Also from the lectures on the Psalms, IV, 191, 15 ff.; III, 44, 33 ff.

thinks of the Holy Spirit in terms of the scholastic tradition as a transcendent cause of a new (supernatural) nature in man producing infused grace (i.e. *caritas*—the sublimated idealistic urge). The Holy Spirit is instead proclaimed as the real presence of God. God himself as the Spirit is really present in the groanings of the anxious and tempted soul held in the grip of death and hell. Luther sternly and firmly contends that everything outside of God himself in the inner conflict allies itself with wrath against the sinner. No form of divine power other than that of God's own presence is available for the sinner in his conflict. No infused grace can groan for man with unutterable groanings. No one but God himself is able to do that.

Already we observe a deviation which we shall have occasion to prove further later on. The thought of a transcendent causality, which in scholasticism and in Lutheran orthodoxy is the fundamental form by which the relation of the Holy Spirit to man is considered, does not give any idea at all of Luther's view of the work of the Holy Spirit. No matter how often Luther uses the expressions that grew out of the traditional idea of causality, he does not consider the Holy Spirit as a transcendent cause of a really new (i.e. one of supernatural origin and power) human nature. Luther naturally thinks of the psychological phenomena as also wrought by God. But the general causality, which of course also must include the religio-psychological area, is not coextensive with the work of the Holy Spirit. The Holy Spirit is for Luther something more than a synonym for God's sole work in the field of religious psychology.

According to Luther the Holy Spirit is God's real, personal presence, not a transcendent cause. A preliminary comparison between Luther and the traditional view is here in order.

The Augustinian and scholastic doctrine of *caritas* has an idealistic structure. The idea of God is considered principally from the transcendental point of view. Whether the basis is the Thomistic, the Aristotelian-intellectual, or the Augustinian-voluntary metaphysics, in scholasticism God is viewed as the highest good, *summum bonum,* and as the highest possible goal for all idealistic urge in man. God is in principle distant, not in the biblical sense that he dwells in light unapproachable and alone from his position is able to conquer the distance, but he is the distant God whom man by nature is endowed to seek and to find and toward whom man's own idealistic striving is directed, even though it cannot reach its goal unless God intervenes and gives his grace. One has no grasp of medieval thought at all unless he keeps in mind how biblical and metaphysical ideas constantly cross and balance one another. But no matter how much the biblical idea of God in scholasticism is permitted to assert itself against the metaphysical basis as a neutralizing factor, the fact is that the fundamental view of the God-man relationship is that of idealistic metaphysics. The biblical thoughts are made to fit into this basic structure instead of the opposite. It is a basic assumption never to be relinquished in scholastic thinking that man's nature is endowed by the supernatural and that it strives toward it. That assumption is not superseded but rather confirmed by the fact that according to the biblical idea of salvation man cannot by his own strength, but only by the aid of grace reach the goal toward which he is naturally aimed. Nature cannot lift itself up to the level of the supernatural, but the supernatural must on the other hand bend down to nature and lift it up to its own level. This means that the basic metaphysical structure remains, and the biblical idea of grace is modified accordingly. This is seen by the fundamental role which the concept of merit plays in the scholastic doctrine of salvation. That man earns his salvation has nothing to do with Pelagianism. The scholastic doctrine of grace—even the Franciscan—is not Pelagian but very Augustinian. Although it is possible in the Franciscan doctrine of grace to speak of a certain merit, it is merit of a lower type. When we speak of the supernatural salvation, everything, really everything, is done by grace. Man is not able to do anything in himself. But that man by the aid of grace—and only by the aid of grace—merits or deserves salvation, simply means that God is the highest aim for the natural striving of man. The idea of merit is only the way in which the idealistic concept of the relationship to God must be expressed, when Old Testament legalistic piety, idealistic metaphysics, and salvation by the law have been combined into one. That man merits salvation means that with the aid of grace he has effectively accomplished the claim of the law and thus gained access to God. But the way of the law to God is the same as the way of the natural striving. The law is the revealed word, which in the form of the commandment sets off the way of idealistic urge to the true God, the highest good, from all the other ways by which the lower urge seeks to obtain the good of the lower type.

The scholastic system holds that God is the distant one, but the distant one toward whom man as man is going. The upward line characterizes the structure of this concept of God. The fellowship with God is brought about when man in harmony with his inner idealistic urge is lifted upward till he reaches God. In this sublimation the grace of God acts as a means. Grace is the God-given power to strive forward and upward to the distant goal of salvation. The scholastic idea of merit is so far from being Pelagian that it is much more correct to say that it is a genuine expression for the Augustinian doctrine of grace. The system of merit is the idealistic concept of God translated into the language of the law. All biblical ideas of grace are put into this fundamental idealistic concept. The incarnation and the atonement are put into the plan by the aid of the doctrine of satisfaction. Because of the objective satisfaction obtained by the atoning work of Christ the sacraments can infuse grace. The satisfactory suffering of Christ is the meritorious cause of the infused grace. The grace of the sacraments springs from the wounds of Christ.

But the real personal presence of God is not found in the grace which is gained by the satisfactory suffering of Christ and mediated by the sacraments. God remains the distant goal. Grace is the gift of God, the supernatural power granted through the sacrament, which lifts man up to the supernatural level where he can strive for the highest good and, thus striving by the constant aid of grace, reach upward on the meritorious ladder toward the distant goal, which is the eternal contemplation of God or the enjoyment of God.

It is very clear in this system how seriously Augustinianism is taken. Not one step may be taken on the way toward God without grace. In the final analysis the Franciscans and the Nominalists take this same stand. Even Biel's Pelagian-sounding doctrine about man's essential ability to love God *e puris naturalibus* has as its necessary complement the doctrine that God demands that every work performed by natural ability be adorned with the jewel of grace if it is to be acceptable to God. The doctrine of grace of the Middle Ages is definitely anti-Pelagian. But—and here the difference from Luther is very distinct—it is an idealistic anti-Pelagianism like Augustine's own doctrine of grace. God is essentially the distant goal for the ideal striving of man, and he remains that in the doctrine of grace, in the doctrine of incarnation, in the doctrine of the sacraments. The doctrine of the atonement is a typical example, for here it would seem most difficult to unite a biblical concept of salvation with idealistic metaphysics. But even here the idealistic point of view is made superior. By the teaching of the objective satisfaction the redemptive work of Christ is relegated into a historic distance. The present relation to the historic Christ is in scholasticism and the whole Middle Ages moved into the category of the imitation of Christ. And the Spirit is moved back into the metaphysical distance of transcendent causality. The act of redemption drawn back into the distant space of history and the work of the Spirit in supernatural causality's remoteness prove the essentially idealistic structure which is contained in the concept of God.

While God is thus drawn back from the immediate reality, there is another development, in that man's own nature is conceived as one essentially fitted for God—not in the sense which all biblical Christianity must hold, that man is created by God for fellowship with him, but in the sense that man's aptitude for fellowship with God is identified with man's higher and ideal nature. With this idealistic concept of God goes an idealistic anthropology, by which man is divided into a lower, sensually directed stratum and a higher stratum directed toward the spiritual realities of our nature. On the background of this anthropology the infused grace becomes synonymous with a sublimation of the higher nature of man. The infused love directs and perfects man's natural love of good. The higher nature of man therefore has a special affinity for the Spirit of God; it is in itself spiritual. This does not mean that it by its own aid can get beyond itself into the world of the Spirit of God, for then grace would be superfluous; it means that grace, when it is infused, is able to melt into the higher nature of man and perfect it in the supernatural sphere. This important contrast between flesh and spirit, a contrast, which as we have seen also has a decisive influence in Luther, is here ascribed to man's own nature as a contrast between its higher and lower strata.

We should not, as Protestants are prone to do, interpret this "synergism" between the Spirit of God and the spirit of man as raw Pelagianism. By its principle of analogy Thomism certainly is able to underscore the chasm between all created spirituality and the Spirit of God more clearly than is generally recognized by Protestant theologians. We Protestants have no right before the Middle Ages or before modern Roman Catholic theology to consider this underscoring of the chasm a mere trifle. But no matter how much the chasm is emphasized, the basic supposition by which the whole scholastic synthesis of metaphysics and faith, idealism and Bible, stands or falls is that both God's Spirit and the spirit of man are spirit, that there in man's own spirit is an urge toward the spiritual, and that it is the task of grace to sublimate this urge and guide it to its high goal. Without the supposition that all of nature strives for and moves toward grace, the whole scholastic doctrine of grace collapses. It is its basic structure we find here, the relation between God and man understood with God as a fixed point and man eternally moving upward toward this point. This is expressed in the well-known words of Augustine in the introduction to his *Confessions* that the heart is restless until it finds rest in God. With his basic structure the whole Roman Catholic interpretation of Christianity stands or falls. The synthesis between idealism and the Bible is only possible with such a basic structure.

However, our cursory examination of Luther's testimony about the Holy Spirit has already revealed to us the development of a completely different basic understanding of Christianity. This understanding we designate realism of revelation in contrast to the *caritas* idealism of the Middle Ages. For Luther God is not a distant God to whom the higher nature of man gradually lifts itself with the aid of grace. When Luther speaks about God's remoteness, as he does in the description of temptation and inner conflict, he is not thinking about the metaphysical concepts of *prima causa,* but God is remote as the one who in his wrath has turned himself away from man and left him in the power of death and hell. To Luther God is remote not as the infinitely high place of the first cause and highest good over *secundae causae* and over the longing of all creation for its source, but remote in the biblical sense, remote as the one who himself only is able to build a bridge over the chasm between him and man, but who also has done that very thing in Christ, and whom we therefore can designate as the remote only without Christ, but who in the form without Christ not only is very remote metaphysically speaking, but whose remoteness is his active, judging and deadening wrath. The concept of God which is presented in Luther's description of inner conflict, such as in *Operationes in psalmos,* cannot be reconciled with any idealistic metaphysics. It does not in its dynamic force permit a synthesis with any type of philosophical thinking.

In Luther God is not remote—except in his wrath without Christ. In Christ, where we meet God in all his grace, God is really and personally present. And God's presence does not mean a special affinity to man's higher nature. Luther's concept of the Holy Spirit eliminates every idea that our so-called "higher" and "spiritual" nature should have any special affinity to the Spirit of God. Luther's testimony about the Spirit takes the precisely opposite direction from all *caritas* idealism. Where man is at the very lowest point, where all man's spiritual and religious powers are paralyzed by the power of death, where all idealistic striving toward the highest good is destroyed by the accusation which is directed by God and all creation against the conscience of man, precisely there it is that God by his Spirit is present as the subject

24

of the unutterable groanings by which man conquers the accusation. This is biblical realism of revelation, and there can be no possible reconciliation between that and any kind of idealistic metaphysics.

In Luther's thought about the work of the Spirit in inner crisis there is a completely different concept of God from the one which is fundamental for the scholastic *caritas* idealism. Luther's view of God is characterized by God's own living and struggling presence in the midst of man's damnation and death. This is the view of God which undergirds Luther's interpretation of Romans 8:26. This is a realistic concept of God. In connection with this view of God salvation is understood as something present and immediate in the presence of God and not as a remote goal toward which one is gradually struggling by the aid of grace. Grace is the real presence of God himself. Where God is, there the whole salvation is already present. This does not mean that it is finished, but it means that it is certain.

The direction in the relation of God and man is here viewed in exact contrast to *caritas* idealism. There God was considered as the fixed point toward which man was constantly struggling. Here it is man who in his perdition is dead and motionless, while it is God who struggles for man and who seeks man in his distress and in the words of Nygren creates "the fellowship of God on the level of sin." This movement in the concept of God—characterized by Anders Nygren's agape in opposition to the upward struggling *eros* movement of *caritas* idealism—completely destroys the scheme of merit and the law. That God is truly present in the perdition and death of man and that he struggles for him signifies the end of the law and the coming of the gospel. But with this break in the order of the law and in the system of merit there is a realistic understanding of the redeeming work of Christ. The death and resurrection of Christ do not for Luther become an objective satisfaction given once and for all time to the Father. But the death and resurrection of Christ are a present reality in the conformity to Christ which is man's condition in the Spirit's work. The relationship to the historic Christ is not understood under the law as an imitation, but by the gospel as a conformity, not as a result of the initiative of man, but as the result of the *opus alienum* and *proprium* of God who is present.

In the same manner the work of the Spirit is realistically understood. In the midst of inner conflict and temptation the Spirit is truly near as intercessor and comforter. That means that God is near in the Spirit as the one who struggles for us and with us against our adversaries. It is not a supernatural force which has come from God, it is not the experience of a mystic sensation of him, it is not a God-produced, supernaturally supported urge toward him in the heart. It is no one and nothing but God himself in person fighting in the battle for us.

But this realism of revelation which characterizes the testimony of Luther concerning the Spirit also harmonizes with the realistic concept of man. The inner nature of fallen man is no longer understood as a religious force which directly points toward God. In the inner conflict every religious force is dead. In this inner conflict it is not just a matter of perfecting man's inner nature and sublimating his idealistic struggle, but he must himself be completely raised from the dead. Luther therefore does not recognize any idealistic division into two parts of man, a higher and a lower nature. The contrast between flesh and spirit is to Luther a contrast between the whole of man without the real presence of God and the whole of man within and under this real presence of God. There is therefore no real affinity between the spiritual nature of man and the Spirit of God. The implications of this thought will be studied later. In the final analysis it is this thought which is back of the different manners in which the enthusiasts and Luther evaluate *eusserlich ding*—the external sign. But this will be discussed in another connection.

In this preliminary account of Luther's interpretation of the scholastic doctrine about the Spirit's work as *infusio caritatis* we have thus been able to see the distinct outline of Luther's teaching about the Spirit in contrast to the traditional ideas. These traditional ideas we called *caritas* idealism, thus indicating the connection of the whole scholastic doctrine of grace with the idealistic-Christian *caritas* speculation. This contrast we shall attempt to define even more sharply as we penetrate deeper into the understanding of Luther's testimony about the Spirit. But already here we are able to conclude that the traditional concepts about the Spirit as the transcendent cause of a new (supernatural) nature infused by *caritas* (that is, sublimated *amor boni*) under no conditions contain the testimony of Luther about the Holy Spirit. A very different attitude in the real understanding of the relationship between God and man is here maintained, which is the reason why the similar expressions get one meaning in Luther and a different one in scholasticism. It cannot just be assumed that the many, often very brief and traditional-sounding references to the Spirit's work are to be understood from the "traditional" point of view. On the basis of the entirely different approach to the understanding of the Spirit's work that is brought out in the exegesis of Romans 8:26, the directly opposite conclusion emerges, the conclusion that the traditional terminology actually covers a new, "realistic" understanding of the Spirit, completely different from the traditional concept.

The Work of the Holy Spirit as Mediator of the Real Presence of Christ

In the preceding part we have learned that during the recasting of the *caritas* concept of Augustine Luther arrived at a concept of love to God which excluded every form of inherent idealistic urge. This love to God is hardened to self-hatred in the fire of inner conflict under the killing wrath of God, and could not be described in any other manner than as conformity to Christ in his cross, conflict, and death. This is a conformity, it should be noted, which is not brought about at the initiative of anything human, and which is not the result of any imitation of Christ or of any mystic technique, but which is nothing else than the work of the Holy Spirit. In the same manner the rescue of the believer from the death and hell of inner conflict is conforming to Christ in his resurrection.

When Luther, retaining the Augustinian terminology of inspiration, describes the work of the Holy Spirit as the infusion of the true love to God and then defines this love as a real conformity to Christ in his death and resurrection, it is because for Luther the work of the Holy Spirit always means a relationship to the living and present Christ. The love which is infused by the Holy Spirit is not an element in the soul but a real relationship to the truly present crucified and risen Christ. This is the contrast between imitation of and conformity to Christ. In the piety of imitation the believer is related to Christ as an idea. The believer himself is the active one who is struggling and seeking to realize the ideal which Christ represents. The activity of the piety of imitation corresponds to an idea of Christ; the passivity of the conformity-idea corresponds to the living and acting Christ.

In the preceding observations we have seen that the realistic understanding of the Spirit's work cannot be separated from the idea of conformity. Not before the experience of the total conformity with Christ in the inner conflict does the real presence of the Spirit become possible and real as the one who in groanings that cannot be uttered struggles for us against death and hell and the wrath of God. There is therefore an insoluble relationship between the real presence of the Holy Spirit and the presence of the crucified and risen Lord. How is this relationship to be understood? Are the Spirit and Christ only interchangeable ideas?

This is the question we intend to raise in this section.

In the two previously quoted passages, where Luther proclaims the Holy Spirit as the source of conformity to Christ, he underscores an expression which gives us direction, and which we must study more thoroughly: *per fidem Christi.*

Quod enim nos odimus et damnamus nunc concupiscentiam et eligimus charitatem, non nostrum est, Sed Dei donum, ideo dicit, quod Deus damnauit et destruxit in carne peccatum Et nos destruere facit per spiritum suum per fidem Christi *diffusum in cordibus nostris.*[22] *'Nisi quis renatus fuerit ex aqua et spiritu denuo, non potest intrare regnum celorum,' ac sic nihil reservat veteris*

---

22 *W. A.*, LVI, 360, 2 (1515-16).

hominis, sed totum destruit et facit novum usque ad odium sui eradicans penitus amorem sui per fidem Christi.[23]

In the term faith in Christ is expressed the connection between the Spirit and the real presence of Christ. Faith in Christ is the medium in which the Spirit does his destroying and creative work. But what does this formula contain?

Fides Christi means to Luther life as a redeemed reality under and by the presence of Christ. The Christian and Christ are one in faith in such a way that faith possesses the redemption of Christ as a direct reality. By faith in Christ we have the reality of his redemption as our own reality. His victory is our victory. This is not to be understood in a figurative sense, but in a real sense. His victory is ours in death. In our death we are by faith just as closely related to the risen and victorious Christ as his human nature in death was related to his living and victorious divine nature. Therefore he who believes in Christ really conquers over death when he enters with Christ into its darkness. Faith in Christ is a real union with the living Christ as a redeeming reality.[24]

We have purposely given first consideration to these very realistic expressions. For it is on the basis of the realistic understanding of the redeeming presence of Christ in faith that we are to understand Luther's often quoted expressions about the happy exchange between Christ and the believer by which Christ takes the sinner's sin and the sinner is given the righteousness of Christ. There are in these expressions no idea of a mere theoretical imputing. On the contrary the real fellowship between Christ and the believer is the necessary basis for the fact that the righteousness of Christ *truly* and not merely in our thinking is reckoned to us, and our sin *truly* is reckoned to Christ. The order is always the same: first faith's real fellowship with Christ, and after that the imputing

---

23 *W. A.*, LVII, Heb., 114, 2 (1517-18). See also LVI, 280, 3 ff. (1515-16); I, 140, 2 ff. (1514-17); II, 458, 24 ff. (1519), 502, 12 ff. (1519); X, 1, I, 49, 1 ff. (1522).

24 *W. A.*, IV, 697, 5 (1516) *per fidem Christo adheretur.* I, 593, 14 (1518) *per fidem Christi efficitur Christianus unus spiritus et unum cum Christo.* II, 146, 14 (1519) *qui credit in Christo, haeret in Christo estque unum cum Christo;* 535, 24 *Credere enim in Christo est eum induere, unum cum eo fieri.* X, 1, I, 319, 16 (1522) *Der glawbe mach auss Christo und dem menschen eyn ding, das beyder habe gemeyn werden.* See also I, 219, 30 ff. (1517) and VIII, 599, 2 ff. (1521).

of the effective righteousness of Christ. Of course "after that" is not a temporal reference but is to be understood from a logical point of view. There is naturally no interval of time between the moment faith lays hold on the real presence of Christ and the reckoning of his righteousness. The two factors are one sole concrete expression of faith. From a logical point of view, however, it is maintained that fellowship with Christ is a prerequiste to the reckoning. Otherwise faith, which lays hold on the reckoning of Christ's righteousness as truth, becomes a human performance—something man does of himself.

The forgiveness of sin and the reckoning of the righteousness of Christ, if it is to be gospel, can only be preached in such a way that Christ, who once finished the work of redemption, now is given to me as a gift, so that what I *first* recognize is that the living Christ is with me and thereby I may *also* know that he is my righteousness. For he would not be with me if he had not taken away the sin that separated me from him. Here faith in the forgiveness of sin is not the work of the law but a direct result of true fellowship with Christ. Our reckoning of the objective redemption as our righteousness must never become a condition for fellowship with Christ but must on the contrary rest completely on the foundation of this fellowship.

This insight into the connection between fellowship with Christ and justification was the essential content of Luther's well-known exegetical discovery with respect to the meaning of the word *justitia Dei,* the righteousness of God. This is especially evident in a sermon from the *Advent Sermon Book* of 1522, in which we find an account of the concept of God's righteousness, which is in complete harmony with Luther's exegetical discovery as this is described in the preface to the Wittenberg edition of 1545:[25] *Merck disses stuckle mit vleys, das, wo du ynn der schrifft findist das wortle: gottis gerechtickeytt, das du dasselb ia nit von der selbwesendenn ynnerlichen gerectickeyt gottis vorstehist, wie die papisten, auch viel heyliger veter geyrret haben, du wirst ssonst dafur erschrecken. Sondern wisse, das es heyst nach brauch der*

---

[25] *W. A.,* LIV, 185 ff.

schrifft die ausgossene gnad und barmhertzickeyt gottis durch Christum ynn uns, davon wyr fur yhm frum und gerecht werden geacht, *und heyst darumb gottis gerechtickeyt odder frumkeytt, das nit wyr, ssondern gott sie wirckt* yn unss *mit gnaden, gleych wie auch gotis werck, gotis weyssheytt, gottis sterck, gottis mund heyst, das er* ynn uns *wirckt unnd redet.*[26]

Here is the new element: the righteousness of God begins with his giving of life instead of demanding it, and thus God fulfills his own claim upon us. In a table talk Luther is therefore also able to describe the content of the discovery as the ability to distinguish between law and gospel. The righteousness of faith is of the gospel, it is not a righteousness of the law. The righteousness of the gospel is a righteousness which in the first place is the gift of God to us. The righteousness of the law is a righteousness which in the first place is our right before God and therefore, by virtue of this right, can lead to the gift of the fellowship of God. The righteousness of the gospel is Christ really present as a redeeming reality. The righteousness of the law is our own religion and morality, perhaps our very orthodox Lutheran religion and morality. Where we do not fully realize Christ's real and redeeming presence as the basis of faith and justification, there we change faith to religion and obedience to morality, i.e. to law, no matter how much we proclaim the orthodox doctrine that salvation is by faith alone because the righteousness of Christ is reckoned unto us. The orthodox doctrine is no guarantee that we have rightly distinguished between the law and the gospel. For the orthodox teaching may also be proclaimed as a law, and it has often been so proclaimed. And the danger of making the orthodox teaching into law grows in direct proportion to the extent that we neglect Luther's realistic message about the indwelling Christ.

The connection of these facts, on which we have dwelt so long because of the importance of having the right conception of *fides Christi*, is clearly formulated in Luther's teaching about *gratia* and *donum*, of which the earliest and most explicit development is found in the *Rationis Latomianae confutatio* of 1521. Luther here

---

[26] *W. A.,* X, 1, II, 36, 22 ff.

differentiates between *gratia* in the sense of *favor Dei* and *donum* in the sense of faith in Christ. The differentiation is noted in an exegesis of John 1:17, where grace is explained as *favor Dei* and truth is explained as *justitia,* i.e. *donum,* i.e. *fides Christi.* The opposite of grace is wrath, the opposite of the gift is sin. Grace and wrath are outside us, sin and faith are within us. Grace and wrath are total, sin and faith are partial. A man is always completely under grace or completely under wrath. But the man who is entirely under grace is never fully faithful, but always also sinful, so that faith under grace is in a constant struggle with sin. In these sentences we have an important contribution to the understanding of the previously mentioned and for Luther so important problem, *totus homo.* That which unifies a man's life and makes him a personality is not man's own inner striving or his own ethical and religious self-estimate, but it is God's evaluation. Man is made perfect and complete under God's grace or God's wrath.

This totality is that which unites *justus* with *peccator,* the gift of faith with sin, *donum (fides)* with *peccatum manens.* The divided nature of man *(simul justus et peccator)* is based on his totality (simul *justus et peccator*). For it is only through absolute unity with grace that faith is in constant struggle with sin. For if faith is to be understood as man's own act (as a religious activity), or if the good in us is to be understood as the work of our own will (as a moral activity), then they belong to the *totus homo* which has found its totality under the wrath of God, that is, "the old man." Everything that is our own, including our morality and religion, is a part of the old man and therefore cannot fight the old man. Only when faith is understood as the gift of God—and by that very term its exclusive source in God and its absolute difference from all religion are proven—is it able as the act of the new man to fight against the total old man.

The gift and grace therefore inseparably belong together. But grace is the greater of the two. For grace is eternal life itself. If the two could be separated and you were to choose one of them, then you would have to choose grace before the gift of faith. But it is impossible to separate them; it must not be done. And it is impossible even to think of a choice between the two. For without grace the gift is not the gift of God, and without the gift grace is not the grace of God. Therefore Luther has definitely stated that this separation and choice between grace and the gift of faith cannot in reality take place but is just an experiment in thought in order to clarify the logical relation between the two. That grace is a greater good than the gift only means that *gratia* is a source of the gift. It is the favor of God which makes faith in Christ the gift of God. If the presence of Christ with us and the faith which comes from this presence were not accompanied by the favor of God, this presence and this faith would not be the gift of God at all, even though Christ was sent by God. For not everything God sends is a gift. What he sends accompanied by his wrath is not his gift but his punishment.

It is very easy to see that there is such a logical connection between the concepts of grace and gift. Gifts come only from a gracious God. But when we understand that Luther is not talking about abstract ideas, but about the reality which the gracious God and faith are, then the relationship becomes more complicated than at first glance. The expression quoted, "accompanying justice," takes a somewhat different direction from the preceding account of the logical connection between grace and gift. Luther states this as follows: *Huic fidei et iustitiae comes est gratia seu misericordia, favor dei, contra iram, quae peccati comes est, ut omnis qui credit in Christum, habeat deum propitium.*[27] It even seems as though *"comes"* is to be understood as "successor" rather than "companion." Here grace is seen as a consequence of faith. He who believes in Christ receives, as a consequence of his faith, a gracious God. This is stated even more clearly in another place: *Gratia quidem nullum ibi peccatum habet, quia persona tota placet, donum autem peccatum habet quod expurget et expugnet, sed et persona non placet nec habet gratiam; nisi ob donum hoc modo peccatum expugnare laborans.*[28] Here grace does not appear as a greater good than the gift; but the gift, which is

---

[27] *W. A.,* VIII, 106, 6 ff.
[28] *W. A.,* VIII, 107, 32 ff.

faith struggling against sin, is a condition for grace. And that which is a condition for something else, must in a certain sense be considered bigger.

How can these complicated ideas be clarified?

If we study to the end the one idea: that grace is a greater good than the gift because it is eternal life itself, then we meet a predestinarian concept of God by which the free favor or wrath changes everything to either gift or punishment. This thought no doubt is intended to convey that the wrath of God, when it is effective, also changes Christ to a punishment instead of a gift. That such a thought is not completely outside Luther's idea is seen in his teaching in the *manducatio indignorum* by which the Christ who is truly present in the Lord's Supper becomes a curse to him who does not accept him in faith. As Luther so often states, on the basis of his experience in the struggles in the monastery, without grace, Christ changes himself into the hated judge before whom the sinner must tremble or whom he must mock. According to this idea, the Christ and his work seem to shrink to a mere symptom of either grace or wrath, and faith to an act that has no real significance.

The other idea: faith as a condition for grace, carried out to its final conclusion, leads naturally to the idea of faith as a sort of meritorious work which must be done by man before grace can enter.

It is evident that neither of these two ideas covers the concept of Luther, though the first undoubtedly is much closer to his view than the second. This much, however, is clear: a logical and complete conception of God and man's relation to him cannot be obtained by reading Luther's reflections about grace and gift. There is a hidden tension in these reflections that you meet in all Luther's theology: the tension between the theology of predestination and redemption.

On the one hand it is clear to Luther that both the grace and the wrath of God are realities. But where the wrath is, there is no gift and no Christ. On the other hand it is just as clear to him that Christ is our righteousness and the gift of God. Where Christ is there is no wrath. This tension you may try to iron out by logical reasoning, by making the wrath an illusion, removing the idea of predestination as a "foreign element" in Luther's thought, and letting the idea of the universality of salvation result in some form of apocatastasis. Or it is possible to retain the idea of the reality of wrath by a logical and clear construction of the relation between objective redemption and justification and thus to let the gulf between salvation and perdition, grace and wrath, be decided by man's own free attitude to the objectively accomplished redemption.

Luther did not take either of the two roads generally traveled by Lutheranism in the sixteenth and seventeenth centuries. Luther's concept of Christianity remained an uncurtailed theology of predestination and an uncurtailed theology of redemption. Therefore it also remained unclarified, logically speaking, just as all theology must be unsettled which does not by a logical short circuit destroy the wall of partition between *theologia viatorum* and *theologia beatorum*. It is therefore no wonder that this tension is so strongly emphasized where Luther develops the two most important ideas of his theology, grace and faith.

However, if we are not looking for a logical solution of the tension we shall discover that Luther does not lack a solution for the problem of grace and the gift. Their relation cannot be solved by logic, but it can be understood christologically. Christ is the connection between grace and the gift. Only in Christ is it possible to realize grace and the gift as reality. Without Christ these concepts are meaningless. We have no idea what grace is without Christ, the Christ who simultaneously is God's gift. The connection between these two obviously contrary thoughts is expressed thus in Christ: *Ita veritas ex Christo in nos fluens fides est, gratia fidem comitatur ob gratiam Christi.*[29]

Here it is seen what faith in Christ is: *veritas ex Christo in nos fluens.* Therefore faith may be described as a gift of God, because Christ himself as God's gift and God's truth (righteousness) is in us as a redemptive reality in such a way that truth (i.e. righteous-

---

[29] *W. A.,* VIII, 106, 30.

ness) flows from him into us. This is what we have expressed by the real redemptive presence of Christ.

In the very expression, *veritas ex Christo in nos fluens,* is stated the relation which we have constantly expressed between the real presence of Christ and the faith which lays hold on this reality.

But this truth of Christ (i.e. righteousness) which by faith flows into us is accompanied by grace by the favor of God. Why? The answer is: on account of the grace of Christ. Not on account of the *truth* of Christ, but on account of the *grace* of Christ. The difference between the two is not without significance. Let us assume that Luther had said, on account of the truth of Christ. We should then find ourselves within the rationally smooth frames of redemptive theology. In this case the righteousness of Christ was considered as a substitutionary, satisfying fulfillment of the law for man, by which he on our behalf earned salvation. We appropriate this merit by faith and in this way, by pure grace since the merit is Christ's and not ours, obtain salvation. The form of merit is not broken by this, the order of the law not conquered, but the work of Christ is understood on the basis of the demand of the law, not the demand of the law on the basis of the work of Christ. Thus faith is also easily understood as a sort of work of the law, that is, as a duty resting upon us which is the subjective condition of the fact that the righteousness of Christ can be reckoned unto us.

We read in Luther: on account of the grace of Christ. The expression permits a double paraphrasing. It can mean on account of the favor of God in Christ—and it can mean on account of the favor of Christ in us. No doubt Luther means both. Christ is not only man, but God and man. Therefore the favor of Christ always means the favor of God. Him to whom Christ turns in mercy, God also turns to in mercy. Yet it is also clear that the expression "favor of Christ" must mean favor of God in Christ since the Son of God is true man and as such is obliged to receive the grace of the Father. As God and man Christ is the Son who always has the favor of God upon him. As the Son Christ does not first as man have to deserve grace by fulfilling the law (a thing which *he* is able to do), but he already as God has grace in fullest

36

measure, long before he may think of fulfilling the law. Righteousness and grace are one in Christ, just as God and man are one (Romans 5:17). The form of merit and the demand of the law are already abolished. That he has never done anything but receive the Father's grace and therefore is not able to think of gaining anything by fulfilling the law is truly the righteousness of Christ.

By faith in Christ, Christ's righteousness flows into us—that righteousness which Christ is by the fact that he as one with his Father's favor and as the valid expression of that favor gives himself to us as a gift of the Father. It is this righteousness and nothing else that faith places before God as a fulfillment of the demands of the law. This righteousness, it is true, is another and an extraneous righteousness; for nothing of it comes from us, but is completely outside of us in Christ. Yet it is simultaneously a redemptive reality in us. For the work of the righteousness of Christ is not his fulfilling a private demand of the law in himself but his giving of himself to us on behalf of God. Christ has no other righteousness than the one he works in us. By that righteousness he fulfills the law. This righteousness is not only *Christi justitia*. Because it always exists in behalf of God and so also may be called God's own righteousness, it is also Christ's grace and Christ's favor, and—since he himself is God and man—God's grace and God's favor.

Therefore it may be written: *gratia (i.e. gratia Dei et Christi) fidem (sc. in qua veritas ex Christo in nos fluit, ɔ: in qua Christus se nobis dat) comittitur ob gratiam Christi (= gratiam patris in Christum et gratiam Christi patrisque in nos).* Here we find the form of merit and the order of the law really broken. Our righteousness is not at all under the sign of the law. As Luther stated in his *Table Talks* of 1542, referring to the experience in the tower, it is not a legal righteousness but an evangelical righteousness. Our righteousness consists in accepting Christ as a gift. For his own righteousness consists in living as the gift of God to us. Therefore to have his righteousness reckoned to us is the same as to receive him as a gift, and in receiving this gift live as the children of God, superior to and independent of all law, just as Christ did. Only in this way is the law fulfilled in us. Just as Christ alone fulfilled the law before he met the law in order to become eternally free and independent of it, so we also fulfill the law by beginning to be free and independent of it, because we in faith are sons together with Christ. The law is fulfilled only in free will. And it can be voluntarily fulfilled only by the one who in eternity has been free and independent of it. Here the form of merit is broken; the law is fulfilled in and with the fact that it has been overcome. In this manner the law and the fulfillment of the law are understood on the basis of the work of Christ conquering the law, not the work of Christ understood on the basis of the demands of the unconquered law.

Now it is clear how grace and the gift are united in the concept "faith of Christ" *(fides Christi)*. Grace and the gift are one in Christ. Even Christ's giving himself to us because of his deity-humanity is both God's own self-sacrifice for us (and therefore the expression of his grace toward us) and our righteousness before God, since Christ's self-sacrifice because of his deity-humanity is so divinely limitless that it permits all, even his own direct relationship of Son to God to be mutual for us and for him. Therefore he who is one with Christ by faith possesses in him both grace, which is God's merciful disposition toward us revealed in the self-sacrifice of Christ for us, and the gift. For the self-sacrifice of Christ means to us that war is declared against our whole old man and that faith stands beside Christ or rather: faith is in Christ and fights against our whole old man.

But what is the significance of this differentiation between grace and the gift? What has that to do with the understanding of the concept "faith of Christ" and the consequent understanding of the work of the Spirit in its connection with the thought of conformity? Is it not all rather an unnecessary complication of something so simple and uncomplicated as the experience of the grace of God?

That Luther in opposition to Augustine and his own former mode of expression gradually learns to distinguish sharply between grace and gift and place the first above the last, has this decisive significance that it makes it possible for him to retain the "foreign"

character of our righteousness without yielding the realistic understanding of the presence of Christ. The thoughts about grace and
gift therefore contain a vital contribution to Luther's understanding of faith of Christ and the work of the Spirit in connection
with the faith of Christ, as we shall presently see.

The Augustinian and scholastic teaching of justification which
Luther opposes in the writing against Latomus permits grace to
be a new nature in man, so that man is gradually changed to a
new man or lifted up from the natural level to the supernatural.
Righteousness in this manner becomes a "formal justice." Perhaps
it can be stated crudely that in the scholastic teaching grace results
in a gradual improvement of the old man until he insensibly has
become a new man. Luther's teaching of justification is characterized by a radical self-condemnation that brutally destroys all
thoughts about a gradual transition from the natural up into the
supernatural level or a slow process of becoming perfect. But this
is a foreign thought to scholasticism. This does not mean that
there is no room for a consciousness of sin in the scholastic system.
The whole system of the sacraments, for example, is orientated
on the basis of the problem of sin. But since for the scholastic the
difference between the sinner and God actually is identified with
the metaphysical difference between nature and supernature, the
consciousness of sin is not, as for Luther, a radical self-condemnation. Therefore it is possible to understand victory over sin and
sanctification as elements in the same smoothly transitory process
which gradually lifts man from the level of the natural to the level
of the supernatural. Man thus gradually becomes more and more
righteous. Grace gradually substitutes the new nature more and
more for the old sinful self. It is impossible in this sense to talk
about something like *simul justus et peccator.*

The Augustinian and scholastic teaching about grace presupposes a *Neoplatonizing* understanding of sin, according to which
sin comes from the lower sensual nature which is gradually pushed
aside by the higher, supernatural, and purely spiritual nature infused by grace. This idea of sin in connection with the corresponding idea of grace permits, even demands, a quantitative under-

standing of the struggle of sin and grace during a progressive process of justification. On the other hand, Luther's concept of sin places the nature of sin in the self-will, which very often is most deeply embedded right in this "higher" and spiritual nature. With such a concept of sin it was impossible to retain the physical* concept of grace. In the monastery Luther time and again experienced that grace did not mingle with his own nature, that although the sensual desire could be subdued, his self-will so much the more stubbornly encased itself in a pious suppression of the "lower" nature. The problem *peccatum manens* (in the sense of the ineradicable self-will that dwells especially in one's own piety) was constantly the stumbling block for him in his relation to the scholastic doctrine of grace. He was not helped until he learned to understand the righteousness of God as Christ himself, given us by God as a gift. This means that our righteousness is Christ, given us by God as a gift, in other words, something entirely outside ourselves, not only at first, but always. By this the judgment is pronounced upon our whole real self. Only that which is entirely outside of us, that is, in Christ, is righteous. Everything in ourselves, the highest as well as the lowest, is judged to the same extent. Simul *justus et peccator.*

Peccatum manens therefore was not a sign that grace was lost, but quite the opposite. The fact that the remaining sin is recognized as sin shows that righteousness is in us and has declared war upon our selfishness. For sin can be acknowledged as such only on the basis of faith; only where Christ is our only and alien righteousness

---

* The word "physical" does not mean a "materialistic" or "magic" concept of grace, though the Catholic doctrine of grace is sometimes so presented by Protestants. The word is used in its scholastic sense, and it has nothing to do with physics or materialism. The "nature" which is infused is, according to the Roman Catholic view, really a spiritual nature. The whole point in the scholastic physical doctrine of grace is based on the teaching that the supernatural grace which is infused is of a higher kind than the lower and sensual nature. It is therefore not only a bad distortion, but a complete lack of understanding of the inner intent of the scholastic doctrine of grace, when it is presented as an impersonal and magic form of religion compared to the personal religion of Protestantism. The infused grace has nothing to do with the dynamic substance which often is described in Protestant expositions of the history of dogma. It is truly very spiritual, for it is supernatural. But it is physical because it is viewed as a higher nature than that of man, a supernatural nature, which nevertheless by the infusion of grace makes a connection with man's natural nature and lifts it up into the level of the supernatural.

does our total selfishness become visible. The acknowledgment of sin, penitence, is the first reaction of righteousness by faith.

But this faith which clings to the alien righteousness of Christ is *in* man. It is there, not passively, but manifested in penitence. And just as we know it from the writing about good works, faith is constantly active in good works toward the neighbor. Faith is a completely new life, not just in theory, but a real, concrete new life with praise and prayer and the work in our calling here on earth.

It would be very easy to understand this new life as a *justitia formalis,* a new nature in us, that is, to go back to the old, scholastic, physical teaching of grace. How easy this is, is shown by the fact that two prominent Luther scholars, Karl Holl and Reinhold Seeberg, arrived at this view of Luther's doctrine of justification.

The distinction between grace and gift prevented Luther from taking that course. It helped him to see that faith and the new life in faith, in the very moment they are made a part of ourselves as our own *justitia formalis,* belong to the old man. For everyone who scrapes together things for himself, even *justitia* is dominated by the old man. But the old man together with what he has been able to gather of formal righteousness is entirely under the wrath of God. To want to own a *justitia formalis,* an outward righteousness, is a result of the inner essence of sin, the self-will, which in the shape of self-righteousness makes us *justitiarii.* It is true that faith in us and its new life are a part of our real self, a *part* of our *totus homo,* and that as such it struggles with the old man as the other *part.* But this is only true as long as faith (and the whole new life in faith) in the strictest sense is a gift of God. To the same extent that faith and its new life become our own possession, they become a part of our old man. That which makes us total human beings, the children of God, is not the gift as a part of ourselves, but grace as the favor of God which is inseparably connected with the gift. The favor of God is completely outside ourselves and continues to be so.

By designating grace as God's favor, Luther has been able to retain the concept of the alien character of righteousness without

41

weakening the present reality of this righteousness. Because Christ in us is an expression of the unchangeable favor of God which makes us into total human beings, we are here and now completely saved by faith which clings to Christ and which is always accompanied by the favor of God. It is not because this faith in Christ is a part of us, or a new nature in us, a better ego which is able to make demands upon God's favor. Luther's distinction between grace and gift makes it possible for him to retain the whole realistic concept of the presence of Christ in us and by faith as a really new life out of this reality. At the same time he is able to claim that this new life is not and never will be our own, but in the sense that it always remains the gift of God it continues to judge our real self as sinful. Faith—with Christ upon whom it lays hold, and with the new life in which it moves—is wholly the gift of God, that is, it points only toward the grace of God (God's favor) as our eternal life. And if faith is viewed from a different point of view, because it is a reality in us, it will be considered as something that belongs to us, and then it is no longer faith. Faith and its life belong to God, it is a gift of God. Therefore faith and its life constantly depend on grace. For the gift of God only becomes a reality through the grace of God.

Popularly the definition of grace is often given as the favor of God. Luther was not satisfied with this but added the idea of gift because a definition of grace as simply favor would change grace to an abstract idea and make faith in such an idea a work of the law. At one time in his lectures on Romans, Luther treats the idea of faith in Christ (Romans 3:22, *per fidem Christi,* by means of Christ's faith). He speaks here of some arrogant people who admit that they in themselves are unrighteous and who understand that they must be justified by God. But they refuse to be justified by God through Christ: "But we do not wish Christ because God can grant us his righteousness without Christ."[30] According to this view justification by grace is an abstract idea. When the grace of God is a universal truth then it is natural that God can forgive and

---

[30] *W. A.,* LVI, 255, 25. *Christum autem nolumus, potest nobis sine Christo Iustitiam suam dare.*

justify even without Christ. But Luther answers these people: "This God neither can nor will do, for Christ also is God. Righteousness is granted only through faith in Jesus Christ. Who shall stand against his will? If this is so, however, then is it an even greater arrogance not to want to be justified through Christ."[31] Luther says that Christ is also God. God is not an idea we have conceived ourselves. God has revealed himself in Christ. God is in Christ. Christ is God. Therefore the grace of God is not a truth which can be separated from Christ but it is an event as the gift of God in Christ. Therefore grace can be had only by faith in Christ as the gift of God. Grace and gift are interdependent on each other. Without grace, the gift, our faith and the new life in faith become a part of our old man and as such worthy of the severest judgment of God. Without the gift grace becomes an abstract idea, a universal truth, the acceptance of which will always be a work of the law.

In summing up these thoughts it may be stated that the separation between grace and gift means that Christ as the living and redeeming reality present in us is seen as the essential purpose and plan in the nature of faith. Grace and gift meet in Christ as the present, redeeming reality. This is the basis for both the separation between them and their mutual partnership. Grace is solely revealed in Christ, and it is revealed in Christ as the gift of God. It is because Christ is the gift of God that faith also is the gift of God. Faith is created as a gift of God when Christ is accepted as the gift of God, and in no other way. It is not created by some secret metaphysical causality. Faith lives completely and alone by the real presence of Christ. To the same extent that Christ is really present, faith is really present, and only to that extent.

By this digression in our thoughts about grace and gift we have been able to show that the thought of Christ's real and redeeming presence is not an accidental definition of the nature of faith, but it is the decisive distinguishing mark of the substance of faith. To

---

[31] *Non vult neque potest. Quia Christus quoque Deus est. Non dabitur nisi per fidem Ihesu Christi. Sic statutum est. Sic placet Deo et non mutabitur. Quis eius voluntati resistet? Hocipso magis superbia est non per Christum velle Iustificari.*

Luther faith is always primarily faith in Christ. Only on the basis of this definition is it possible to understand the other qualities of faith.

We would not, however, give a really clear picture of the faith of Christ as the medium by which the Holy Spirit makes us conform to Christ if we stopped with the above explanation. So far we have purposely, in a one-sided manner, emphasized the last part of the genitive construction, *fides Christi,* faith *of Christ.* It is, however, just as important for our understanding of the work of the Holy Spirit in this connection to emphasize the first part of the construction: *faith* of Christ.

Although we consistently have emphasized the real presence of Christ in faith, we have not thereby denied, but rather substantiated that here we have a type of reality which is different from all other reality. It is not a distortion of Luther's concept of faith to say that the reality of Christ is so totally different from all other forms of reality that, from an ordinary view of reality, it must appear as an illusion. Our general understanding of reality is brought about by the senses—human experience based on observation and reason. The understanding of reality by faith is contrary to that of the senses. It is absolutely opposite to all understanding by experience. *Ideo arduissima res est fides Christi, quia est raptus et translacio ab omnibus, que sentit intus et foris, in ea, que nec intus nec foris sentit, scil. in invisibilem, altissimum, incomprehensibilem Deum.*[32] The real redeeming presence of Christ in us is God's reality, the invisible, high and incomprehensible reality of God. Therefore it must be at war with every reality which is visible, manageable, and comprehensible. Faith of Christ is not just a "religious experience." This modern category would no doubt be characterized by Luther as inner knowledge from which faith actually is a transfer and result. Faith is a strenuous affair, because it is always *argumentum non apparentium.* It does not have the reality of Christ in the feeling but in the word. This other mark of distinction of faith is just as decisive as the first one. If it is not constantly placed together with the first, all talk about the

---

[32] *W. A.,* LVII, Heb., 144, 10 (1517-18).

real presence of Christ is changed to an unclearly formulated and in every sense unevangelical Christ mysticism. The many-sided and too much emphasized phrase "Christ mysticism" should in any case be kept as far away as possible from Luther's presentation of the real presence of Christ. Luther does not know of any other reality of Christ than that of faith. And faith is a strenuous affair, *argumentum non apparentium*. But—and this must never be forgotten—faith, as *argumentum non apparentium*, is in contact with God and with Christ as a present reality, not just as a mere idea. The *res non apparentes* of faith is simultaneously *res valde praesentes* of faith.

The second decisive characteristic of *fides Christi* (faith of Christ) is that which we meet in the definition of the reality of Christ as *justitia aliena* or *extranea*, a definition which we already touched during the study of Luther's thoughts about *gratia* and *donum*. This definition must not be overlooked if we are to get the right impression of what Luther understands by the real presence of Christ in faith. Already in the first comments on Romans 1:1 in Luther's great lectures on Romans we meet this conception. The fact that he places it there proves how important it is to him that this aspect of the reality of Christ be not overlooked. "But God does not wish to save us through our own righteousness and wisdom but through a righteousness and wisdom that comes from outside us—that has not had its source in us and come to us from ourselves, but comes instead from somewhere without—that does not spring from our earth but comes from heaven. Thus any righteousness that comes completely from outside and is totally strange to us must be learned."[33]

The concept *extra nos* has its origin in the fundamental characteristic of the concept of the righteousness of God: in Christ. Our righteousness is outside us only because it is in Christ. "As he says through the prophet Jeremiah, 'that thou root out, pull down, and destroy' all that is in us, i.e. all that stems from us and is found in

---

[33] *W. A.*, LVI, 158, 10. *Deus enim nos non per domesticam, sed per extraneam Justitiam et sapientiam vult salvare, Non que veniat et nascatur ex nobis, Sed que aliunde veniat in nos, Non que in terra nostra oritur, Sed que de celo venit. Igitur omnino Externa et aliena Justitia oportet erudiri.*

us."[34] What alien righteousness is, is seen in the stories of the calling of Abraham and of Israel's exodus from Egypt. These stories not only show our escape from vice to virtue but rather our escape from our own virtue to the grace of Christ. A Christian should not call anything his own. It is not even permissible for a Christian to consider the spiritual virtues his own, making him worthy of being justified by God because of them; the Christian must always stand before God as the one who has nothing.

Here we meet the idea which we know from the writing against Latomus, that the alien righteousness in Christ, that which is named *donum* by Luther, is present for us only in the grace of God. Only in the expectation of the naked graciousness of God can we "possess" the righteousness which is "alien" and which is in Christ. That Christ is our righteousness means that he is the gift of God to us. But a gift is only possessed through the grace of the giver. Therefore to possess this righteousness is the same as possessing nothing which may be called righteousness, but to be directed to the graciousness of God. That God for the sake of Christ's righteousness considers us as righteous is only another way of saying that he gives us Christ as a gift. But receiving Christ as a gift and living in the expectation of God's graciousness must therefore of necessity be accompanied by self-condemnation and the renunciation not only of the material but also the spiritual benefits. There are many who as Jews and heretics readily renounce material benefits for God's sake. But, Luther continues, *qui dextraria bona i.e. bona spiritualia et opera Iusta velint nihil reputare propter Christi Iustitiam acquirendam, pauci sunt. Hoc enim Judei et heretici non possunt. Et tamen nisi fiat, nemo salvabitur.*[35]

These sentences implicitly contain Luther's understanding of the double concept *caro-spiritus,* flesh and spirit, with which we previously have become acquainted through the development of Luther's thoughts about hatred of oneself and about grace and the gift. The righteousness from the outside qualifies the new man as

---

34 *W. A.*, LVI, 158, 6. *Sicut per Iheremiam dicit: 'Vt euellas, destruas, dissipes et disperdas' Scil omnia, que in nobis sunt (i.e. que nobis ex nobis et in nobis placent).*

35 *W. A.*, LVI, 159, 17 ff. (1515-16).

a man completely under the grace of God. Only when the new man's righteousness in the strictest sense is outside of himself in Christ is it possible to distinguish the new man from the old man. The new man's character consists in his possessing nothing in himself but all things outside of himself, in Christ. Only so is the new man able to condemn himself and forgive himself. The new man is at the same time both righteousness and sin, because his righteousness is Christ, and as faith lays hold of Christ it forces the new man to recognize his own flesh, his old man, as completely condemned by the presence of Christ as his outside righteousness.

This presentation of the idea of an alien righteousness (*justitia aliena*) on the basis of the lecture to the Romans is further proven by Luther's writings the following years. These thoughts are especially clearly developed in the sermons from that part of the postils in 1522 which is edited by Luther himself. Here the thought of an alien righteousness is developed in a very rich and broad presentation. Christ is the hen under whose wings we as the chicks seek protection. He alone is our righteousness. Nothing of our own, not even what we have from God, not even faith itself, when it is considered our own piety, will be recognized by God. Only the vicarious Christ is our righteousness, our atonement, and our protection against the wrath of God.[36] *Drumb hutt dich fur falschen predigen, ya, auch fur falschem glawben, kreuch inn Christum, hallt dich unter seyne flugel, bleyb unter seynem deckel, las nit deyn, ssondern seyne gerechtigkeyt unnd seyne gnad deyn deckell seyn, das du nit durch deyne empfangene gnade, sondern, wie alhie S. Pau. sagt, durch seyne gnade eyn erbe seyist des ewigen lebens.*[37] The grace which has been received, faith itself as a living power in the heart, is not righteousness before God, but only Christ, comprehended by faith. *Denn wer fur gottis gericht bestehen solt, ist nit gnug, das er sagt: ich glewb und hab gnad; denn allis, was ynn yhm ist, mag yhn nitt gnugsam schutzen, ssondern er beutt demselben gericht entgegen Christus eygene*

---

[36] *W. A.*, X, 1, I, 48, 9 ff.; 124, 18-128, 10; 281, 4-284, 17; 291, 10-292, 9; 475, 10 ff. Also II, 146, 29 ff.; 491, 13 ff. (1519); VIII, 606, 37 ff.; 608, 19 ff. (1521).

[37] *W. A.*, X, 1, I, 126, 13.

gerechtickeyt, die lest er mit gottis gericht handlen, die besteht mit allen ehren fur yhm ewiglich . . . Unter dieselben kreucht, schmuckt unnd duckt er sich, trawett und glawbt on allen tzweyffell, sie werd yhm behallten; sso geschichts auch alsso, wirtt durch denselben glawben behallten, nicht umb seynen oder solchs glawben willen, ssondern umb Christi und seyner gerechtickeyt willen, darunder er sich ergibt.[38]

We learn that the two chief marks of distinction in faith of Christ meet in the concept alien righteousness (*justitia aliena*). Our righteousness is an alien righteousness and as such an invisible righteousness, which we are unable to possess as a quality of distinction in ourselves. But an alien righteousness can be retained only in utter dependence upon God's grace alone. Our alien righteousness is real and actual only in faith. And faith is *arduissima res* because it is removed from all that which is visible and thrown upon the invisible, upon the most high incomprehensible God. In the very moment the difference between alien and legal righteousness was removed, in the very moment grace according to Augustinian and scholastic views was understood as an infused quality, righteousness would no longer be an object of faith, but it would be an object of *intus sentire*, of a religious experience. It would no longer be an *arduissima res* to keep this righteousness. This righteousness would be viewed from the rational point of view which would make it acceptable to our ethical consciousness. For it is no *arduissima res* to claim that God accepts us as his children because he in advance sees the completion of a true germ of perfection, whose present and living power we already here and now are able to experience. This would mean that we could build a good conscience on the basis of a definite psychological quality and its potential expansion. But Luther has, as we have seen, clearly prevented such a weakened interpretation. God is gracious and reckons us justified not because of the grace received and not because of faith, but because of the alien righteousness of God. The message of alien righteousness preserves the characteristics of faith of Christ as faith, as *argumentum non apparentium*, as

[38] *W. A.*, X, 1, I, 281, 16, 21.

arduissima res. Our righteousness is as alien righteousness always a hidden righteousness, hidden with Christ in God, hidden under its visible contrast. Righteousness is not visible to us, but sin is.[39] In a hidden sense our righteousness belongs to that world of *non apparentia* which, as opposed to all experience and feeling, can be comprehended only in faith.

But the expression "alien righteousness" proves at the same time the characteristics of faith in Christ as Christ's faith. Our righteousness is alien because it is in Christ, yes, is Christ himself personally. *Ideo Recte dixi, quod Extrinsecum nobis est omne bonum nostrum, quod est Christus.*[40] *Solus Christus est et Justitia et veritas eius.*[41] In this connection it should be noted that the two words, *aliena* and *extranea,* do not in Luther signify our righteousness as a mere theoretical imputation of Christ's substitutionary satisfaction understood as an actual contribution which is different from the living Christ himself. The view of alien righteousness which is based on the system merit and law, and which is known in later Lutheran orthodoxy, is not found in Luther. Our alien righteousness is to Luther the living personal Christ, not a certain abstract contribution of Christ. And this Christ is not away from us somewhere *in foro coeli* but dwells in us by faith. Therefore it is possible for Luther in describing the alien righteousness to use the form *aliena justitia ab extra infusa,* or *Que aliunde veniat in nos.*[42] As one with Christ himself, alien righteousness belongs simultaneously to *non apparentia* and to *valde praesentia.*[43]

This account of the important parts of Luther's concept of faith in Christ is in no way an exhaustive analysis of Luther's concept of faith, but its purpose has been to indicate the most important points regarding the concept which Luther uses to show the means by which the Holy Spirit makes us conform to Christ. This is done through faith in Christ *per fidem Christi,* says Luther.

---

[39] *W. A.,* LVI, 392, 28 (1515-16). Also I, 140, 13 ff.; 148, 35 ff.; 543, 25 ff. (1514-17, 1516, 1518).

[40] *W. A.,* LVI, 279, 22 ff. (1515-16).

[41] *W. A.,* LVI, 247, 1 ff. (1515-16).

[42] *W. A.,* LVI, 247, 1 ff.; I, 140, 8 ff. (1514-17); 219, 30 ff. (1517).

[43] *W. A.,* I, 219, 30 (1517) and I, 140, 8. Also LVI, 247, 1; I, 149, 33 (1516); I, 191, 23 ff. (1517).

We are now able to see what this answer contains. We can now go back to the main question, our point of departure in this section: What does it really mean that the Holy Spirit does its mortifying and regenerating work by making us conform to the death and resurrection of Christ? Luther's answer, *per fidem Christi,* is no longer a strange unintelligible phrase, but we have through the preceding analysis gained an understanding of the extent to which this short phrase contains Luther's whole interpretation of the gospel. Faith in Christ is the real presence of Christ in us as a redeeming reality, which as an invisible and incomprehensible but divine reality tears us away from and places us in contrast to all other reality.

After this account of Luther's concept of faith in Christ, we learn that the idea of conformity is simply another expression for faith in Christ. Luther does not hold that conformity to Christ and faith in Christ are two different attitudes which we might possibly place in a cause and effect relationship to one another, but that they are simply identical. We have previously observed the sharp distinction between imitation and conformity. The only way in which conformity with Christ is real as something different from the imitation of Christ is in faith in Christ. All conformity with Christ which is not identical with faith in Christ is imitation.

He who is taken away from all other reality, away from all inward and outward experience, away from all legal righteousness and who is called to rely on the pure mercy of God alone, to rely on an alien righteousness, to a life which is hidden with Christ in God by its invisible contrast, while everything he can see in himself as good and strong is relegated to the state of "flesh" by this alien righteousness, as captured by the sinful self-will, such a person is poor as Christ was poor. He is exposed to the vicissitudes of life in the same way Christ was, he is defenseless and in the grip of death and inner conflict in the same manner as Christ was. The description of faith in Christ as a very strenuous affair is identical with the description of hatred of self and the conformity of inner conflict with the suffering Christ. This identity of faith in Christ and conformity to Christ is contained in Luther's description of

faith as a *suspendi in cruce*. But in this poverty and defenseless-
ness, death and inner conflict, the believer in Christ is rich and
strong and alive just as Christ was. For he possesses the redeeming
reality of Christ as present in himself just as Christ in his defense-
lessness, death, and inner conflict had in himself the living presence
of God the Father. In the very poverty and impotence of the
Christian faith the fusion of God's alien and God's very own work
takes place, just as it did in the death and resurrection of Christ.

The conformity to Christ is not created by any form of imitation.
The imitation of Christ is a result of human endeavor. But all
human endeavor and strength belongs to the flesh, that is, it seeks
that which is of man. And he who tries to be pious by imitating
Christ will not be Christlike at all. For Christ was not one who
endeavored. He who in his endeavor to become Christlike tries to
build up his own piety will not become like unto Christ, for Christ
does not build anything up for himself. To be like Christ is therefore not something we may will or aspire toward. All such desire
and aspiration is the very opposite of what Christ wants. To be
like unto Christ is something which one arrives at without merit
or premeditation, by faith alone. For faith is not something pre-
meditated but the redeeming presence of Christ which overpowers
man. Faith in Christ is the only likeness with Christ that is not
infected with piety of imitation.

In the first lecture on the Psalms and the lectures on the Letter
to the Romans, this identity of faith in Christ and conformity to
Christ is not so often clearly expressed. But it is implied everywhere in the way both ideas are developed. By the constant reference to the Holy Spirit as the source, the Lutheran idea of
conformity is clearly distinguished from every form of imitation-
piety based on the law. The content of conformity to Christ is for
Luther in this first period less marked by outward tribulations,
even though they also belong to *Crux*, than by spiritual conflicts
culminating in the tropologically interpreted descent to hell. In
this manner the conformity to Christ in his inner conflict and fear
of death really harmonizes with that condemnation of the old man
which is the content of the concept "faith in Christ," understood

as the insistence of alien righteousness. In the same manner, conformity to Christ in his resurrection must become harmonious with faith in Christ, understood as the gift of God, as the reality of the new man. Conversely, where faith in Christ is described as a real faith, as a strenuous affair and a separation from all visible reality, from all that which is controlled by outward as well as inward experience, such a faith with its hatred of oneself is really the same as conformity to Christ in his suffering, inner conflict, and cross. Gradually the word "faith" gains prominence in Luther and supplants the words about the conformity concept which are a little too strong a reminder of imitation-piety and mysticism. But this does not mean that that content in the concept of faith which is identical with the idea of conformity disappears. On the contrary, this content is an indispensable part of the concept "faith in Christ." This shifting toward a stronger emphasis on faith and the fusing of the content of the idea of conformity into the very concept of faith can be seen in the second lectures on the Psalms, 1519-21. The similarity of conformity to Christ and faith in Christ is emphasized much more in the second lectures than in the first and in the lectures on the Epistle to the Romans. *Coniungit enim fides animam cum invisibili, ineffabili, innominabili, aeterno, incogitabili verbo dei simulque separat ab omnibus visibilibus, et haec* (NB!) *est Crux et phase domini.*[44] This unity of faith and conformity can be called *living Christ. Non enim que loquitur, sed qui vivit Ihesum Christum crucifixum, salvus erit. At vivere Christum, hoc est crucifigi, ut Gal 1. dixit 'Christo crucifixus sum, vivo iam non ego, vivit vero in me Christus.'*[45]

We are then finally able to summarize the result of the study of the relationship between faith in Christ and conformity to Christ. That the Holy Spirit is doing his creative work by making us conform to Christ in his death and resurrection can signify only one thing: the Holy Spirit makes the crucified and risen Christ such a present and redeeming reality to us that faith in Christ and con-

---

[44] *W. A.*, V, 69, 29. See also V, 72, 38; V, 108, 17; V, 128, 37; V, 176, 22; V, 639, 2; I, 141, 11 (1514-17).
[45] *W. A.*, V, 81, 7.

formity to Christ spring directly from this reality. The description in the previous section of the work of the Spirit in inner conflict is continued here. The work of leading us into inner conflict, which tempers our faith, leads us to hatred of self, and gives us perseverance under the alien work of God, in order to prepare us to receive Christ as our alien righteousness, this work the Spirit does by making the crucified and risen Christ a living and redeeming reality for us. It is this reality of Christ which makes it possible for a sinner to do the impossible: to lay hold on Christ as his alien righteousness. It is this reality of Christ which makes it possible for a sinner to hate and judge himself because the reality of Christ has overpowered him and permitted him to live by Christ as his alien righteousness. It is because of the reality of Christ alone that not all faith and all self-condemnation are a desperate struggle to become like Christ. There is only this difference between faith and works, between conformity and imitation: in the first case, when we speak of faith and conformity, it is the reality of Christ who overpowers the sinner and enters into an active relationship with him so that both faith and conformity are a state of suffering in this active reality of Christ; in the other case, where the question is that of imitation and works, it is the sinner who is active and who by his endeavor to be like Christ tries to approach God. It is the real presence of Christ which alone unites the grace and the gift into an unbreakable unity, in such a way that the grace of God does not become a timeless general truth which faith is duty bound to regard as truth, but becomes an event in and with the real presence of Christ, and this in such a way that our new life in faith is not considered as a part of an improved old man, but is a gift outside us in the living Christ.

But it is the work of the Spirit to realize this real presence of Christ. In the last section we observed that Luther's view of the Spirit was realistic. Luther holds that the Spirit is God himself who is near and struggling in us right in the midst of our condemnation and death. He is near in the sense that he takes the crucified and risen Christ out of the remoteness of history and heavenly glory and places him as a living and redeeming reality in the midst of our life with its suffering, inner conflict, and death. The very fact that our life is able to contain suffering, inner conflict, and death that are not a mere series of events in our life but the entrance to restoration and to life, is because of the fact that the Spirit has put the crucified and risen Christ into our life as a present reality. The groanings which cannot be uttered are themselves the most elementary manifestation of the faith in Christ which flees from all its own to God, that is, to Christ, through whom alone God has graciously come to meet us. We shall later see how even these groanings are produced by the real presence of Christ. The connection Luther has made between the Holy Spirit and conformity to Christ—and thereby also faith in Christ—shows that Luther knows of no influence of the Spirit which is not Christ-centered. The Spirit always works by making Christ present. But the Spirit is not identical with Christ. For it is the Spirit alone who makes a distinction between Christ and Christ—between the distant Christ of imitation and history and the present Christ of faith and conformity.

Without the work of the Spirit, Christ is not a redeeming reality. Without the work of the Spirit, Christ remains an example and faith a historical faith. Without the work of the Spirit with our faith, with our Christ, and with our new life, we remain under the law, which ultimately means under the wrath of God. And there all our faith and all our Christian piety, our whole new life, no matter how beautiful it may look, are nothing else than a desperate bondage under the law and the wrath of God. But where the Spirit does its work and makes Christ really present, there man is under grace because Christ as the gift of God is near. And under grace man is completely saved and becomes entirely well-pleasing to God, wholly believing and wholly certain, because all his righteousness and all his salvation are outside himself in the present Christ as the alien righteousness. And there under grace, in Christ, everything is gospel, everything life and blessedness, even though no new life is visible at all, but all the new life is hidden with Christ in God, even though there is no other righteousness than the alien, which can only be possessed in the faith which is a strenuous affair and leads us away from all things visible. There man is at peace and happy in God, even though he finds nothing in his soul but the pangs of inner conflict and the groanings which cannot be uttered. These groanings are a much greater, stronger, and purer faith and holiness than the most perfect sanctification under the law where the Spirit is not present. For the Spirit and Christ are truly present in these groanings, but in the imitation only man himself and his strenuous slavery under the law are present.

The difference between the true faith and the mere form of imitation, between the truly present Christ and the Christ who is only imagined, is a difference which in no way can be demonstrated psychologically and experimentally. It is a difference which in no way is open to observation or feeling. The Holy Spirit alone by its presence makes this difference. It is this that Luther describes by the concept "experience." In order to understand what it means that the entire work of the Spirit is making the crucified and risen Christ truly present in us, we must study this problem in more detail. We shall do so in the following section.

The Holy Spirit and the Experience of Christ

The subject, "faith and experience," is one of the most frequently discussed problems in the modern study of Luther.[46] Nevertheless, the treatment of the theme has often been marked by the introduction of an attitude that is foreign to Luther. One example of this is the attempt that has been made to make Luther responsible for a "religious transcendentalism" (R. Seeberg and also in part Karl Holl and Torsten Bohlin) or for a dialectic anti-psychological attitude (Emil Brunner). The problem whether faith is a psychological experience or not—as if it is possible to talk of a faith which is not also a psychological experience—is a sham prob-

---

[46] Torsten Bohlin, pp. 431-483. H. M. Müller, *Erfahrung und Glaube bei Luther.* R. Seeberg, *Lehrbuch der Dogmengeschichte,* 4th ed., IV, I, pp. 272-294. W. v. Loewenich, pp. 96-147. S. v. Engeström, *"Tro och Erfarenhet,"* pp. 76-92, and the same author's *Luthers trosbegrepp,* pp. 172-228. Emil Brunner, *Die Mystik und das Wort,* as well as *Erlebnis, Erkenntnis und Glaube.*

lem which is of no consequence in Luther's thinking. Luther is thoroughly convinced that faith is in opposition to natural experience, and that it is a *true experience*. But the decisive point in understanding Luther in this matter is that his thoughts must not be pressed into a concept of experience brought in from other sources. If Luther's own concept of experience is used, it will readily be seen that the two "lines" which students so often try to find in Luther's idea of faith and experience, the line of criticism and the line of experience, are not two lines at all, but one. The experience of *faith* is first produced as distinct from *all* other experience, the religious experience included, but it is still *experience*.

That which is first observed when one studies the comments of the young Luther on experience is the close connection Luther finds between experience and inner conflict. These two words seem almost to be synonymous. Already here we notice the unity of the two "lines." For the inner conflict signifies the crisis for *all* natural experience (not least the religious!), for every form of *"sensus,"* feeling. He who wants to attend the school of experience will first be led out into the darkness of inner conflict.

Experience belongs to inner conflict, because experience signifies a confirmation of reality in contrast to imagination, to that which is merely thought or pictured or mere words. That faith is experience means that it is concerned with reality and not with mere thoughts, words, or pictures.[47] The inner conflict, however, is that test which proves whether faith and its objects were just a fancy, an imaginary affair, or reality. That which is able to stand the fiery test of inner conflict is confirmed as reality and thus is experience. But this experience under the test of inner conflict is given only by the Holy Spirit. We have already seen that, through Luther's life and thinking, his conception of the inner conflict became so radical that nothing but the groanings of the Holy Spirit on our behalf to Christ and the Father can survive the attacks of death and

---

[47] *W. A.*, IX, 611, 6; VII, 546, 24 (1521); also VIII, 385, 28 ff. (1521) and X, 1, I, 302, 1 ff. (1522).

hell during the inner conflict. Experience means that the intercession of the Spirit for us proves that the Christ, in whom we take refuge and with whom we are made to conform in the groanings that cannot be uttered, is a reality and not a dream. What belongs only to our own piety is lost in the inner conflict as a dream. The witness of the Holy Spirit, however, will stand in the midst of the test of inner conflict as experienced reality. Therefore Luther in a sentence often quoted from the exposition of the Magnificat describes experience as the school of the Holy Spirit.

The content of Luther's concept of experience is very clear. Experience means a proof of reality in opposition to a dream, word, fancy. Thus when Christ by the witness of the Spirit is proven to be reality as apart from a mere idea (thought, word, fancy), this is the experience of faith. But since the object of faith is Christ as God's revelation in the flesh, the experience of faith must necessarily appear as a contrast to all other experience. In the experience of faith the witness of God's Spirit struggles with our own reason and senses. But the experience of faith is a true *experience*. In the man in whom the experience of faith by the witness of the Spirit is produced, there is no doubt that he is face to face with reality, yes, face to face with a reality which is over and above all other reality. Therefore Luther does not hesitate to say that he who believes in Christ shall feel the Holy Spirit in himself. For the feeling of the Holy Spirit is nothing else than to hear his groanings that cannot be uttered and to have part in them.

Hereby the meaning of the concept "experience" in understanding Luther's view of the work of the Holy Spirit is clarified. That experience and the Holy Spirit may be used interchangeably means that only the Holy Spirit is able to take all that which is proclaimed and heard of Christ from the sphere of idealism into the palpable reality. No one but the Spirit is able to make the proper distinction between the mere historical faith and the genuine and justifying faith. Time and again Luther emphasizes that it is not sufficient to accept the teaching of the Scriptures and the church about Christ as correct. Even the demons and ungodly men believe in this manner. But it is all useless if I am not able with complete certainty to claim that it has been done for me.[48] But whether the one or the other type of faith becomes mine depends solely on whether the Holy Spirit himself bears witness in me.[49] No one but God the Holy Spirit is able to unite the certainty of experience to the outward acceptance of the truth of the gospel story. Without this experience given by the Holy Spirit the whole content of the gospel remains in the sphere of history and the ideal. The whole thing is then just an idea, just words and pictures, just the recollection of a distant past, at best an example which may be imitated. It may also be expressed in this manner: only the Holy Spirit can make the message about Christ into the gospel. Without the experience which the Spirit alone can give, the message about Christ remains law; without the experience given by the Spirit our relation to the Word is simply imitation.

Luther's ideas about experience as the school of the Holy Spirit are therefore closely connected with the whole set of thoughts which are summed up in the pair of words *spiritus-littera. Littera* is the word and our relation to it as long as the Spirit of God is absent. Then the word and our relation to it are completely dominated by the law, which emphasizes our own performance. The law is designated "letter" because it does not give that which it signifies; it is content to describe that which it demands but is not able to produce. The law may well be called spiritual in so far as it *characterizes* the Spirit. But it must be satisfied to characterize it; it cannot give the Spirit. The law (*lex litterae*) and the gospel (*lex spiritus*) divide themselves from each other as the symbol from that which it symbolizes and as the word from the thing described by the word.[50] The law can never of itself give more than the mere word and symbol. It may beautifully describe the life we shall live. But the description does not have within itself the power to realize that which is described. The law is only a symbol, but it is not the

48 *W. A.*, LVII, Heb., 169, 10. Also LVI, 370, 10 ff. (1515-16); II, 693, 21 ff. (1519); IX, 440, 22 ff.; 442, 23 ff. (Poliander's codex, 1519-21); X, 1, I, 71 ff. (1522).

49 *W. A.*, LVI, 370, 7 (1515-16). Also LVII, Heb., 169, 18 ff. (1517-18); IX, 632, 1 ff., 11 ff. (Poliander's codex).

50 *W. A.*, II, 552, 3 (1519). II, 500, 6 *Lex literae et lex spiritus differunt, sicut signum et signatum, sicut verbum et res.* Also IV, 58, 15 ff. (1513-15) and LVI, 408, 6 ff. (1515-16).

thing which it symbolizes. The law can describe the ideal. But the ideal described remains a mere word so long as the Spirit is absent. Only where the Spirit is, do the words become alive, the symbol, the thing itself, and the law, the gospel.[51] The distinction between law and the gospel therefore is not a distinction between two stages of development of history of religion—for instance, it is impossible simply to identify the law with the Old Testament and the gospel with the New Testament, since both may become either law or gospel to us according to the concrete situation in which we meet them. The distinction between law and gospel is a distinction between letter and spirit, between a mere description of the life which is demanded of us and the realization of the life which is described. Even the message about Christ may become law if the Spirit does not turn the content of the message into present reality, into experience. Where this does not take place, the message about Christ remains *letter*, which describes an ideal which judges us, but which does not help us reach this ideal.[52] Using the concept of experience, the same idea may be expressed thus: Without the Spirit the message of Christ remains an idea (*Bild, Geschwätz, Traum*), but with the Spirit it becomes an experienced reality. Law-letter-idea are placed over against gospel-spirit-experience.

After the foregoing study and description of Luther's understanding of the concepts "faith in Christ" and "experience," we see more clearly the type of connection which exists between the work of the Holy Spirit who creates the new life and conformity to Christ, and faith in Christ which is the whole content of the new life. In other words, we see clearly the relation between the truly present Holy Spirit and the truly present Christ in the work of the Spirit.

When the real presence of Christ in the faith in Christ and the conformity to Christ was so strongly emphasized as in the previous section, it might seem as if the idea about the Holy Spirit was pushed into the background at the expense of the thought "Christ

---

[51] *W. A.*, LVI, 338, 18 (1515-16); 338, 27; 338, 25; also III, 456, 14 ff. (1513-15).
[52] *W. A.*, LVI, 336, 25; 338, 20; II, 551, 28; also III, 457, 4 ff.; IV, 174, 21 ff. (1513-15).

in us." It might seem as if the idea about the Holy Spirit either became a mere duplication of the thought of the indwelling Christ or a superfluous interpolation between the believer and the truly present Christ. The more formal and traditional manner in which Luther often speaks of the Spirit in contrast to the strong witness of Christ found in his theology of the cross may seem to make such a view natural. However, we are now able to see that this is not the case. On the contrary, it is the real presence of the Holy Spirit alone which determines whether Christ is *truly* present in faith, or whether it is the idea about him to which man adheres. It is only the presence of the Spirit which determines whether our presumed faith and our new life are that which they pretend to be or just a copy, an imitation, under the dominion of the law. For there is no difference in the psychological description between true and copied faith, the truly new life and the imitation. It is true that it is psychologically possible to point out the contrast between the spontaneous joy which marks the life based on the reality of redemption and the bitter necessity which marks the bondage under the law. But the psychologist who looks at things from without—and this includes the religious psychologist who looks at his own piety from without so long that it becomes to him a psychological object—cannot see that when the man in inner conflict groans, "My God, my God, why has thou forsaken me?" it is true joy and willing obedience, because it is the Spirit himself who groans within him and thereby makes him conform to Christ. Nor is he able to see that the willing fasting and joyful church attendance of the Pharisee is nothing but compulsion and bitterness because the Spirit is absent and it all takes place without the reality of redemption. This is because, psychologically speaking, the exercise of piety carries with it a certain joy and inner satisfaction when it becomes flesh and blood in a man through the habit of many years. The psychologist is as little able to distinguish between real and depicted faith as the logician is able to see the difference between the content of the concepts of one hundred real and one hundred imagined dollars. That which makes the difference, the presence of the Holy Spirit, will never be evident to the observation of the psychologist, but only to the experience of faith.

Thus the connection between the work of the Holy Spirit and the real presence of Christ is the fact that there never can be a real presence of Christ except in and by the work of the Spirit. Without the work of the Spirit, Christ is only present as an idea. That which without the work of the Spirit may call itself the real presence of Christ in contrast to a mere idea of Christ is not Christ himself but mysticism's mistaken substitution of "a life in Christ" for Christ himself.

Luther's realistic concept of the work of the Spirit thus signifies a limitation on two sides. First of all, the work of the Spirit as a mediator of the experience of Christ reveals every relation to Christ which is not experience, which does not rest on the mediating, real and redeeming presence of Christ, as imitation, as a relation to Christ as an idea, as law. In the second place, the work of the Holy Spirit as mediator of faith in Christ reveals any identification of the present Christ with certain psychological qualities as a falsification of the witness of Christ. The Christ present in faith is Christ himself, who as our alien righteousness is completely different from every substantiated psychical quality. The idea of the Holy Spirit is therefore not a rather superfluous interpolation but is on the contrary an underlining of the fundamental thought of all Luther's views of the presence of Christ in faith. To Luther the Holy Spirit, viewed realistically, is the sphere wherein Christ alone can be truly present because of faith. All other talk about the presence of Christ outside this sphere is either spiritualistic mysticism of Christ or moralistic imitation of Christ.

The connection between the thought of the Holy Spirit as creator of the new life and faith in Christ and conformity to Christ as its content can be concisely formulated in this way: the Holy Spirit is a real and divine sphere of revelation in which the risen Christ alone is present as a present and redeeming reality. Outside of this real and divine sphere Christ is only an idea. Thus we understand that Luther does not permit the Spirit and Christ to be separated. Luther does not know any other Spirit than the Spirit of Christ, that Spirit in which the living Christ is with us. And the living Christ manifests himself to us only in the Spirit; there is no other living Christ.

In this connection between the Spirit of Christ and the "pneumatic" Christ, Luther's close relationship to biblical realism of revelation becomes very evident. But this also proves how far the study of Luther has deviated from Luther himself. So much of this study has shown no interest in Luther's witness of the Holy Spirit. It has been taken as a matter of course that what he said about the Spirit should be understood on the basis of "tradition." And all this proves that the concept which has been given of Luther's theology has been marked by the attitudes that Luther critically resisted. The new Luther research has been moving between an interpretation based on imitation and moralization (Karl Holl is the classic representative of this type) and an interpretation related to a mystical and psychical concept (Erich Seeberg is the main spokesman here). Both of these tendencies are based on the traditional orthodox concept of Luther which is characterized by the forcing of Luther's original realism of revelation into a strongly intellectual, forensic idea of justification, in which Christ himself becomes merely the ideological content of the doctrine of objective satisfaction with its legalistic demand of acceptance in faith, and into a theological formula about the mystical union, which often becomes almost a nonevangelical mysticism of Christ. In the orthodox conception the real presence of Christ and justification, which in Luther's thinking were a complete unity, became two opposing tendencies which it became a problem to reconcile, that is, the *religious* interest of the doctrine of justification and the *ethical* interest of the doctrine of sanctification. That it was possible in our heritage from Luther to find such opposing tendencies was because Luther's realism of revelation had been lost. When it was no longer understood that Christ is only present in the Spirit, all ideas of "Christ in us" were understood on the basis of a mystical Christ, as one with substantiated psychical qualities, and not as Christ himself—our alien but living righteousness. Therefore all ideas about Christ in us had to be kept strictly apart from the doctrine of justification so that these presumed psychical qualities should not become the motive of justification. A consequence of this was that the doctrine of justification in its extreme forensic form threatened to become an abstract doctrine, which operated by the weight of the law, and which made Christ a mere idea, that is, the main content of the pure doctrine of the objective satisfaction, while the living Christ was relegated to a special doctrinal point in the presentation of sanctification or regeneration. It was not seen that in spite of all polemics against Catholicism this was a concept which was very close to the medieval idea of love. Nor was it noticed that faith, in the sense of appropriating an objectively finished atonement, came to hold a position equal to that of justifying grace as a means by which man might be united with the truly distant Christ. But the consistency with which the doctrine of the mystical union forced itself forward as a reaction against the abstractly considered, forensic doctrine of justification indicated that the orthodox doctrine of justification was no longer saturated with Luther's realism of revelation.

This split in the orthodox transmission of the heritage of Luther has had its aftereffects even in the newest concept of Luther. One group supports and defends the real intention in the forensic doctrine of justification (W. Walther, J. v.Walter, Fr. Gogarten, H. M. Müller, Werner Elert, S. v.Engeström, etc.), while the reaction against this interpretation of Luther is the mystical union idea, claimed by its proponents to be the integrating part of Luther's evangelical view (E. Hirsch, E. Vogelsang, E. Seeberg, etc.). As a rule it is hopeless to judge between the conflicting parties, because both sides start their thinking from a viewpoint that is not Luther's at all. The only way out of this very unfruitful question is found in the rediscovery of Luther's realistic understanding of the Spirit. In this realistic understanding all idealistic and "mystic" interpretation of Luther is eliminated, and thereby the unfruitful struggle between the tendencies of Melanchthon and Osiander in Luther research is revealed as the result of a question that is entirely foreign to Luther. Therefore we believe that the correct understanding of Luther's account of the Holy Spirit will mean more than a correction of a single point in Luther's theology. It will mean the elimination of a long series of unfortunate problematic positions which have constantly retarded students of Luther in the attempt to penetrate into Luther's own thoughts. In this way it also will provide a new and fruitful addition to a more true and complete understanding of Luther.

The Holy Spirit and Empirical or Actual Piety[53]

Our presentation of Luther's thoughts thus far contains in itself an inner contradiction, which we must study more closely. We started by demonstrating that the basis for Luther's presentation of the work of the Spirit in the period we are considering was the Augustinian view that the Spirit is the source of the love infused in the heart by God and that this is the cause of the new life. Then we showed how these Augustinian forms were filled with a new content, which made Luther's message about the Holy Spirit entirely different from the Augustinian and the scholastic. We saw how the traditional idealism of love was replaced by a biblical realism of revelation. In the account of the concepts "faith in Christ" and "experience," it was clearly seen that the new life which the Spirit produces is concentrated in the living Christ as our alien righteousness and thus in a sense completely outside of ourselves. But then there arises the problem of all that which we generally understand as "the new life," and which in some way or other must be found in the Augustinian forms used by Luther. If

---

53 In this section we use the expression "empirical piety" in a very definite sense. The word "piety" is selected in place of "righteousness" to show that the reality which it covers is ambiguous in its relation to the concept of righteousness (that is, before God). By "empirical *righteousness*" we are to understand a real psychical quality which without any question may be regarded as righteousness before God, a "formal" righteousness. (In this sense Luther knows of no empirical righteousness. When Luther nevertheless is able to speak of an empirical righteousness as distinguished from the righteousness reckoned to us from Christ, he does not thereby mean a righteousness which in itself possesses the God-pleasing quality, but an empirical piety, which by being covered with the alien righteousness of Christ shall be able to stand before God.) Furthermore, the word "piety" is supposed to express man's relation to God (the religious, "faith") and also the definite relation to the neighbor which is brought about by the relation to God (the ethical, "love"). Our language does not have a word which directly expresses the unity of faith and love (religion and morals) which is fundamental for Luther. We have selected the word "piety" to convey this meaning.

it is true that the work of the Spirit as shown by the previous presentation is so exclusive and that it is limited to mediating the real presence of Christ, the question may be asked if it then is at all possible to speak about the Spirit as the source of a new life, a *really* new life. The really new life must be more than the groanings of the inner conflict, the faith that takes refuge in the alien righteousness of Christ as a subjective correlate to the thought about Christ's real presence in the Spirit. It seems as if the definition we have used thus far for Luther's understanding of love infused by the Spirit has been rather negative. We have seen that love to God was hatred of self, that it was conformity to Christ in inner conflict, that it consisted in taking refuge to an alien righteousness. But is it possible that all those negative statements fully describe what Luther means when, in his Augustinian manner, he states that love and the new life by the Spirit is poured into our hearts? Is our contention correct when we say that the traditional Augustinian forms in Luther shall be understood on the basis of a new realistic view of the Spirit's work? Does it not rather signify a not permissible systematizing of truly disparate elements in Luther's thought? Would it not be simpler just to register that in the young Luther there are different ways by which the Spirit is understood, ways independent of one another and impossible to unite? Could we not say that the traditional Augustinian view, a theology of the Spirit which is related to mysticism, and possibly a third view, which springs from Luther's own experience, seem to be struggling in the young Luther without ever being fused into a complete whole? Must we not admit that the positive element of the idea of conformity (not only with Christ in his death but also in his resurrection) has not come into its own, nor has the positive content of the concept of faith (that it is not only a taking refuge in Christ's alien righteousness, but also the author and perfecter of all good works)? And must not therefore the previous presentation of the Holy Spirit's place in connection with the idea of conformity and with the concept of faith in Christ be considered out of line?

These questions cannot be overlooked. They compel us to study the problem of Luther's view of the connection between the Holy Spirit and empirical piety, that is, faith (and the life in which it moves) as a psychical reality. That Luther truly reckons with such an empirical piety as inextricably bound up with the relation to God, that the faith of which he speaks, while it takes refuge in the alien righteousness, yet expresses itself in prayer, praise, and service, this needs no further documentation. We need only think of the classic presentation of this in the "Sermon on Good Works." But when empirical piety is not to be understood as man's own endeavor, is it not then necessary to understand the Holy Spirit as a sort of supernatural causality which produces this piety? And does this not lead one into thoughts that are very close to the Augustinian idealism of love and the scholastic doctrine of grace, to which we placed Luther in such strong opposition? Is it really true that such thoughts are not found in Luther, or that he regards them of no value?

We must attempt to clarify these questions by submitting to a thorough investigation Luther's whole view of empirical piety and the relation of this view to the previously described realistic understanding of the work of the Spirit.

In order to get into this problem more easily, we shall use a different method from the previous one. We shall first attempt to analyze the problem from a deductive point of view on the basis of the thoughts we have come to know in the previous study. We shall especially consider the thoughts about grace and gift, about faith in Christ and alien righteousness. Then by referring to the sources we shall determine to what degree our deductions may be justified.

First we recall what we previously proved, that Luther sharply distinguishes between Christ in us and all empirical piety. Christ in us is not identical with all real divine influences in the soul. On the contrary, Christ in us is constantly an alien righteousness clearly separated from all our own empirical piety. This piety is only righteousness before God to the same degree and extent that it is covered by Christ's alien righteousness. Viewed independently of Christ's alien righteousness our own empirical piety is solely an expression of the old man, that is, "flesh." It is "Spirit" and an expression of the new man only when it lives and moves in faith, which signifies a taking leave of all things visible and thereby also of our own righteousness in favor of Christ's alien righteousness. Or stated somewhat differently: viewed as *appropriation* our own empirical piety is flesh belonging to the old man and thereby under the wrath of God. Viewed as *donum* (gift) it is Spirit belonging to the new man and thereby under the grace of God. Viewed as appropriation our righteousness is passive or resting (that is, in the old man), and thereby it is doomed to death. Viewed as a gift it is struggling against the old man, and thereby it lives in the hope of resurrection.

It is this understanding of the contrast between the old and the new man which constitutes the difference between Luther and all pietism. In the pietistic preaching of conversion and sanctification the new man is identified with the converted man. The new man is himself the real, psychologically changed, new individual which the conversion has produced in man and which sanctification has continued to establish. According to this view, the new in the converted man is a psychological reality, a legal righteousness. According to Luther the "new" in the new man is the living Christ himself who as alien righteousness classifies the whole old man, including both his conversion and sanctification, as flesh and old man, if it is not covered by the alien righteousness of Christ.[54] In the pietistic preaching of conversion, the struggle between the old and the new man is a struggle between two different strata in man, the lower strata which comes from the life before conversion and the higher strata which comes by the life created by conversion. The struggle between the old and the new man is in Luther a struggle between Christ truly present in faith and our whole real self, including both the lower and the higher strata, both the converted and the unconverted parts of man. For the pietist neither the old man nor the new man is the whole man, but each is a part of man. According to Luther, one cannot understand what the new

---

[54] *W. A.*, LVI, 280, 8 (1515-16). Ragnar Bring, *Gesetz und Evangelium*, pp. 49-71.

and the old man are until it is understood that each one of them in the strictest sense is the whole man.

However, this does not mean that Luther denies the presence of real works of grace in the soul. Luther sufficiently emphasizes that faith and the new man live and move in praise, prayer, and the works of the vocation to which man is called. But empirical piety is not in itself the new man (as pietism holds) nor is it our righteousness before God; it is only a fruit of the Spirit, an expression of the new man. Therefore it presupposes faith and the new man. In the very moment man as a whole man is flesh and not Spirit, in the very moment that man seeks his own, empirical piety is changed into self-righteousness, to a merit by which the sinner tries to justify himself before God, that is, to the fundamental sin which is pride. No quality of the soul whatever, no religious experience at all, no pietistic conversion, for example, possesses in itself a definite value before God. Its value in every moment depends (as do all other human qualities) upon man's actual attitude to God as a person and as a whole man. If a man is sinful, then his other qualities are all sinful. If a man as a person is righteous, is Spirit, that is, if he in that very moment is leaving all his own in favor of Christ's alien righteousness, all his good qualities are the fruits of the Spirit, and his sins are forgiven and removed, because Christ's alien righteousness covers man. If man as a person is flesh, that is, if he at that very moment is seeking his own, then all his qualities, including the good ones, are the fruits of the flesh. His sins are then without the forgiveness of Christ because the egocentric man in his flesh pushes Christ away and wants to be just in himself. In this case his ethical and religious qualities become merits by which he seeks to cover his own sins and be just before God; that is, they become the sophisticated sins of pride. This selfsame empirical quality, for instance a pietistically understood conversion or sanctification, may in the same man in one moment be the fruit of the Spirit, as when in faith he leaves all his own (including this state of conversion or sanctification) in favor of the alien righteousness of Christ, when he lives trusting solely in the pure mercy of God and therefore views all his own religious and

ethical qualities, if he is able to find any such at all, as the undeserved gifts of God. But in the next moment the same empirical
quality, the same state of conversion and sanctification, may be the
fruit of the flesh, as when he seeks his own and thereby changes
this real quality from being the undeserved gift of God to being
his own appropriation, by which he justifies himself before God
and man.

Once this difference between Luther and all pietism has been
realized, it becomes clear that it is impossible to agree with
Karl Holl and R. Seeberg in speaking of a gradual real *Gerechtmachung* (process of justification) as the content of Luther's doctrine of justification. The source of Holl's and Seeberg's presentation, as we shall see later, is the pietistic fundamental attitude
which the "positive" theology of the nineteenth and twentieth centuries inherited partly from Schleiermacher and partly from the
revivalistic pietism of the nineteenth century. How far removed
this presentation is from Luther's thinking is revealed by the fact
that for these scholars the progress of sanctification is identified
with a real progressive process of justification. Luther speaks both
of empirical piety (faith, which is man's righteousness before God,
and in which man lives and moves in real praise, prayer, and work)
and of progress in sanctification (the Spirit becomes more and
more master over the flesh). But in Luther these two lines of
thought are not so blended that the progress of sanctification can
be forthwith identified with the increase in empirical piety as is
done in Holl's and Seeberg's interpretation of Luther. In Luther
empirical piety is always ambiguous. It may in every moment be
either an expression of the Spirit or of the flesh, according to
whether the man in that particular moment is either Spirit or
flesh. Therefore it is impossible to speak of an unambiguous
growth in the plan of real justification. When Luther speaks about
the progress of sanctification, he thinks of something entirely different. He thinks of the fact that man on the way between baptism
and resurrection constantly and anew takes leave of himself to take
refuge in Christ's alien righteousness. In this refuge of faith in
Christ, man is *Spirit*, new man, and all his past life up to this

moment is at once considered as flesh, as old man. In this manner the Spirit, who knows only Christ's alien righteousness, is constantly struggling against the flesh, which wants to hold on to its own past life as an appropriation, its own righteousness. In the resurrection man shall be completely Spirit. Then the Spirit shall no longer struggle against the flesh. But on the way between baptism and resurrection man is Spirit and flesh. But the closer man gets to resurrection, the more the old man is destroyed and annihilated, and the new man, which has only Christ's alien righteousness, is the only possibility left. Therefore sanctification is a constant progress, a growing mastery of the Spirit over the flesh. But *this* progress is not the same as the increase of empirical piety. For empirical piety is ambiguous. It may constantly be qualified in two ways, and therefore so may its growth. The progress of sanctification is not, as is the increase of empirical piety, an object of psychological observation, but an object of faith and hope. It is not evident to oneself and others, but it is hid with Christ in God.

After this purely deductive presentation, which has been a mere repetition and further development from the previous sections, we turn to the sources to see if they use the same language. We are particularly interested in two points in the previous deductive presentation: first, the sharp distinction between the growth of empirical piety and progressive sanctification; and secondly, the emphasis upon the Spirit's creation of the new life as consisting alone in the mediation of Christ's real presence as our alien righteousness. Does Luther himself speak in this manner?

That the young Luther (and the older too) speaks about a progress in sanctification cannot be denied. Luther gives expression to this matter in several clear illustrations, such as the patient who gradually is healed, the soldier who is in constant struggle, the leaven which gradually leavens the dough, etc.[55] The Christian's life is described as a constant progress and not a standing still. This constant progress makes justification something that

---

[55] *W. A.*, LVI, 258, 20 ff.; 272, 3 ff.; 350, 27 ff.; 351, 17 ff.; 441, 14 ff.; 513, 17 ff.; 347, 11 ff.; (1515-16). III, 453, 22 (1513-15). VII, 338, 29 ff. (1521). R. Hermann, pp. 10-18.

cannot be obtained and possessed once and for all, but which again and again must be sought and prayed for anew. "He that is righteous, let him be righteous still" (Rev. 22:11) is a passage to which Luther constantly refers in this connection. The progress in the Christian life is identical with the struggle that is always going on between righteousness and sin, between the Spirit and the flesh in every man, because every man is at the same moment just and sinful.

But what kind of righteousness is it which struggles in the believer against sin and gradually overcomes it? Is it the empirical piety? Luther has some expressions which might be so interpreted. As an illustration, Luther may state that sin in the Christian is daily decreasing by the renewing of the mind.[56] This expression could indicate that Luther conceives of sin as being decreased by the gradual progress of empirical piety. Luther may express it in this way that sin, when the Spirit comes into power, no longer is *peccatum regnans*, but *peccatum regnatum*. The "good works" are not works which in themselves are without sin, but those works that are struggling against sin.

But when the good works are not without sin, how can they struggle against sin? And can these works really be the same as a real righteousness when they are not without sin? After all, it was the actual struggle against sin that made the works good and not the indwelling goodness of the works that caused the struggle against sin.

But what then is it that struggles against sin? It is righteousness. But this righteousness is not a legal righteousness, not an empirical righteousness, but it is the righteousness which is the gift of God, the faith in Christ. Therefore the empirical piety is not in itself unambiguous. The front on which the empirical piety is carried in the struggle between the flesh and the Spirit cannot be determined by an investigation of its own quality, but is entirely dependent upon the root from which it springs. It is faith in

---

[56] *W. A.*, I, 534, 13 (1518) *peccatum manet usque ad mortem, licet quottidie miniatur per renovationem mentis de die in diem.* Also I, 555, 1 ff. (1518); VI, 27, 13 ff. (1520).

Christ, understood as a gift of God, which alone struggles against sin. And only by being united with faith in Christ can empirical piety itself struggle against sin. Faith in Christ as a gift of God is, according to the previous analysis of the thoughts of grace and gift, inseparably united with the grace of God *(gratia—favor Dei).* It is the grace of God accompanying faith in Christ as a gift which alone is able to justify our real self. A so-called real "righteousness" is really a concept which cannot at all be made a part of Luther's whole view; for this concept presupposes that the content of our real self can be given an unambiguous valuation in relation to God and once and for all time be designated by the name righteousness. But this is not the case at all. The whole content of our real self is constantly exposed to a double evaluation from God's point of view, namely from his severity and from his kindness. There is no real righteousness at all under the severe judgment of God. Under the kindness of God, even our real self is just, but only by the grace of God. Here we recall that Luther thought of grace and wrath as total reactions from God. When man is entirely under grace, he is of course simultaneously both just and sinful. But because he is fully under grace, righteousness is solely the gift of God, and sin is mastered and dead, yes, even harmless, according to Luther. For under grace there is no wrath at all. Conversely it is true that man, when he is fully under wrath, in the same sense is a mixture of good and evil. But just as sin under grace is dead because of the gift of God in us, in the same sense our whole empirical piety under wrath is infected and impure because of that part in us which is opposed to God, and which is accompanied by his wrath. This last situation is the one we have learned to know through the description of inner conflict. In inner conflict man is completely under the wrath of God, and therefore his whole real self, which includes also his empirical piety, is judged by the severity of God. Sin is entirely in the power of death and hell. In inner conflict it is the law that rules in the conscience. From its mastery, only the Spirit can deliver us, as we have previously seen. When the Spirit delivers us, it does not mean that sin and death cease to exist. On the contrary, they continue and remain. But it means that he delivers us from the law of death and sin and from its tyranny. He moves us with all our sin and death from wrath to grace.

By this we understand the difference between *peccatum regnans* and *peccatum regnatum*. *Peccatum regnans* is sin under the wrath of God. By the power of the law it governs the conscience in inner conflict as a tyrant, so that no real righteousness is permitted to live. But the power of the law is broken by grace, so that sin must yield itself to be placed under righteousness. It becomes a dead sin because it becomes a sin without law. Sin under grace becomes a sin which is not reckoned unto us. Nonimputation is an expression for the mastery which grace and gift work in us. Under this mastery, sin becomes *peccatum regnatum* and thereby also *nonimputatum*.

Whether the struggle against sin takes place in us or not is not determined by our own real qualification in general, but by our *situation*: whether we are under grace and there possess as the gift of God that faith in Christ which can struggle against sin, which under grace is degraded to be sin that is not imputed and not mastering; or whether we find ourselves under wrath and thereby the power of the law in the conscience is robbed of every iota of real righteousness. But since our empirical piety in itself is ambiguous and does not receive its qualification as righteous or sinful except through its situation under grace or wrath, then it is clear how impossible it is to understand Luther's idea about progress in sanctification as identical with an increase in "real righteousness." Such an increase is itself ambiguous. It might be either an increasing pharisaism or an increase in the fear of God. In the situation of inner conflict it is revealed as a deception.

But how then shall "growth" and "progress" be understood? We must constantly maintain that righteousness which grows and struggles and thus overcomes sin is a gift—faith in Christ—in other words, the alien righteousness on which faith in Christ lays hold. It is *this* which grows and overcomes as it struggles, not a supposedly empirical piety. This alien righteousness on which faith in Christ lays hold is the living Christ himself. He it is who in a living and struggling presence overcomes sin. It is not something that his presence has made to grow in us.

This is seen in the first place by the fact that the progress of which Luther speaks in these connections is equivalent to losing all that is our own and starting anew again and again: *proficere, hos est semper a novo incipere*. This constant starting anew which embodies the essence of progress embraces the constant taking refuge in the righteousness of Christ. Luther says in his first lecture on the Psalms that every "righteousness" is sin in relation to the righteousness which must be won in the next moment. *Terminus a quo* for progress in sin, which is our whole real self in any one moment; *terminus ad quem* is righteousness, which is in Christ. Therefore progress may also be said to be a constant seeking and praying, not only in words, but also in works. Thus all just works ("real" righteousness!) are a preparation for the next step in justification. Therefore this progress and movement are also characterized by the fact that no saint can reckon himself as just, but he must pray and hope to be justified by that God who looks to the humbled ones. Thus God is marvelous in his saints when he reckons as righteous sinners who admit they are sinners and judges the righteous who consider themselves righteous. It can also be put this way: "The saints are inwardly always sinners, therefore they are always being justified outwardly. The hypocrites, however, are always holy within themselves and, for this reason, outwardly they are always sinners.

"Inwardly, I say, as we are in ourselves, in our own eyes, in our own opinion—outwardly, however, as we are with God and as we stand in his judgment. Thus we are outwardly justified not from within ourselves, not from our own works, but solely through the power of divine imputation. . . . Within yourself is nothing but perdition, but your salvation is without."[57] The *semper* with which

---

[57] *W. A.*, LVI, 268, 27. *Sancti Intrinsece sunt peccatores semper, ideo extrinsece Justificantur semper. Hippocrite autem intrinsece sunt Justi semper, ideo extrinsece sunt peccatores semper. Intrinsece dico, i.e. quomodo in nobis, in nostris oculis, in nostra estimatione, extrinsece autem, quomodo apud Deum et in reputatione eius sumus. Igitur extrinsece sumus Justi, quando non ex nobis nec ex operibus, Sed ex sola Dei reputatione Justi sumus . . . intra te non est nisi perditio, Sed salus tua extra te est.*

this passage begins has a direct relationship to the *semper* we meet in the formula *Semper a novo incipere.* Since we are *always* sinners in ourselves and *always* have our only hope in an alien righteousness, the progress in our Christian life is a constant beginning anew, *semper a novo incipere.*

In the next place Luther's view of the growth of sanctification is seen in his frequently used illustration of the convalescent man who is both sick and well at the same time. Where this illustration is most clearly presented the emphasis is not on the progressive process of recovery, but on the physician's promise of complete recovery, and on the faith of the patient in this promise and his consequent obedience to the rules of the physician. The emphasis is on the certainty of the promise, which in Christ corresponds to promise of eternal life. There is little reflection on the continuity of the process of recovery which would correspond to Holl's and Seeberg's view about a gradual growth in empirical holiness; but the emphasis is upon the absolute certainty of its completion, because this certainty rests upon the unfailing promise of the physician. Accordingly the illustration is so interpreted that the convalescence is not described as a constant increase in health but rather a paradoxical simultaneous existence of both illness and health. The whole connection into which the picture is put (Notes on Rom. 4:7; LVI, 271, 2-277, 3) describes how concupiscence always continues to dwell in the righteous man. Therefore in the use of this picture it is stated that the justified is *peccator in re, sed Initium habens Justitiae, ut amplius querat semper, semper iniustum se sciens.*[58] The justified man may thus fall to two sides. He may, as sometimes happens to a sick person, lose the will to be healed. This happens to all who do not fear God, and therefore do not pray and request the forgiveness of sin. These are all those that do not *will* their righteousness. Or he may, as sometimes happens, deny that he is sick and therefore ignore the advice of the doctor. They who want to be justified by their works are in this class. The emphasis is on the fact that a sick man must recognize his illness *(semper iniustum se scire)* and trust in the

---

[58] *W. A.,* LVI, 272, 19 ff. (1515-16).

promise of the physician. The healing is therefore not described as something belonging to this life but to the resurrection. Finally Luther has a description of the situation in which his view is clearly presented: "See then, it is as I said above: at the same time the righteous are justified, they are sinners; justified because they have faith in Christ whose righteousness covers them and is imputed to them. But they are sinners because they do not fulfill the law; they are not without concupiscence. They are like sick people in the care of a doctor—people who are really and truly sick but who are hopefully beginning to get well, or, more exactly, are made well. That is, they are at the point of becoming well."[59] The health which the convalescent man possesses as a hope together with the reality of his illness is not a beginning "real" righteousness, but the alien righteousness of Christ which covers him. Therefore the illustration states that we always are both righteous and sinners at the same time. Righteous in Christ, sinners in ourselves. But when this simultaneousness is expressed in the illustration about the convalescent man, that means the simultaneousness is not dialectic, but of a historico-eschatological salvation. When faith takes refuge in Christ's alien righteousness, the hope of resurrection is included, when our righteousness no longer shall be a mere alien righteousness but our own personal being. It is by taking refuge now in Christ's alien righteousness (which corresponds to the ill person's trusting in the promise of the physician and obeying his advice) that the sinner gets the hope about an eternal personal righteousness in the resurrection. If in the place of this he were to build his hope on the presence of a certain germ of "empirical righteousness" within himself, it would be the same foolish conceit, as it would be if the sick man believing that he could feel the power of health in himself, began to trust in this beginning of health instead of following the advice of the phy-

---

[59] *W. A.*, LVI, 347, 8 ff. *Vide nunc, quod supra dixi, Quod simul Sancti, dum sunt Iusti, sunt peccatores; Iusti, quia credunt in Christum, cuius Iustitia eos tegit et eis imputator, peccatores autem, quia non implent legem, non sunt sine concupiscentia, Sed sicut egrotantes sub cura medici, qui sunt re vera egroti, Sed inchoative et in spe sani seu potius sanificati, i.e., sani fientes, quibus nocentissima est sanitatis presumptio, quia peius recidiuant.*

sician. It is not possible to understand Luther's parable of the convalescent man if one overlooks this important point, that the sick man's hope of healing rests solely on his trust in the promise of the physician and in following his advice. The daily progress in healing takes place when the ill man commits himself over and over again into the hand of the physician and does not trust in his own health just starting. This should be interpreted in this manner: the believer's progressive sanctification comes about when he again and again in faith yields to the alien righteousness of Christ and condemns all his own. In this way he has placed his whole sanctification in the hand of Christ. His walk forward in the way of sanctification consists in this that he again and again takes leave of himself and takes refuge in Christ.

The parable of convalescence thus expresses with all possible clearness that the progress in sanctification is not identical with the definite increase of empirical piety but, by a constant repetition of the beginning of justification, is a constant taking refuge anew in Christ's alien righteousness. It is, of course, marvelous that such a progress, which consists in constantly starting anew, can lead to the goal which is known as the resurrection and the perfect righteousness. But this matter is also very wonderful to Luther. The parable of the convalescence shows that the healing of which he speaks is a *miraculous healing*. In the background of this description is the interpretation of the parable of the good Samaritan according to which man is the lost and unconscious man, and the Samaritan who pours oil and wine on his wounds is Christ. It is this "illness" and this "physician" Luther has in mind where he uses the description of the convalescent man. Luther has in mind, not a modern physician who with well-balanced technical knowledge gradually brings the ill man forward toward the cure, but the good Samaritan who in a wonderful way found the dying man and saved him from death after which he left him with the innkeeper with the promise that he would soon be back again. The healing which is started is therefore not the idea of the gradual increase of empirical piety, but the total expression for all man's existence under grace in the hope of the coming resurrection.[60] This paraphrases the content of faith in Christ.

Thus the analysis of the parable about the convalescent man has proven our thesis that the progress in sanctification is not the same as the increase in empirical piety, but it is the constantly repeated flight from all empirical piety and the taking refuge in Christ's alien righteousness.

In the third place, Luther's view of the progress of sanctification is underscored as a constant taking refuge in Christ's alien righteousness by the relation in which he places the Spirit, understood as that principle which struggles against the flesh, to the Holy Spirit. Sanctification consists in this that the Spirit overpowers the flesh. *Flesh* is the whole of man when his conscience is under dominion of the law, by which it is forced to seek its own righteousness. This is the situation we know from its culmination in inner conflict, by which man is driven to wish that God did not exist. Spirit is the whole of man, when he is driven by the Spirit of God, so that he does not seek his own, but lives by the mercy of God and thereby is in conformity to his will. Flesh and Spirit can by this definition also be distinguished by the terms *sensus* and *fides*. The principle of the flesh is *sensus,* that of the Spirit, *fides.* The mind of the flesh always looks more to works than to the Word, the mind of the Spirit always looks to the Spirit and not to the works. And the Word, which must be believed, is this, that Christ is dead and risen (Rom. 10:6). Spirit and flesh are the two ways of existence, under the law and wrath (the existence by works) and under the gospel and grace (the existence by faith). But how does man become Spirit? The answer is, by the Spirit of God. The Spirit is man when the Spirit of God dwells in him. Man is flesh when the Spirit of God is absent. The struggle between flesh and Spirit is therefore a struggle between the flesh of man and the Spirit of God. Therefore the gospel about Christ's work and alien righteousness to be accepted by faith is lined up in this struggle against the conceit of the flesh with its faith in works stimulated by the law.

---

[60] *W. A.,* LVI, 347, 8 ff.; 351, 17 ff.; 272, 11 ff.; 513, 11 ff. (1515-16). A. Hamel, pp. 116 and 119.

But it certainly is very evident that the Spirit of God can never be the same as man's empirical piety. This piety can only be the fruit of the Spirit, it can never be identical with the Spirit of God. But for Luther it is very decisive that it is the Spirit of God which struggles against our flesh. If the principle which struggles against the flesh is not completely outside man himself, just as the Spirit of God is, the flesh can never be understood as *totus homo.* The principle in man which struggles against the flesh must in this case be subtracted, and then the flesh is not *totus homo,* but *totus homo* minus man's empirical piety, which struggles against the "flesh." Only when the principle which struggles against our flesh is God's own Spirit, is it possible to call man's flesh *totus homo.* God's Spirit is not identical with our empirical piety, but he is that Spirit which testifies of Christ and that means Christ himself, the living Christ outside ourselves, Christ as our alien righteousness. Therefore Luther is able to identify the living Christ with our spiritual life. *It is the risen and living Christ himself who vicariously lives that life which alone deserves to be considered as our spiritual life.* But this has so little to do with our empirical piety that Luther maintains that when man sins, it is not his spiritual life which dies, but it is man himself who dies and falls out of his spiritual life, while it lives on in the living Christ. Progress in this connection can only mean that the sinner, as often as he falls out of his spiritual life, which is Christ, returns to him again in faith and penitence. The leading of man to Christ is the work of God's own Spirit. But this progress, which consists in constantly going back to Christ, is not therefore a state of marking time. It has its unchangeable beginning in baptism and its destination in the resurrection. The movement in this progress and the direction of this movement cannot be measured in man's own religious life, but the movement is in God who is acting in baptism and resurrection. God begins his active work in our life in baptism. Our life thus begins with the death of Christ and ends in the last day. In baptism our life takes on eschatological quality. Our progress consists in this, that we in baptism are becoming a part of God's progress toward his own goal. But this only takes place when the Spirit calls us away from ourselves and our empirical piety and makes us rely on Christ as our alien righteousness and our eternal life. Thus the Spirit gains power over the flesh. Thus sanctification moves forward.

These three glances at Luther's view of sanctification teach us that sanctification is not an increase in empirical piety, but the constant return of alien righteousness. This is clearly stated in Luther's sermon on *Duplici Justitia*, 1519. In this sermon Luther differentiates between essential righteousness and actual righteousness. The first is alien righteousness, Christ's imputed righteousness; the other is the real piety which is a fruit of the first righteousness. Concerning the struggle between righteousness and original sin it is stated that it is the alien and not the actual righteousness which directs the struggle: *Haec igitur iusticia aliena et sine actibus nostris per solam gratiam infusa nobis, trahente intus scilicet patre nos ad Christum, opponitur peccato originali, quod alienum similiter est sine nostris actibus per solam generationem nobis cognatum et contractum. Et ita Christus expellit Adam de die in diem magis et magis, secundum quod crescit illa fides et cognitio Christi. Non enim tota simul infunditur, sed incipit, proficit et perficitur tandem in fine per mortem.*[61] Here it is clearly stated that it is the alien righteousness which struggles against original sin, and this alien righteousness is the living Christ himself to whom the Father by the Spirit (i.e. *intus trahente*) leads us. It is clearly stated that faith is not a possession gained once and for all but it is infused in a constantly forward-moving process till the time of death. What we have partly seen previously through the different passages, is here shortly summarized in a few sentences which clearly prove the preceding exegesis.

We have now clearly documented that the concept "real" righteousness, as it is seen in those interpretations of Luther's doctrine of justification which consider this as "real" justification, cannot be harmonized with Luther's ideas because our whole real self constantly remains ambiguous in its relation to the concept of

---

[61] *W. A.*, II, 146, 29. Similarly, I, 186, 25 (1517). *Nu ists mit unss alsso, das Adam auss muss und Christus eyn geen, Adam zu nichte werden und Christus allein regiren und seynn, derhalben ist waschens und reynigens kein ende yn disser tzeit.*

righteousness. And the righteousness whose growth *signifies the progress of* sanctification is not such a real righteousness, but it is an alien righteousness, the living Christ himself present in us by the Spirit, struggling against our whole real old man, our whole real self, in so far as it is under the law. The empirical piety, the reality of which Luther at no time has thought of denying, does not come under the category of righteousness before God. Luther is able to describe it as righteousness only in the sense of actual righteousness, as a fruit of essential righteousness. The true righteousness before God is always, at the beginning as well as at the end of the way of sanctification, alien righteousness, the living Christ himself. Hereby it is also proven that the young Luther certainly makes a sharp distinction between the growth of empirical piety (in the sense of a visible increase of faith and the life of faith as a psychological reality) and the hidden progress of sanctification. And it is proven that his theology and piety form a clear contrast to the pietistic identification of the new man with the converted man and to all views of Christianity and interpretations of Luther which have been formed by this fundamental view of pietism.

The other question which we were compelled to answer by a more thorough documentation in order to set forth Luther's view of the relation between the work of the Holy Spirit and empirical piety was this: does Luther as a rule speak in such a way about the Holy Spirit as a source of the new life that he is content to proclaim the Spirit as the mediator of Christ's redeeming presence, so that our whole new life is simply depending on the fact that Christ is really present? Is this view of the Holy Spirit of as great importance as we have asserted in the preceding study?

It would be very easy to quote a long series of passages where Luther directly describes the work of the Holy Spirit as that which brings Christ to us or unites us with the living Christ.[62] We have already quoted passages to that effect. However, the question demands a more comprehensive and systematic answer. To

---

[62] For example: *W. A.*, III, 553, 28 ff. (1513-15); I, 219, 26 ff. (1517); I, 593, 16 ff. (1518); II, 504, 7 ff. (1519); VII, 509, 13 ff. (1521); X, 1, II, 245, 39 ff. (1522).

this end we must return to the traditional forms in the writings of the young Luther where he plainly states his view about the work of the Holy Spirit. It was these Augustinian-like forms which might indicate that Luther perhaps had more to say about the new life and the Spirit as its source than the reference to the truly present Christ as our alien righteousness and to the faith, which takes leave of all empirical piety and constantly takes refuge in Christ. Is it possible that these Augustinian-like forms may be harmonized with this realism of Christ and the Holy Spirit? Or do they point in an entirely other direction, into a totally different line in Luther's thinking?

We therefore come back to the Augustinian formula used by Luther about the Holy Spirit as a source of infused love. We have previously analyzed Luther's understanding of this formula and we have shown that Luther's understanding was very different from that of Augustine and scholasticism. But we hardly got farther than negative ideas such as love and hatred of self and conformity to the will of God in the tempted and suffering Christ. We now ask, what is the positive content in Luther's new concept of love which is characterized by the idea of conformity and of inner conflict? What does Luther consider positive in the idea of the Holy Spirit as a source of a love to God, whose negative demarcation is described by expressions such as hatred of self, conformity to Christ, resignation, and so on.

The Augustinian concept of love from its *eros* point of view is first of all an expression for the yearning of creation for God as the highest good. The concept of love is therefore characterized by the fact that it uses man as subject and God as object. The Christian love to God according to Augustinian thinking is a sublimation of man's idealistic aspiration. This gives the Augustinian idea of love a very decided anthropocentric character. However, the idea of conformity in Luther is definitely theocentric. It demands that the concept of love must be understood as God's act of agape and not from the point of view of *man's idealistic aspiration*. The Lutheran idea of love has God as its subject and man as its object. (This is true also when it is a love of one's neighbor.) Thereby

Luther's idea of love becomes theocentric. It is characterized by agape and by its direction from above downward, not from the earth upward; by God's act in man, not by man's yearning for God. This means that love toward one's neighbor becomes most prominent in Luther's idea of love,[63] while love directed toward God completely dominates the Augustinian idea of love. This Copernican expression in Luther gradually results in love to God being identified with and substituted by faith,[64] while the word "love" is more and more filled with the content of agape directed toward one's neighbor. Luther's idea of faith and love (that is, faith in Christ and love of one's neighbor) therefore replaces the Augustinian concept of love. The scholastic development of the Augustinian idea of love also recognized such a unity of faith and love, *fides caritate formata,* but in that unity it is love that gives substance to faith. In the Lutheran idea of unity—faith active in love—it is faith which carries and nourishes love which without faith is dead and saturated with selfishness. We shall study more closely what this shift in the interpretation of the infused love means in understanding the Holy Spirit's relation to empirical piety. Now let us look at the sources.

We have previously referred to a number of passages where Luther expresses himself in a completely Augustinian sense about the Holy Spirit as the source of the new life. The Holy Spirit infuses love to God, a love which is simultaneously love to the law of God, so that the bondage of the law is replaced by the liberty of the gospel. However, we may observe that in these statements the Christian faith, in the sense specifically used by Luther, gradually dispels the Augustinian idea of love.[65] That joy in God which is the motivating force in love both to God and man, and which makes free and spontaneous the will to do the good, is only produced by faith and through the trial of faith in inner conflict. The new life is not infused directly by the Spirit, but is produced only

---

[63] *W. A.,* III, 210, 36; 396, 17 ff.; LVII, Heb., 59, 12; I, 365, 1; II, 575, 31-582, 34.

[64] *W. A.,* LVI, 307, 4 ff.; 338, 14 ff.; 136, 7 ff.; 107, 11 ff.; 514, 7 ff. Eduard Ellwein, p. 152 ff.

[65] *W. A.,* II, 498, 25 ff. (1519); V, 33, 25 ff.; 118, 1 ff.; 459, 29 ff.; 460, 37 ff. (1519-21); X, 1, I, 102, 8 ff.; 259, 7 ff.; 455, 20 ff.; 467, 11 ff.; 476, 1 ff. (1522).

when man in faith, tried in inner conflict, is compelled to rely on Christ. In this sense faith is the work of the Holy Spirit.

But this change in the description brings with it a certain tension between the usual and the new formulation. In this period we often find in Luther a formulation which seems to indicate that faith must come first and constitute the condition so that the Holy Spirit can be infused with love and its fruits. In this connection Luther generally uses the adverb soon *(mox, sobald)* in order to describe the relation between faith and the outpouring of the Spirit. When faith is there first, love is infused soon thereafter.[66] There is a very definite order in the relation between faith in Christ and the outpouring of the Spirit which cannot be changed: the preaching of the gospel, faith in Christ, the outpouring of the Spirit with love and its fruits.

However, it is not correct to construe Luther in such a way that the method of expression just mentioned comes to mean that he considers faith a kind of provisional merit which brings about the infusion of the Holy Spirit, even though there are certain sentences that certainly could be understood in this way. The fact is that what we previously have heard about Luther's view of the work of the Holy Spirit in inner conflict and as a source of faith is thoroughly opposed to this. And then a closer examination of the passages shows that rather the opposite is the true meaning. It should first be noted that the words *mox* and *sobald* (soon) not only signify a separation in time but also fully as much a logical dependence. In the second place Luther states clearly enough that when he says it is faith that brings the Holy Spirit, he does not think of faith as a human achievement, but as a result of the promise of the Word of God. Therefore it is just as often stated that it is the Word of God and the promise of God which bring the Spirit. This is often stated in such a way that the Word of God (or the gospel) is placed in the strongest opposition to all human endeavor or preparation. It is often underscored in connection

---

[66] *W. A.*, II, 490, 27 (1519); VI, 206, 28; VI, 356, 13 ff.; 210, 5 ff.; 515, 29 ff. (1520); VIII, 504, 25 ff.; 468, 24 ff.; 509, 13 ff. (1521); X, 1, I, 49, 1 ff. (1522); IX, 633, 1 ff. (Poliander's codex).

with Galatians 3:2, that the Spirit is not received by the works of the law but by the hearing of faith.[67] *Alsso das nit muglich ist, das ein mensch auss seiner vornunfft und vormugen solt mit wercken hynauff genn hymel steygen und gott zuuorkumen, yhn bewegen zur gnade, sondern gott muss zuuorkumen alle werck und gedancken und ein klar aussgedruckt zusagen thun mit worten, wilch den der mensch mit eynem rechten festen glauben ergreyff und behalte, sso folgt den der heylig geyst der yhm geben wirt umb desselben glaubens willen.*[68] It is an expression for God's unconditional anticipation that the Spirit comes through the promise of God and by faith in this promise. God's promise must precede the coming of the Spirit in order to eradicate every human preparation for the reception of the Spirit. It may also be stated thus that the Spirit is given to us because we already are children of God and not slaves (Gal. 4:6, 7), even though it also is true that it is only the Spirit which can make us God's children. This apparent contrast Luther resolves by showing that in God's anticipation we are already children the moment the promise is given to us. By promise we are *future* children even when we yet are under the bondage of the rudiments of the world. When God gives us the Spirit which makes us his children (that is, to those who know they are children and live as children) he does it because beforehand in his mind we are already children (that is, by virtue of the promise of *future* children). When it can be said simultaneously that faith is wrought by the Spirit and yet is a condition for the work of the Spirit, that the Spirit can be given only to them who already are children of God, and yet alone can make slaves into children of God, it is because the unity and the relation in the Christian life are not given us as a possession, but found outside ourselves in God in the unity of God's promise and fulfillment.

The contradiction we face here is exactly the same which we met when we discussed the relation between grace and gift. On the one hand it was grace alone which made faith in Christ into the

---

[67] *W. A.*, X, 1, I, 49, 1 ff.; 101, 19 ff.; 328, 7 ff.; 337, 6 ff.; 363, 1 ff.; 365, 8 ff.; 367, 19 ff. (1522).
[68] *W. A.*, VI, 356, 13 ff. (1520).

gift of God. On the other hand faith in Christ was the condition of the grace of God. We saw then that the difference in this case contained the inexplicable tension between Luther's theology of predestination and theology of redemption. This is also the case in the difference we meet here. If we emphasize the promise of God as immovable, we are led in the direction of theology of predestination. If we emphasize faith as a necessary condition in order that the promise might be made effective in the individual, we are moving in the direction of theology of redemption. But when we discussed the relation between grace and gift we also learned that the unity in this tension could only be christologically understood. This is also the case in the difference we meet here. When it is said that the promise and faith must precede the coming of the Spirit and his work in us, then faith is considered as the reception of Christ who in the promise is the revelation of God's eternal and changeless grace. That is why the Spirit works only under this grace; which again means—only in laying hold of Christ revealed in the promise. Therefore it is said again and again: you must first hear the gospel, after that faith comes and with faith the Spirit with his gifts. But when on the other hand it is said, faith is itself a fruit of the Spirit and only that faith which is the fruit of the Spirit is a genuine faith, then faith is considered united with Christ who by the Spirit is truly present in us and who as our alien righteousness struggles against our old man. Faith must precede the coming of the Spirit and his work. Only he is able to receive the Spirit as an experienced and guaranteed possession who is made to rely completely on the grace of God and who in himself has no qualification at all that he might expect the coming of the Spirit and his dwelling in him—only he who has nothing but the promise of God. (This means that he who wants to have the Spirit without Christ as the gift of God will inevitably lose him.) Faith is succeeded by the coming of the Spirit and his work, which means that we cannot of ourselves take refuge in the eternal and changeless grace of God. This is only possible when Christ is present in us as a redeeming reality and as the alien righteousness which carries our faith. And Christ is only present through the Spirit.

Thus the two modes of expression in their mutual tense relationship describe the rhythm in the progress in sanctification itself as something that constantly must begin anew. We are constantly moving from the state of faith, which grasps nothing else than the promise and the alien righteousness, out into the activity of faith struggling against the old man and thence again through the state of self-condemnation back to the alien righteousness. The progress of sanctification constantly moves in this circle. But even in this circular movement it is true that the same faith always can be considered both as wrought by the already present Holy Spirit and on the basis of the future coming and work of the Spirit. If faith in itself had life, if in accordance with the scholastic understanding of the doctrine of infused grace it was viewed as a supernatural substance which by the mediation of the sacrament assumed an unbreakable connection with our own nature and lifted it up in the position of the supernatural, then the relation between the Spirit and faith could be presented without any logical contradiction. In this case it would be possible to consider faith partly from the point of view of man's own work, which as a matter of course would merit the infusion of grace, or else to consider it as an infused faith, as a part of the supernatural grace, which in reality changes the nature of man, so that an unambiguous real righteousness begins to grow. There is no tension and no logical contradiction in such a plan. Everything is made rationally smooth. Faith as a forerunner of grace is always just an imperfect faith, while faith as a fruit of the Spirit is a real work of grace in the soul, whose supernatural power unambiguously substantiates its supernatural source. It is not possible for Luther to present the relation between the Spirit and faith as rational and smooth without any logical contradiction because for Luther faith is not a supernatural substance of which the Holy Spirit is the supernatural cause. It is the personal gift of God which is constantly depending on God's renewing and gracious giving. Faith never becomes a possession, and the Spirit never becomes a divine cause. For Luther faith is the life which is brought about by the really present reality of Christ mediated by the Spirit, which is simultaneously an escape from one's own empirical piety.

Therefore faith, to Luther, is a movement which never stops. It cannot be viewed as a property reposing in the soul, an *otiosa qualitas,* but faith is a constant movement away from myself to Christ. Therefore faith is not to consider itself an unambiguous psychological quality whose relation to the Spirit may be defined metaphysically without contradiction. In its movement away from myself toward Christ faith may be said to be a condition of the gift of the Spirit, for not before the mediation of Christ's real presence is the Spirit really present in us. When it moves away from Christ back to the concrete reality of my life, to my sin, to my calling, to my neighbor, faith is the fruit of the Spirit. For the consciousness of my sin, the sense of my calling, and the love to my neighbor becomes possible only through the reality of Christ which the Spirit mediates. *But this is that same relationship of faith in God through Christ which moves in both directions.* It is seen here that to Luther faith is an encounter with the living personal God. It is not an infused substance. *Therefore faith must always be considered from both directions if it is to be correctly understood.* It must be seen both as our flight toward the reality of the Spirit and our life lived out of the reality of the Spirit.

The relationship of faith in both of these directions is solely the work of the Spirit. But it is easily observed that this expression cannot be understood from a general, physical, cause and effect point of view. The Spirit is not only a supernatural cause of faith as a psychological phenomenon. The Spirit is a mediator of the reality of Christ which is the cause of faith in its ability to move both toward Christ and out of Christ. For both of these directions of moving are possible where Christ by the Spirit is really present. But faith certainly always contains both of these directions when it is a personal life with Christ who is truly present in the Spirit.

It is this double movement of faith which causes Luther to differentiate between faith and love in a completely different way from that of theology before him. Luther speaks of faith in a more restricted sense (i.e. the movement of faith toward Christ) as *ingressus in Christum* and love (i.e. the movement of faith out of Christ) as *egressus*. Luther varies this theme again and again in his sermons. The true faith which makes man righteous before God receives from above and gives out of itself here. The more man gives to his neighbor the more God gives to man. Luther compares the Christian man to a tube through which the benefits of God are poured out to the neighbor. By faith we are children of God and heirs of all his divine benefits. In the state of love we are ourselves gods, for the divine nature consists of constantly doing good. It is therefore impossible to speak about separating faith and love. The two directions, into Christ and out to our neighbor, belong to one and the same spiritual totality.

Luther has given the classical presentation of the theme "Faith and Love" in *Evangelium von den zehn Aussätzigen,* of 1521; *Nu ist glawb unnd liebe das gantz wesen eynisz Christlichen menschen, wie ich oft gesagt habe. Der glawbe empfehet, die liebe gibt. Der glawbe bringt den menschen tzu got, die liebe bringt yhn tzu den menschen. Durch den glawben lest yhn wol thun von got, durch die liebe thut er wol den menschen. Denn wer do glawbt, der hat alle ding von got und ist selig und reych. Darumb darff er hinfurt nichts mehr, sondern allisz, was er lebt und thut, das ordenet er tzu gut und nutz seynem nehisten und thut dem selben durch die liebe, wie yhm gott than hat durch den glawben, als schepfft er gutt von oben durch den glawben und gibt gutt von unten durch die liebe.*[69]

The two movements of faith correspond respectively to prayer and work. In this connection Luther refers to a passage of Scripture which is of importance for the understanding of his view of the work of the Spirit, Zechariah 12:10: "And I will pour upon the house of David, and upon the inhabitants of Jerusalem, the spirit of grace and of supplications." Luther often uses this passage when he wants to describe the work of the Holy Spirit as an intercessor and comforter in inner conflict in connection with Romans 8:26. It is *spiritus gratiae* which accompanies the sermon about grace and mercy, about redemption in Christ from sin and death. But

---

[69] *W. A.,* VIII, 355, 20 ff.

when grace which is mediated by *spiritus gratiae* shall be preserved and kept against all the attacks of the devil, it is necessary that *spiritus precum* step in to intercede for us with groanings which cannot be uttered, when we are in the darkness of inner conflict. We must know the Holy Spirit both as *spiritus gratiae* and as *spiritus precum,* if we are to keep him. The two aspects of the Spirit's work cannot be separated at all. But both of the two aspects of the work of the Holy Spirit are concerned with the mediation of Christ's real presence. The Spirit of supplication drives us toward the truly present Christ, while the Spirit of grace causes us to live on the basis of his reality.[70] The same thoughts are contained in the quoting of Zechariah 12:10, and in the development of the relationship between faith and love in the gospel about the ten lepers. This makes it possible to get a clearer vision of both faith and love. The movement toward Christ and the movement out from Christ are both the work of the Spirit. Faith and love correspond to prayer and work. Faith is the refuge which he who is poor finds in the riches of God in Christ. This taking refuge is the constant prayer of the poor and the lost for salvation. The movement of love is Christ's own work in the sinner, which because of his wretchedness has taken refuge in him. When it is said that the movement of love is work and that of faith, prayer, it is very important to remember that the work of love is not the believer's own work, but is the work of Christ wrought by Christ with the believer as his instrument. The works which he speaks of as *our* works are always the works of law, never the works of love. *Opera legis audivimus dupliciter fieri, aliquando per nos, ut nostra, aliquando per Christum in nobis, ut Christi, cuius sunt donum. Aliquando per nos ut nostra: tunc sine dubio omittenda sunt et damnanda, ut quae a Christo avellunt conscientiam piam et in opera laceratam dispergunt. Docent enim iustitiam et peccatorum remissionem extra Christum operari. Aliquando fiunt per Christum in nobis spiritu libertatis, dum voventur et servantur*

---

[70] *W. A.,* XLVI, 166, 10; 165, 2; also according to the older Luther: XXXI, 2, 117, 11 ff. (Lauterbach, 1527-30); XXXI, 1, 274, 1 ff. (Veit Dietrich, 1530); XLII, 275, 2 ff. (Commentary on Genesis, 1535-45).

*gratis, ut nec peccatis per ea satisfiat, nec iustitia nec salus quaera-
tur. Verum impossibile est hac conscientia voveri, nisi ab iis, qui
mirabiliter spiritu Christi intus ducuntur et servantur, hoc est, ab
electis.*[71]

Therefore it is not that the two movements in faith which are
described as prayer (faith) and work (love) are in opposition to one
another. Such an opposition exists only between prayer and the
works which we do ourselves, the works of the law. But these works
are not only opposed to prayer, as an active attitude toward a
passive, but they are just as much opposed to truly good works,
to right activity, because they are directed toward God and not
toward our neighbor. . . . *die blinden leytter wollen die werck
alszo leren und nottig machen, das yhr der wircker bedurffte tzur
selickeyt: das ist die hewbt vorkerung unnd yrthum aller yrthum,
denn damit vorstoren sie beyde, glawben und liebe, das gantz
Christlich wessen und exempel. Sie nemen die werck von dem
nehisten und geben sie der person selbs, als die da yhm nott seyn:
da kan der glawb nit bleyben, der da weysz, das seyne werck nit
yhm selb, szondern dem nehisten nott unnd nutz sind. Alszo sind
sie widdereinander. Der glawb wirfft die werck von sich auff dem
nehisten durch die liebe. Szo reyssen sie die blinden meyster von
dem nehisten und treyben sie auff die eygen person, ersticken
und vordempffen alszo beide, liebe und glawben, machen, das der
mensch nur sich selb lieb gewinnet und nur seyn selickeyt suche
und auff seyn werck sich vorlasse.*[72]

The attitude of the righteousness of work is simultaneously
opposed to both faith and love. It is opposed to faith because by
considering its own works meritorious it becomes too rich to pray
and take refuge in Christ. It is also opposed to love because by
usurping the works for itself as necessary for its relation to God it
steals them from the neighbor. But it is also true that real faith,
whose attitude is that of the poor constantly praying for righteousness simply because it has nothing in itself and never will have anything, can afford to give to the neighbor all that God grants it. That

---

[71] *W. A.,* VIII, 609, 27 (1521).
[72] *W. A.,* VIII, 363, 3.

the "passive" attitude of prayer is opposed to the "activity" of works is not the case at all. On the contrary it is only in the eternal *passive* attitude of prayer before God that the real work in behalf of the neighbor can be accomplished.

Real faith is however only the faith which in the midst of inner conflict is preserved by the Spirit of prayer as the constant cry to Christ: Lord, help! And real love is only that love in which Christ is so truly present that the works of love are Christ's own works performed by the believer as the instrument of Christ. It is therefore evident that faith and love cannot be separated at all. They are both the result from the reality which the Spirit creates when he makes Christ truly present in us. This real presence of Christ mediated by the Spirit is that which produces both the unutterable groaning about help, which is the movement of faith, and kindness to the neighbor, which is the movement of love.

This connection between faith and love clarifies the work of the Spirit as the Spirit of grace and prayer. It is seen here how misleading it is simply to consider the Spirit as a supernatural cause. The Holy Spirit is God himself present in us, but present in such a way that his presence takes Jesus Christ out of the remoteness of history and heavenly exaltation and places him in the midst of our concrete life as a living and redeeming reality which constantly calls upon both the groaning of faith and the work of charity. The relation of Jesus Christ to the work of the Holy Spirit is not a physical-hyperphysical relationship of cause but a personal relationship of faith. When it is said that the Spirit produces faith and love and that the Spirit is the source of the new life, these expressions are to be understood as metaphors. These are used because by virtue of our thinking we are compelled to use such expressions in order to visualize the personal and spiritual relationships. The relationship of cause which such expressions postulate between the Spirit and the new life can only be understood as a personal fellowship of the truly present Christ into which the Spirit leads us. It is Christ, present and living by the Spirit, who "calls forth" (this word is used in its personal meaning: to call upon someone just as God called upon Adam in the Garden of

Eden) both faith and love. If we ignore this realism of faith and attempt to explain the connection of faith and love psychologically we entangle ourselves in problems impossible of solution. The connection between faith and love cannot be directly explained. If that was the case it had to be presumed that faith and love were for Luther fixed psychological dimensions whose mutual relations could be made the object of a simple psychological observation. But Luther does not at all understand faith and love in this manner. The connection between faith and love is only a reality in the living and present Christ, in the movement toward him and out from him. If we ignore this decisive factor, we falsify in the most essential point both faith and love and their mutual relationship.

This "realistic" concept of faith and love based on the idea of Christ's real presence mediated by the Spirit is also corroborated by the way Luther speaks about the new life as a real participation in Christ's death and resurrection, as in the first lecture on the Psalms and the lectures on the Epistle to the Romans. The previously traced, positive aspect of the idea of conformity is here clearly evident. This way of speaking about the new life no more signifies another phase of Luther's theology of sanctification than does his view of faith and love. The idea is not that the "reforming" Luther should have yielded the pre-Reformation supernatural view in favor of a more psychological view. The fact is that the two modes of expression cover the same idea. Luther rejects every purely symbolic exposition of Paul about being conformed to the death and resurrection of Christ. The death and resurrection of Christ not only illustrate but produce the righteousness in us.[73] It is not a question of an isolated series of thoughts but about one and the same idea considered from several points of view. The double movement of faith, seen in relation to our old man, is a real death and a real resurrection. We again recall the identity of faith in Christ and conformity to Christ in Luther which was indicated previously. This identity does not only apply, as previously indicated, to the negative aspect of faith and conformity,

---

[73] *W. A.*, LVI, 296, 60 (1515-16); E. Ellwein, pp. 78-127.

that is, the death of the old man and his crucifixion with Christ. This identity also applies to the positive aspect of faith and conformity. The fact that I am righteous before God by taking refuge in Christ through faith and that, by the movement of love toward my neighbor, I become an instrument in the hand of God is the real resurrection of the new man. This resurrection is directly united with the resurrection of Christ. For it is only by virtue of his resurrection that Christ can be truly present as our refuge and as the active cause in love's work for the neighbor.

The realistic understanding of faith and love is finally established by the way in which Luther speaks of the royal state and the priesthood of the Christians. The use of these two expressions to signify the double movement of faith indicates how realistic and Christ-centered Luther always is when he describes faith and love.

The investigation of the positive content of Luther's view of love to God has produced the same result as the interpretation of the negative demarcation of his idea of love. Back of Luther's view of the Holy Spirit as the source of true love to God there is a totally different concept of charity from that found in the Augustinian and scholastic concept. As the negative demarcation separated Luther's concept from all idealism of love but demonstrated a realistic concept of the work of the Spirit in the experience of inner conflict, so Luther's positive addition to and filling out of the idea of love means a continuation of this realism. Just as it is solely the real presence of Christ which calls forth the groaning from the soul in inner conflict, it is also only the real presence of Christ which makes possible the work of love for the neighbor. For only the work which is done by the truly present Christ, using man as his instrument, is a real work of love. All other works for the neighbor, which have only man himself as the subject, are just works of the law performed in behalf of the doer and not in behalf of the neighbor. There is no part of the Christian life at all which does not belong to the movement of faith toward Christ or to the movement of love out from Christ. By this it is proved that Luther really has said *all* that may be said about man's empirical piety when he has announced how the Holy Spirit makes the crucified and risen Christ truly present as a redeeming reality. By this *everything* is actually said. For this presence calls forth an incessant double movement of faith, the constant prayer to Christ and the constant work of love for the neighbor. This double movement includes all empirical piety. But the Holy Spirit does not directly produce this piety by some mystical causality. He produces it by making the crucified and risen Christ a present reality in the believer.

In summing up we may now describe Luther's view of the relation between the work of the Spirit as a mediation of Christ's living presence and man's empirical piety. The preceding investigation has shown that empirical piety, by Luther's realistic understanding of the Spirit's work, is brought into a double presentation, a critical and a positive.

The critical presentation of empirical piety consists in the revelation of its ambiguity in relation to the concept of righteousness. In our description of Luther's view of the progress of sanctification we saw that any fragment of empirical piety at any time may be defined either as Spirit or as flesh. It is defined as Spirit when man in this very moment lives in the reality of the Spirit of God. It is defined as flesh when man lives outside the reality of the Spirit of God.

The positive presentation consists in this: the whole empirical piety, in the moment that man lives in the reality of God's Spirit, becomes an expression for the Christ's real presence either as the movement of faith to Christ, or as the movement of love from Christ.

This double presentation, which interprets empirical piety by the idea of the Spirit's mediating work through Christ, further emphasizes the realistic understanding of the work of the Holy Spirit as the discussion in the preceding sections of this chapter have proven.

In the last section we saw how Luther's concept of the Holy Spirit best can be designated as the real divine sphere of revelation in which only the risen Christ can be present with us, and outside of which Christ exists only as an idea, as law. It is the same realistic concept of the Spirit we have met in this section. The Holy Spirit is also considered here as the sphere within which empirical piety alone can live. Outside of the sphere of the Spirit all piety is only an activity of man himself. It is flesh, a bondage under the law, man's proud attempt to justify himself before God. Within the sphere of the Spirit the same empirical piety, however, is an activity of the living Christ himself which calls forth and directs both the movement of faith toward himself and the movement of love out from himself.

The idea of causality cannot express this relationship. When Luther uses expressions seemingly influenced by the idea of causality about the Spirit's relation to the new life—and he cannot avoid this because of tradition and also because of the limitations of language—these expressions must be understood in a figurative sense, as expressions of the fact that they as the phenomena caused by the Spirit move about within the sphere of the Spirit.

We are now able to see the decisive defect in the Luther interpretation of such scholars as Karl Holl and Reinhold Seeberg when they have understood Luther's view of justification as a gradual progressive *reale Gerechtmachung* and therefore, as far as Karl Holl is concerned, were able to describe God's pronouncement of justification as a proleptic and analytic judgment.[74] The error in these presentations is not found in the emphasis on the fact that there is a decisive difference between Luther's development of the evangelical doctrine of justification and the later Melanchthonian view. We have had several occasions to point out that such differences exist. It is therefore impossible to refute Holl and Seeberg just by repeating as stubbornly as possible the old orthodox Lutheran concept of the doctrine of justification, colored as it is by the Melanchthonian and forensic views. Over against such an orthodox reintroduction (repristination), Holl and Seeberg are correct in maintaining that justification and sanctification—or as Luther generally stated it, the nonimputation of sin and the expul-

---

[74] Karl Holl, pp. 111-154; Reinhold Seeberg, *Lehrbuch der Dogmengeschichte*, 4th ed., pp. 124-134, 294-307.

sion of sin—are woven together in Luther in such a way that the Melanchthonian, forensic doctrine of justification cannot anticipate it. But the mistake is that sanctification in Holl's and Seeberg's Luther research is seen in the idealistic perspective. The new life, in spite of the fact that Seeberg often refers to the thoughts about the Spirit and Christ in us, is not considered as an existence within the sphere of the Spirit in which Christ himself at the same time is both the alien righteousness, which qualifies all man's righteousness as flesh, and the active subject of all the activity of man. But instead of this the new life is considered as identical with man's gradually increasing empirical piety. By this concept it is inevitable that Luther is placed very close to the Augustinian and scholastic doctrine of justification. For when the perfected real righteousness is able to form the basis of a proleptic and analytic judgment, it means that the whole process of justification is seen from the point of view of the law. It makes no difference at all whether that means that the pronouncement of justification is a proleptic and analytic judgment, or whether it is preferable to state that God, when he gives his salvation by virtue of the merit realized through grace, simply honors his own gifts. The idea behind the concept of Holl and Seeberg is the pietistic identification of new man with converted man, the idea of the unambiguousness of empirical piety and that of sanctification as a constant progress toward a greater and greater perfection. These thoughts cannot be harmonized with Luther's view. The idea of law is forever removed from Luther's concept of piety. Sanctification for Luther does not mean that man by the aid of God becomes better and better, stronger and stronger, and more pious and more pious, until he of goodness, strength, and piety gets into heaven. But Luther holds that man in his totality comes into the sphere of the Spirit of God and therefore, in a certain sense, day by day becomes more weak, more sinful, and more helpless, so that he more and more comes to rely on Christ alone as his only righteousness and as the one who takes him and uses him as his instrument in his work for our neighbor. Luther has no room for any independently evaluated, divinely supported, and independently growing empirical piety. Man according to Luther is in every moment, even on the last day, completely dependent on the pure mercy of God. If in this moment he is outside the sphere of the Spirit of God, he is a lost and condemned creature even though he may be resplendent with much empirical piety and great holiness wrought by God. But if in this moment he is within the sphere of the Spirit of God, he is blessed even though he has a stench from his past sins. Salvation in the evangelical sense is not, as legalistic piety claims, gradually becoming better and better and better and finally becoming good enough before God, but it is getting *immediately* and *completely* within that sphere where God in Christ receives the unworthy and does his work in them. This last point must be included as a contrast to the purely forensic, abstract doctrine of justification. The sinner is never received by God without being used as an instrument by God simultaneously with the reception. Faith is never without love, forgiveness of sin is never without the expulsion of sin. But this expulsion of sin is not to be understood in the legalistic sense that the good part of our real self is gradually increased while the bad part is proportionately decreased. But the expulsion of sin means that our whole real self with both its good and its bad parts— by referring to Christ's alien righteousness as our only security and by having our neighbor's need as our only task—is completely torn out of the disease of self-seeking and our constant preoccupation with our temporal and eternal advantage in favor of something more useful.

The questions raised in the introduction of this section have already been answered by the account given of the relation between work of the Spirit and empirical piety. There is in reality no contrast in the discussion of the work of the Holy Spirit as a mediator of Christ's real presence and the work of the Spirit as a source of the new life in the sense of empirical piety. For empirical piety is only genuine when it lives and moves within the sphere of the Spirit in which Christ alone is truly present. It may sound as a paradox, but it is nonetheless the real fact that empirical piety can exist only within the sphere of the Spirit where there is a constant flight away from one's empirical piety to Christ as the alien righteousness. Only within this sphere is it possible for the movement of faith to live as a true prayer to God, and for the movement of love to live as Christ's spontaneous work of love to the neighbor. Outside of this sphere, and that means under the law, both faith and love are changed to pious self-justification. The exclusive message about the work of the Spirit as a mediator of Christ's real presence does not take the place of the statement about the Spirit as a source of empirical piety, but on the contrary it prepares the way for it. The real new life is of course more than the unutterable groanings of inner conflict and faith taking refuge in Christ's alien righteousness. It is also the work of love toward the neighbor. But these works can live only in the sphere of the groanings of the Spirit and where faith constantly takes refuge in Christ. The negative "definitions" of love to God therefore in an eminent sense have a positive direction. There is no reason whatever to interpret Luther's view of the Holy Spirit as Augustinian "leavings." This of course does not exclude the fact that an Augustinian understanding of the concept of love, especially in the earlier writing so strongly influenced by Augustine, to some degree struggles with the new understanding.[75] But the fact that the Augustinian terminology of inspiration is retained by Luther until he is advanced in years suggests that care must be taken that an Augustinian understanding not be postulated every time the word *infundere* is used. And in this presentation in which we are more interested in the systematic connection of the thoughts than in their historic genesis, it is clear that, as far as possible, we must try to understand the thoughts as a unity, that is, that the Augustinian expressions must be understood from the point of view of the new realistic understanding of the Spirit and not in the opposite sense. The guiding viewpoint must always be that Luther never thinks of the Spirit as a transcendent cause, but as the present sphere of revelation in which Christ is truly present, and in which the believer incessantly is driven into the double motion of faith and

---

75 *W. A.*, I, 66, 9 ff. (1516); VII, 6, 12 (1522); XLVI, 405, 10 (Rörer, 1538); also XXXIX, 1, 321, 12 ff. (*Disp. de veste nuptiali*, 1537); XXXIX, 1, 373, 1 ff.; 375, 4 ff. (1. *disp. ctr. Antinom.*, 1537); XX, 769, 7-770, 10 (Rörer, 1527); XX, 394, 27 ff. (Rörer, 1526); XXXI, 2, 69, 23 ff. (Lauterbach, 1527-30).

love. That love is "infused" does not really say anything else than that the whole of man is brought into the sphere of the Spirit in which the motion of love (and of faith!) necessarily takes place, and yet this motion is made in the greatest sense of liberty. However, it does not say that supernatural powers are put into man which lifts his nature into a supernatural plan.

Chapter II

THE MEANS USED BY THE HOLY SPIRIT

The Spirit and the Word

In the first chapter we have tried to obtain a rather comprehensive picture of Luther's view of the work of the Holy Spirit. One question, however, was always left out. It was the question of *how*; that is, by what means does the Spirit do his work? We have spoken about a realistic concept of the Spirit, that the Spirit is the real divine sphere in which Christ is truly present and in which alone empirical piety can live. How is this divine sphere of revelation recognized? By what means does he manifest himself? This is the question we shall discuss in the present chapter.

It is generally known that Luther's answer to the question about the means of the Spirit is *the Word*.[1] The Word is the means of the Holy Spirit. But this answer also raises the question about the relation between the Spirit and the Word. Are they so connected with each other that the Spirit is always present where the Word is? Or is it possible for the Word to be without the Spirit, or may the Spirit work independently of the Word?

What does Luther really understand by the Word?

That Luther finds the Word in the Scriptures needs no further proof. By this he simply followed the tradition of the church. But this tells only very little about his concept of what the Word really is. We have already seen in the discussion of Luther's concept of

---

1 *W. A.*, II, 509, 13 (1519). *Si vis gratiam consequi, id age, ut verbum dei vel audias intente vel recorderis diligenter: verbum, inquam, et solum verbum est vehiculum gratiae dei . . . stat fixa sententia, ex auditu fidei accipi spiritum (Gal. 3:2). Hoc modo acceperunt spiritum, quicunque acceperunt.*

experience that the contrast *littera-spiritus,* law-gospel, is of decisive importance for Luther's attitude to the Scriptures. The
distinction between law and gospel goes through the *whole* of
Scripture. It does it in such a way that it is really only as gospel that
the Scriptures can truly be called the Word of God. The Word as
spiritus in opposition to *littera* is compared to the Word as God's
own Word in contrast to the mere word of man. The word *spiritus*
can even be directly identified with God himself.

Luther also expresses this contrast by the aid of the Augustinian
distinction between the outward and the inward Word. The outward Word is the Word of Scripture (or *verbum vocale,* or the
sacrament), the inward Word is God's own voice by his Spirit.
Without this inner Word of God the outward Word remains a
letter, the word of man.[2] Luther often uses I Corinthians 3:7 in
this connection. God alone can give increase to the Word. The
outward Word is only the means which God uses when he writes
his own living Word into the heart.[3] Man is able to bring the
Word to the ear, but not into the heart. This work belongs to
God.

Hereby we really state this one thing: the Word of God—or the
gospel—is not just present in Scripture in such a way that it can be
unmistakably pointed out. If God does not speak into the heart
while the ear listens to the outward Word, the outward Word remains the word of man and law.[4] When we hear the Word of the
Scripture, we are compelled to wait on the Spirit of God. It is God
who has the Scripture in his hand. If God does not infuse his
Spirit the hearer of the Word is not different from the deaf man.
No one can rightly understand the Word of God unless he receives
it directly from the Holy Spirit. The sermon and the sacrament

---

2 *W. A.,* III, 250, 4; 255, 28 ff.; 256, 4 ff.; 259, 13; 261, 5; 262, 30; 347, 37 ff.;
348, 11 ff.; 456, 5. Also LVII, Heb., 196, 4 ff. (1517-18); II, 469, 18; 499, 22; 551, 33
(1519); V, 266, 2, 24; 554, 13 (1519-21); IX, 462, 12, 17 (Poliander's codex, 1519-21);
X, 1, I, 456, 18 (1522); XI, 111, 19 (Rörer, 1523); XV, 460, 9 ff. (Rörer, 1524); XVII,
137, 11 (Rörer, 1525); XVII, 1, 269, 33 (Rörer, 1525); XVI, 328, 10 ff. (Rörer, 1525);
XXXIII, 273, 2 ff. (Aurifaber, 1531-32); XLV, 150, 3 (Rörer, 1537); XLV, 230, 2
(Rörer, 1537); XLVI, 405, 13; L, 626, 18 (1539).

3 *W. A.,* III, 256, 10 (1513-15); 259, 13; also III, 250, 4 ff.; 256, 1 ff.; II, 469,
17 ff.; 499, 20 ff. (1519).

4 *W. A.,* III, 348, 1 (1515); also III, 347, 25 ff.; 466, 9 ff.; IV, 9, 36 ff.

are here placed together with the Word of Scripture. They are all outward words which must necessarily wait upon the inward Word of God.[5]

If we thus take our point of departure in the concrete form of the Word of Scripture, in the sermon and in the sacrament, we easily get into the situation in which the Word threatens to disappear from us. The Word indeed is "only" the outward Word. It does not become the Word of *God* until the inward Word is added to it. But this is the concern of God alone. It seems as if we have to pause to observe a concept of the relationship between the Spirit and the Word, according to which the outward Word becomes a mere symbol, a signpost which directs us to the point where the Spirit is, but does not itself mediate the Spirit.

However, as the passages so far have indicated these thoughts are not found only in Luther's first lectures on the Psalms and on the Epistle to the Romans, when he was strongly influenced by Augustine. They are also found in the writings of the following years. To evaluate these thoughts rightly they must be compared with other statements which seem to take an exactly opposite direction. If we use the thoughts about the freedom and sovereignty of the Spirit as our point of departure, we get into the same situation as when we used the outward Word. The Spirit and the inward Word seem to vanish into nothing if we do not hold on to the outward Word as the means of the Spirit. Luther emphasized that the Word is the instrument of the Spirit,[6] that the outward Word is the incarnation of the Spirit, and that it corresponds to the Spirit as the voice corresponds to man's breathing, or as the rays of the sun correspond to the warmth of the sun. It seems as if the connection between the Spirit and the Word is much stronger here than in the first quoted series of passages. It even seems to be in direct opposition to what we just observed with respect to the sovereignty of the Spirit and the insufficiency of the outward Word. It seems as if the outward Word of necessity brings the Spirit with it. The illustra-

---

[5] *W. A.*, I, 632, 9 (1518); also III, 259, 3 ff.; 372, 4 ff.; IV, 243, 18 ff. (1513-15); II, 108, 1 ff. (1519).

[6] *W. A.*, III, 262, 30 (1513-15); IV, 189, 22; also III, 259, 13 ff.; LVII, Heb., 143, 3 ff.; X, 1, II, 92, 15 ff. (1522).

tions about the light and warmth of the sunbeam and of the voice and breathing prove this. Where the Word is, the Spirit inevitably soon follows. But the Spirit does not come before the Word has preceded it. It is not without significance to note that this order cannot be changed. It is always first the outward Word and then— soon—the Spirit with the inner Word.[7]

How may this contradiction be solved? On the one side there is such a strong emphasis on the sovereignty of the Spirit that the outward Word seems to be reduced to a comparatively insignificant accompanying phenomenon of the free work of the Spirit. On the other side there is so strong an emphasis on the connection of the Spirit to the outward Word, on its being a necessary consequence of the Word, that the Spirit seems to become a mere attribute to the Word.

The attempt may be made to solve the tension between these two series of thoughts by supposing a "development" in Luther's thinking. Among the quotations above, the majority of those that shall prove the first idea are taken from the earlier writings, especially from the first lecture on the Psalms, which has been used very little in this book. The majority of the quotations which explain the second idea are taken from the writings after Luther became a reformer. This fact justifies our suggesting a shift of emphasis, which no doubt is a result of the fact that the direct influence of Augustine is stronger in the first lecture on the Psalms than in the later writings. But the problem cannot really be solved by this method. The indicated difference in accentuation in the younger and the older writings is also only partially relative. We have seen how the instrumental view of the Word is not only found in the later writings but also in the first lecture on the Psalms, even though it does not stand out as clearly as in the later writings. But the point that is even more important is that the strong emphasis on the dependence of the Spirit on the Word as its instrument does not cause the earlier Augustinian emphasis of the sovereignty of the Spirit and the insufficiency of the outward Word to be pushed

---

[7] *W. A.*, IX, 632, 25 ff.; also IX, 403, 13 ff. (Poliander's codex, 1519-21); VII, 504, 25 ff.; 509, 13 ff. (1521); X, 1, I, 328, 7; 337, 6 ff.

into the background, which it certainly would be if the new accentuation signified a decisive *change* in Luther's view of the relation between the Spirit and the Word. The Augustinian method of expression is strongly retained along with the more forceful accentuation of the Spirit's dependence upon the outward Word. This is true not only for the period to which this first part of our work is limited, but it is true also for the older Luther.[8] If we may speak about a "development" it certainly is not a development away from the Augustinian emphasis on the sovereignty of the Spirit and insufficiency of the outward Word. In other words this means that the tension is taken into the development. But in this case the development can of course not be used as a means by which to solve the tension. Over against the hypothesis of a "development" in Luther's view of the relationship between the Spirit and the Word is also the fact that the strong emphasis on the dependence of the Spirit on the outward Word is already prevalent before the fight with the enthusiasts. If there is any possibility of a decisive change in Luther's view of the relationship between Spirit and Word from that of the young Luther's Augustinian attitude toward a view more related to Thomism (and the problem is at times understood in this manner) it would seem most natural that this change began when Luther, by the theology of the Spirit of the enthusiasts, had been confronted with the dangers of the sharp distinction between the outward and the inward Word. But the fact is that this accentuation is already present several years before Luther encounters the enthusiasts. We are not therefore to understand that the struggle with the enthusiasts has caused a change in Luther's view on this point. The view of the relationship between the Spirit and the Word which Luther later used against the enthusiasts was fully formed before that struggle. The struggle with the enthusiasts only developed a more polemic keenness in the formulation of the expressions but no real change.

No progress is made by attempting to divide the two opposing

---

8 *W. A.,* XVIII, 602, 11 ff.; 753, 25 ff. (1525); XIV, 726, 33 ff. (1525); XVII, 1, 151, 7 ff. (Rörer, 1525); XX, 396, 25 ff. (Rörer, 1526); XLI, 601, 19 ff. (Rörer, 1536); XXXIX, 2, 356, 15 ff. (*Promotions-disp. Petr. Hegemon,* 1545).

ideas into two different stages in Luther's development. And it is just as impossible to try to reduce to trifles either the one or the other of the two, as Karl Holl and Rudolf Otto try to do. But in order to understand Luther it is necessary to be assured that a genuine tension exists between the two tendencies, one that cannot be glossed over. This is really the very same tension which we found when we discussed the idea of grace and gift, and the relationship between Spirit and faith, namely the tension between the theology of predestination and redemption. And it is impossible to smooth out this contrast by logic. It can only be resolved christologically.

The idea of the sovereignty of the Spirit and the insufficiency of the outward Word, if consistently carried through, will lead to a predestinarian concept of God. The idea of the dependence of the Spirit on the outward Word will, if carried through with the same consistency, lead to the view that the responsibility for the insufficient effect of the Word must be placed on the man who hears it. The Word in itself is indeed the mediator of the Spirit and his power. When it does not succeed in influencing all, the reason must be found in the varied reaction of different people to the Word. Neither of these two points of view belongs to Luther. His view is found only where both ideas are united in the mutual tension and where this tension is not logically glossed over, but is retained and resolved in Christ alone.

If it could be proven that in Luther's view the Word of God, in the strictest sense, was only Christ himself, then it would not be difficult to see why neither of the two opposing ideas can be pushed aside. When the living Christ himself is the Word, then the outward Word as such, whether we find it in the Bible, in the sermon, or in the sacrament, can never directly be identified with God's own Word. Only when the Holy Spirit makes Christ present in the Word does it become God's own living Word. If this does not happen the Word is only a letter, a law, a description of Christ. From the opposite point of view it is true that the Spirit, when it undertakes to make Christ present, is not able to work independently of the Word. For Christ is indeed the incarnated Logos in the person who appeared in history, Jesus of Nazareth, who by the Old and New Testament writings is proclaimed as the Christ. It is therefore only by the Word depending on Scripture that the Spirit can make Jesus Christ present. A spirit who would work independently of this definite outward Word about the incarnated Logos would not be the Spirit of Jesus Christ. We are always referred to this definite Word. But we are not referred to it as our guaranteed possession, but as the place where we expect the Spirit to make Jesus Christ present for us. Without the work of the Spirit the Word may continue to be the Word which speaks of Jesus Christ, but it is not the Word which bestows Christ on us.

The two ideas thus meet one another in Christ. Where he is merely present as the ideological content of the Word, as part of the law, as a description, there the Word is dead. Where he, however, is present in the Word as a living person, as the gift of the gospel, there the Word is alive. And whether Christ is in the Word in the one way or the other, depends solely on the Spirit. Only in the moment when the Spirit, by the outward Word, makes Christ truly present are the Word and the Spirit directly one. But this free intervention of the Spirit is not an incidental event which might just as well, or even rather, not take place. It is an event promised by the Word itself, because it concerns itself with Christ. Even though the Word and the Spirit are separated so that where the Word is we are asked to pray about the Spirit and wait on him, they are not separated as two categories which are not concerned with one another and which only incidentally are brought into connection with each other, but they are separated as promise and fulfillment, as prayer and the answer to prayer, as a sign and as a reality. The two ideas meet in Christ himself as a unity of the promise and the fulfillment, of the ideological content of the Word and its realization, and of prayer and the answer to prayer. Before Christ we are simultaneously poor and rich, begging and possessing, and we learn and we know. We are asked to pray about the Spirit without whom the Word about Christ remains dead letters, and yet at the same time we are in this prayer assured that the Word about *Him* never returns void. The tension between the two ideas is not merely a logical contradiction but it contains the dynamis of faith itself. When faith is *faith in Christ* it contains as we have previously seen a constant motion, the motion away from ourselves to Christ. It is this motion of faith, which we know from the ideas about *gratia* and *donum*, and *Glaube und Liebe,* that we find again in the tension between the two ideas of Luther's view of the relation between the Spirit and the Word. Where the attempt is made rationally to gloss over this tension as is done in the orthodox doctrine of inspiration, where the Spirit is bound to the Scripture (even without its use), or as is done also, to use an example, in the so-called "historic" view of the Bible, where the so-called religiously valuable parts of Scripture are considered one with the real Word of God, then there is no longer any connection with the view of Scripture of Luther's Reformation. The tension in the concept of the relationship between Spirit and Word is inevitable as long as this concept is to be an expression for the motion of faith itself.

Now we need only to show that it really can be proved that Luther holds that the Word of God, in the strictest sense, is Christ alone and that, on the basis of this assumption, the explanation of the tension between the two ideas in Luther's concept of the relationship between the Spirit and Word is correct and can be deepened by a closer observation of the sources.

It is natural to start with the trinitarian ideas of Luther under which he embodies the Logos Christology of the ancient church. In his doctrine of the Trinity Luther takes the prologue of John and the whole tradition of the church and identifies God's eternal inward Word with the incarnated Christ. The Word of God which brings a message from his heart cannot come from him and to us in this world except in a body of flesh. The incarnated Christ himself is the outward Word of God. Yes, he is literally *Words* when in the sermon he falls as rain upon the dry meadows, either to be accepted by faith or to be rejected by unbelief. In the *Church Postil* Luther takes strong opposition to the scholastics who want to make the Logos Christology of the prologue of John into the work of man and into Platonic and philosophical ideas which lead us away from Christ into ourselves, while the gospel writer intends to lead us from ourselves and to Christ. The gospel writer does not treat the almighty, eternal Word of God in any other way than by pointing us to the Word clothed in flesh and blood walking here upon the earth. He does not scatter our thoughts over the whole creation of God that we should try to run after him out there and seek him there and speculate our way to him just as the Platonic thinkers do. He wants to take us away from all these protracted and scattered thoughts and lead us to Christ just as if he would say: Why do you seek so far away? Behold, in the man, Christ, you have it all. Christ is the ladder to heaven by which we alone have entrance to the Father. He is not found in the heaven where the commentators seek him in flighty speculations. He is in the manger and in the bosom of the woman. We must start from below and not from above. Christ—or rather the humanity of Christ—is the sign by which God will draw us to himself. Therefore the eyes must be directed toward this sign and not toward mere speculations.

But these fluttering thoughts may not only be found outside of Scripture. Even in the Scriptures it is possible to flutter past Christ. But as for the Scripture it is true that the whole Bible—its entire content—speaks of Christ.[9] If we do not grasp this sole meaning of Scripture, we have only heard the outward sound, the flesh and the shell of Scripture, and not its spirit and kernel. In the midst of the multiplicity of single words of Scripture there is the one word about Christ as *verbum abbreviatum et consummatum* (Isa. 10:22 ff., Rom. 9:28, 36). God speaks in three ways: (a) in himself and with the saints in glory, (b) in the saints in this life by the Spirit, (c) into the ears of man by the outward Word. This corresponds historically in a reverse order: God's Word by the prophets, God's Word in his Son, and God's Word to us in eternal glory. The word by the prophets was clothed in many figures of speech and shadows, but all that of which the law speaks in many words has been fulfilled in Christ. Therefore the word which speaks through him is *verbum abbreviatum et consummatum*.

In contrast to *verbum abbreviatum et consummatum* there is

---

[9] *W. A.*, LVI, 414, 15 (1515-16); V, 542, 21 (1519-21); X, 1, I, 628, 2 (1522).

verbum inconsummatum (dilatum) et imperfectum, which is drawn out and imperfect because of the many individual words and the many figures and shadows. In the interpretation of Romans 9:28 in the lecture on Romans this contrast is developed in detail. *Verbum abbreviatum et consummatum* is *verbum fidei, verbum spiritus et absconditum*, that is *abbreviatum ab omnibus significatis, sensibilibus ac figuralibus*,[10] which is cut off and separated from all visible things, out of which it promises and produces nothing. Just because of that it is *consummatum* (perfect) for it does not proclaim any of these visible and imperfect things, which do not satisfy the whole man, but only a part of man. On the contrary it proclaims that which is perfect, that is, God alone. *Verbum imperfectum et dilatum* is *verbum legis carnaliter intellectae*, that is, the law, while *verbum abbreviatum et consummatum* is *verbum spiritus* or *verbum legis spiritualiter intellectae*, that is, the gospel. The first is an imperfect word, since it only signifies but does not give that of which it speaks. The other, however, is a perfect word because it truly gives that which it signifies, the grace of God. But that which the law signifies and which the gospel gives, is Christ.

In Luther's exegesis of Isaiah 10:22 (Rom. 9:28) we have the well-known distinction between the law and the gospel, *littera* and *spiritus*, between the word which only signifies and that which also gives that which it signifies. But what is of greatest importance in the manner in which Luther in this exegesis treats this well-known contrast is the fact that it is not made into a separation between different parts of Scripture which may be objectively limited, but is absolutely attached to the motion of faith away from man himself toward Christ. Those who understand the gospel in a proud and false way are selfishly changing it to a *verbum imperfectum et longum*, to an empty and useless and false word, no matter how the word itself is the high and holy gospel. The word, however, which truly is *verbum spiritus*, eliminates all pride and all egotism in the hearer. But such a word is only understood by faith. In this manner faith itself becomes a parabolically expounded, living *verbum abbreviatum*. For all things visible have been eliminated;

---

10 *W. A.*, LVI, 406, 27 ff.

it is *argumentum non apparentium*. But it is also a *verbum consummatum*, because it is *substantia sperandarum rerum*. The distinction between law and gospel is understood by this parabolic interpretation, not as a rigid dialectic point, but as the dynamic contrast which includes both the beginning and the end of the motion of faith. The peculiar Word of God, the Word of the Spirit, is only found in Scripture when faith itself within Scripture (as in all other places) makes the motion away from self-righteousness to Christ. But that again means away from the humanly understood law, from the word which only describes righteousness (and thereby leaves it to us to realize it), toward the gospel, to that Word which gives the righteousness which by the Spirit presents us with Christ truly present in the Word as the gift of God.

That this motion of faith gets started depends solely on the Holy Spirit. The Holy Spirit works in such a way that Christ is present in the outward Word just as he once was present in the flesh of Jesus. Luther even considers Scripture as Christ's spiritual body. The outward Word is that body by which the risen Christ is here and now present among us. Therefore not before Christ's presence in the Word by the Spirit is his resurrection publicly proclaimed. In connection with Romans 1:4, Luther often points out that the work of the Holy Spirit is to proclaim the divinity of Jesus Christ in the resurrection. By the incarnation the Son of God humbled himself and assumed the *forma servi*. He became *humiliatus* so that his divinity was emptied out and hidden in the flesh. In this state of humiliation he was, of course, always the Son of God, but this was not as yet *destinatum, declaratum et constitutum hominibus*. He had authority over all things even though he did not exercise it and was not deemed the one he was. But the public proclamation of the divinity and power of Christ is done *per spiritum sanctificationis*, which was not given before the resurrection of Jesus, but which by the resurrection should glorify him.[11] But this public proclamation and glorification is directed toward men. The miracle of the resurrection is not in itself the glorification of

---

11 *W. A.*, LVI, 6, 3; 168, 8-13. Also IV, 101, 13 ff. (1513-15); V, 251, 35 ff. (1519-21); IX, 458, 16 ff. (Poliander's codex, 1519-21).

Jesus. This miracle would be of no value to us unless succeeded by the outpouring of the Spirit by which Jesus Christ through the message of the apostles is exalted and glorified among men in the whole world. The real glorification and exaltation does not take place in heaven but here on earth by the message of the gospel. The resurrection of Jesus and the enlightening of the Holy Spirit cannot be separated. By the work of the Holy Spirit the resurrection is really taken from the hidden sphere of God into the message of the gospel, so that *the risen Christ lives his risen life in our midst in this message.* The enlightening work of the Holy Spirit is responsible for the fact that the resurrection of Jesus Christ is not a distant metaphysical phenomenon but a redeeming reality in us and for us. This means that the earthly life of Jesus is not mere history, but by the Holy Spirit the risen Christ's present life is in our midst by the gospel. All these thoughts, which are often overlooked when Luther's concept of the relationship between the Spirit and the Word is discussed, clearly demonstrate that the center in the Word of God is the risen Christ himself, and that the outward Word does not become the Word of God until the Spirit causes the risen Christ to live his life in that Word. It is this living presence mediated by the Spirit which produces the previously mentioned motion of faith from the law to the gospel, from *verbum imperfectum et dilatum* to *verbum abbreviatum et consummatum*, from the imitation of Christ as an ideal to the accepting of Christ as a gift.

It is hereby established that to Luther the Word in its real sense is Christ. He is God the Father's eternal and inward Word which by the incarnation was spoken into our world. He, in his humanity, is our only way to God. But in his humanity we meet him only in the outward Word, when this is not understood as law but as gospel, as *verbum abbreviatum et consummatum.* In this Word the risen Christ is present as God's gift to us and thereby directs the motion of faith from all self-righteousness to Christ as our alien righteousness.

By this it is clear that this Christocentric concept of the Word of God not only establishes what we have designated here as the first thought in Luther's concept of the relation between the Spirit and the Word; that is, it qualifies the outward Word as dead letters when it is separated from the living Christ as God's gift to us, but it also underscores the second thought in just as great a sense that the Spirit cannot work except through this definite outward Word. For the outward Word is necessary in order that Christ, who is the content of the Word, can be presented to the individual as a gift. The gospel by which the Spirit makes Christ present must have sacramental quality. Otherwise Christ is changed to an idea to which we are related as imitators of a pattern. Without such a sacramental Word, Christ is understood purely historically, and the gospel is a general story of something that has passed. But the gospel is not past history. It is sacramental, for it gives what it claims. This sacramental character of the gospel is expressed in the fact that the Word is an outward Word. Everything sacramental always contains an outward sign. The outward Word can and shall be the means of God's sacramental message to man, while the absence of the outward Word leaves the man alone with himself and his own recollections and ideas. Jesus Christ, who is the bread of life, cannot be obtained by anyone through his own efforts, neither by studying, by hearing, by asking, or by seeking. The Father himself must give Christ to us. It is the work of Word and sacrament.

If the sacrament were without the Word, it would be of no value that Christ was truly present, for without the outward Word he would not be given to us. And the incarnation of Christ, his life on earth and his suffering, would be of no value if it was not included in the outward Word, to which faith is able to attach itself. In the bread of life Christ and the outward Word are the same thing.

The outward Word is therefore the servant of the Spirit in this way that it can direct itself to the individual and assure him of the presence of Christ. The outward Word has, when it is used as an address, the characteristic of a promise, to which the inward Word corresponds as a fulfillment. *Allso das nit muglich ist, das ein mensch auss seiner vornunfft und vormugen solt mit wercken hynauff gen hymel steygen und gott zuuorkumen, yhn bewegen zur gnade, sondern gott muss zuuorkumen alle werck und gedancken und ein klar ausgedruckt zusagen thun mit worten, wilch den der mensch mit eynem rechten festen glauben egreyff und behalte, sso folgt den der heylig geyst der yhm geben wirt umb desselben glaubens willen.*[12]

This last quotation shows clearly how the outward Word by its alien character comes to oppose all that may be designated one's own thoughts and works. *Opus factum* and *verbum creditum* signify two opposite ways to righteousness. This opposition to all self-righteousness and work of the law is found in the fact that the Word is an outward Word. By its very alien characteristic the outward Word works as a promise of the alien Word of God.

It is in this connection that Luther's strong emphasis on the spoken Word, the living Word, must be seen. Just as eagerly as any Grundtvig[13] he emphasizes that it is not sufficient that someone writes and reads books in the church. It is necessary that a spoken Word be proclaimed, a Word that can be *heard*. Christ wrote nothing and the Apostles only a little, but they all spoke very much. The ministry of the New Testament is not written in dead stone tablets. It is placed in the sound of the living Word. It is by the living Word that it perfects and fulfills the gospel. Almost with the voice of Grundtvig Luther says of the church that it is a house of the mouth *(Bethfage)* and not a house of the pen. It is really contrary to the spirit of the New Testament and a sign of spiritual decadence that in the era of the New Testament it became necessary to begin to write books. It really should have been sufficient that there at all places should be good, learned, spiritual, and industrious preachers, who could draw out the living Word of the Scripture and constantly proclaim it to the people. The law is a *dead* writing, written in books, but the gospel is a living voice.

There seems to be a special connection between the law and the letter on the one side, and between the gospel and the preaching on the other side. Luther himself expresses it in this manner that the living Word shall extract the gospel which is hidden in Scrip-

---

12 *W. A.,* VI, 356, 13 (1520).
13 Bishop N. F. S. Grundtvig (1783-1872), Danish theologian and poet. Founder of the Folk School movement, he was the strongest single influence in Danish religious and social life in the nineteenth century.

ture (i.e. the law). As we have seen before there is a special connection between the law and the flesh and between the gospel and the Spirit. Therefore it seems natural that there also is a special connection between the living Word and the Spirit and between the written Word and the flesh.

Luther's view of the Scripture can therefore be summarized thus: the Word as letter is law. As the letter it simply places us before a history which can only call us to be imitators. As the letter it places us alone on our own resources. As preaching, however, the Word is gospel. In the form of preaching it presents Christ to us as a gift. In the form of preaching the Word is a promise of the coming of the Spirit of God and his work in us.

The difference between the written and the preached Word is not a difference in content but in form. The content of the law and the gospel is the same. Luther describes the content of both as Christ. But the content of the law is Christ as a demand. The content of the gospel is Christ as a gift. It should be mentioned again that the law is not just certain parts of Scripture (e.g. the Old Testament), and the gospel not certain other parts (e.g. the New Testament). The law is *verbum dilatum et imperfectum*, that is, the content of all Scripture understood as a demand (thus also the New Testament and even the Gospels!). The gospel is *verbum abbreviatum et consummatum*, that is, all of Scripture understood as that which gives us Christ (also the Old Testament and even Moses!). But these different forms which the law and gospel place about the same content, have both outward and inward sides. The outward form of the law is the written Word, its inward form the wisdom of the flesh. The outward form of the gospel is the preached Word, its inward form the Spirit of God.

May it truly be said that there is a special connection between this outward and inward form in the law and the gospel? Is there a special connection between the Word as a written Word and the wisdom of the flesh of man?

In the second lecture on the Psalms, Luther at one point mentions that the gospel is not put into letters and books, but into an open and living confession, so that it not only shall be an object of knowledge but shall be publicly preached. This point should be compared with the previously mentioned points where the outward Word is placed in opposition to everything that is classified as our own thoughts and works. The outward form of the letter corresponds to knowledge—that which the wisdom of the flesh can make into its mastered object. In this sense all of Scripture, as the written Word, can be made into inward knowledge. But to the same extent that the Scripture is made an object of knowledge it also becomes law. It places us on our own resources to realize this knowledge. Outward preaching is something entirely different from this inward knowledge which is an expression of man's own ability. In the outward preaching the Word meets us as something over which we never become master; it meets us as an alien power, which gives us what we never could take of ourselves: the living Christ as a gift. This applies not only to the hearer but also to the preacher. It is the impossible he does when he preaches the gospel; it is not the display of his own knowledge and power. In the study of books there is often hidden a proud will to make oneself master over the Word without the aid of the Spirit. Therefore it is not those who have read the most books who are the best Christians. As far as the written Word is concerned this fact applies, that he who does not have the guidance of the Spirit does not in the written Word find anything more than he already has. It is possible in this connection to refer to Luther's well-known doctrine about *lex naturae,* which is written into the heart. When man meets the Scripture as law it tells him no more than what is written into every human heart. That which goes beyond the law of nature is really not law, but "figures" that promise Christ. Because the law, when it demands Christ, can be said also to promise him, it is said that the Spirit is hidden in the letter,[14] and that the law may be spirit-

---

[14] *W. A.,* III, 256, 28 (1513-15) *Spiritus enim latet in litera, que est verbum non bonum, quia lex ire. Sed spiritus est verbum bonum, quia verbum gratie. Et ideo illud educere de litera est ipsum eructare . . . Eructat ergo propheta, sed effundit euangelista et apostolus.* IV, 58, 15 *litera et omnis figura totius legis est velut sermo quidam transitorius. Spiritus autem in illa latens et per eam significatus est velut sensus illius sermonis.* II, 499 (1519) *Igitur spiritualis est (lex) quia spiritum fidei requirit.* 552, 3 *Lex in se semper est spiritualis, id est Spiritum significans, qui est plenitudo eius.* Also IV, 314, 22 ff.

ually understood, that is, not in the sense that we are left with our own resources to fulfill it and thereby to stimulate self-righteousness of the flesh, but so that the law judges us and makes our own fulfillment impossible in order that grace (Christ) becomes our only possibility. In a spiritual sense the law thus becomes one with the gospel. But as long as the written law is not spiritually understood, it is identical with the law of nature. It throws us completely on our own resources. It tells us nothing but what everyone knows and leaves it to each one to realize what he knows. When the written law is understood in this manner it becomes a mere image of the writing which is found in the heart. And therefore as long as man only knows the Word as a written Word, as a letter, he continues to be his own master.

In the same way there is a special connection between the Word as preaching and the Spirit of God. Where the outward Word is to be the bearer of the Spirit of God it must come in the manner of preaching. In its essence the gospel is always a message. From this point of view must be judged the peculiar thoughts about *totus Christus* from the lectures on Romans, often considered typical Roman Catholic remnants. In the interpretation of Romans 3:21, 22, Luther takes issue with the heretics who are willing to believe in Christ, but not in everything that belongs to Christ, that is, who will not accept as Christ's own Word the spoken Word which is being proclaimed by the ministry of the church. He who will not listen to the preached Word thereby shows that he follows his own *sensus*; but how can the one who follows his own *sensus* believe in Christ? His faith is only a knowledge of the fact that Jesus is born and that he suffered, but not a trust in the living Christ who *now* speaks. Such a man divides Christ and does not believe in the whole Christ (that is, not only in the historic Jesus but also on the exalted Christ who speaks in his church *now*), but only in that part of Christ which belongs to the past (the historic Jesus). But he who wants only a part of Christ, denies him entirely. Some scholars rightly address this polemic to the imitation-piety of the Middle Ages. For it is the peculiarity of imitation-piety that it is satisfied with a part of the whole Christ, that is, the ideal of Christ, the earthly life of Christ understood as law, as a demand. The essence of Christian faith in contrast to all imitation-piety is defined thus: *Ita, Quando, 'fides Christi' dicitur, fides in Christum et in verbum cuiuscunque, in quo ipse loquitur, intelligitur.*[15] The relation to *verbum vocale* is that which makes a distinction between the piety which is of the law and is satisfied with man's own resources, his *sensus* and his *opera*, and the faith which, by accepting the spoken Word in the church as Christ's own Word thereby signifies that the believer is in a flight away from all his own to Christ, to the Spirit, to grace. Even by its outward appearance as *verbum vocale* the preached Word produces a challenge to *sensus,* to the self-sufficient knowledge and experience of man, and thereby it proves itself to be a fit instrument for the gospel which certainly is opposed to all reason and experience. When Luther here speaks of *verbum vocale* in the mouth of the prelate or the brother he is not speaking of some casual command or order which demands blind obedience. But the *verbum vocale* here is that which alone bears the *gospel.* We are only speaking of that Word which is necessary that faith may live. He who proudly thinks that he has faith as a certain possession and therefore does not need to listen to any outward Word, is not able to hear the Word of God, since he must consider it false because it is opposed to his own opinion, which he deems to be true. The Word which is spoken by the mouth of the "prelate," or by the mouth of any good believer, is a Word which creates and nourishes the justifying faith. It is not just any kind of word with any kind of content which a "prelate" may think of speaking, but it is a Word which Christ himself speaks, and which therefore has Christ as its content. It is a Word which is not of the law and which works without the aid of the law. But this Word which brings us Christ, and in which Christ himself speaks, we always find *in specie peregrina, in humilitate* and not *in specie gloriae.* The reason for this is that God in his revelation hides himself under his contrast so that Christ as God's revelation appears hidden under death and inner conflict and pain of hell. Because *we* live in a lie, the truth, when it shall come to us,

---

15 *W. A.,* LVI, 256, 8.

must appear *adversaria specie*. Therefore, if we want to hear, we must permit our own thoughts to be corrected by the Word, which comes to us as a message from the outside. In this humble readiness to hear *verbum vocale* the expectation of hearing the gospel—Christ's own voice—makes itself known just as, inversely, the proud feeling of being above the necessity of listening to *verbum vocale* is an expression of the self-sufficiency of work-righteousness.

There is in these thoughts no special emphasis on hierarchical authority. Luther was not interested in exhorting to obedience toward the superiors in the church. His concern was to make known to the representatives of the imitation-piety—just as he later did to the enthusiasts—the character of the gospel as a message. Therefore he wanted with all his power to underscore the significance of *verbum vocale*. Only the Christ who is expected as speaking in *verbum vocale*, no matter from whose mouth it is spoken, is the Christ of the gospel, the present Christ who lives and gives himself in the gospel. Only the Christ whom we again and again expect in the gospel just as often as a man proclaims it (and we must be ready to hear the gospel at any time proclaimed by anyone) is the whole Christ, *totus Christus*. The Christ, however, whom we think we possess because we know what the Scriptures state about him, is not the whole Christ but only a "historic" Jesus, the ideal of Christ in the imitation-piety. The gospel is not only an account of a Christ in the past. It is a message about peace in Christ *now* to those, who now are under the condemnation of the law. But this peace in Christ is something that is so completely hidden for the world, that it must be proclaimed by the oral Word. It is not something that can be seen or experienced. It can only be received as a message proclaimed in words to be accepted by faith.

Here we find the real reason why the living Word is especially suited to be an instrument of the Spirit in his work of mediating Christ. We have previously in the discussion of *fides Christi* seen that the idea of the real presence of Christ by faith is in danger of gliding into an unevangelical mysticism of Christ if we do not maintain that the reality of Christ is totally different from all other reality, a *hidden*, an invisible reality. The reality of God cannot exist otherwise for us. God must hide himself under his absolute contrast, if he is to get near us. When faith maintains this reality of God it is placed in an absolute contrast to all natural experience and reason. And this contrast to *sensus* is most clearly seen in this, that faith—in contrast to all *sensus*—relies only on a message about something that cannot be seen. Christ is *really* present by the Spirit, but this reality is by faith. He does not permit this real presence to be comprehended by *sensus*, but only by the faith which relies on the *message* about his presence, the message which we are not to expect as a voice from heaven, but which meets us here and now in the spoken Word in the church.[16]

We have thus seen that the spoken Word points in a double sense to the living and present Christ and by this reveals itself as the actual instrument of the Spirit. In the first place, the *living* Word proves by its contemporaneity and by its personal form of address that Christ is a risen Christ who lives and speaks and gives himself in his church. It is the reality and presence of Christ which the living Word in this manner directly expresses. In the second place, the living Word expresses the fact that Christ is only really present as the Christ of *faith*, as the hidden, as the one who is opposed to all *Greyffen und fulen*, all *sensus*, all natural experience, as the one who can be apprehended only by the fact that the message about him is believed. The living Word expresses the unity of the reality of Christ both by revealing and hiding it. As a living Word it pushes aside all certain possession of Christ, whether this takes the form of a scholastic control of the Scriptures or by the imitation-piety of isolating the historic Christ as an ideal of life, and it directs again and again to the real presence of Christ mediated by the Word. The *living* Word is the revelation which comes again and again. But as a living Word it brushes aside all attempts to apprehend the present Christ in experience and emotion, all attempts of a greater or smaller degree to identify him with a Christ living in us, whether that takes place in an Osiandric mysticism of Christ or in a post-pietistic formulation of Christian

---

16 *W. A.*, LVI, 424, 27 (1515-16); LVI, 416, 9 (1515-16); IX, 632, 14 (Poliander's codex, 1519-21).

moralism. The living Word is as a veil—it brings only the Christ who is hid, the Christ of faith, of the message, and of the alien righteousness.

We are now able to understand that the double form of the Word as writing and as *verbum vocale* depends on its function as a means of revelation and as the instrument of the Spirit mediating Christ. The Word became flesh as the Messiah of Israel. Therefore the Word, because he is present, is a historic Word, it is the Word about the history of Israel and its fulfillment in the life of Jesus, his death and resurrection, and as such a historic Word it provides a contrast to all human wisdom. The history, which the written Word certifies, is the saving intervention of God into the life of humanity. Therefore this history must be proven as all other history by written sources. It is characteristic for Luther's view of Scripture—as well as the view of the New Testament and that of the ancient church—that the historic proof of Christ is first all the *Old Testament* of which the New Testament is the "opening." But the Word is not only writing. It is not like a historic narrative of Livius. For the Word which has become flesh is not only history, it is revelation. Therefore the written word must become living in preaching as of the present. In the living, present Word of preaching the Christ of the Scripture is really present. And if the Word of Scripture is not in this manner made contemporary, it cannot become gospel. If it remains a written Word without becoming alive in a contemporary proclamation, its testimony of Christ will remain a dead past, law, and become simply an ideal of Christ to imitate in our own strength. But it is the message of the Scriptures that must form the content in all real preaching and not just any kind of beautiful Christian thoughts. They who permit the living message to contain anything beyond the testimony of the Scriptures, that is, they who preach their own philosophy and piety, preach heresy. This mutual connection between the written Word and the living preaching is the synthesis of the historic and the risen Christ. And it is this synthesis or unity the Holy Spirit makes real when he makes the risen Christ truly present.

We have now reached the point where we are able to view in its entirely Luther's complete concept of the relationship between the Spirit and the Word. At the beginning of this section we asked this question: Is it possible for the Word to work without the Spirit, or may the Spirit work independently of the Word?

We are now able to state it in this manner: the Word may exist without the Spirit. When the Word is without the Spirit it is just a letter. It is a letter in the sense that it only gives us a description of the life we are to live, but does not give us the life it describes. As a letter the Word is law and not gospel. And as law the Word is essentially the written Word, that is, the Word understood here as the letter of the Scripture, in its separation from the contemporary oral message in the church as the instrument of the Spirit. As a letter the Word does not take us farther than to that which is written in the heart of every man. As a law the Scriptures do not contain more than the natural law, which is written in the heart of every man. For this natural law, which is in the heart of every man, is the law of love. And there is no higher law. In so far as the Scriptures, as letter, speak of Christ, that is, just describe him separated from the contemporary oral message which presents to us the Christ thus described as a gift, such a description of Christ does not get us beyond the natural law. For a description of Christ as a model can never reach higher than to a concrete description of the love which the natural law already demands. The Word may therefore well be without Spirit, and when this happens the Word is only outward Word. The outward then stands as a contrast to the inward in the sense of the work of the Spirit of God in us, that is, the "inner Word." But if the Word is to be God's own living Word to us, it cannot be so without the Spirit; for it is the Spirit alone that makes the Word God's own saving Word.

In the same manner it is true that the Spirit can exist without the Word. The Spirit is not bound *in* the Word. The Spirit is God's own high majesty and he has his own existence in God's eternal glory, away from the Word and from our world. But as the revealing Spirit, as the Spirit which is come to us, he cannot be without the Word. For it is the Spirit's work to make the risen Christ real and present among us. And the risen Christ can only be present among us in his humanity. But the risen Christ's humanity in our midst now is the Word in which he gives us himself as a gift. As the instrument of the Spirit the Word is therefore always the proclaiming Word, a contemporary and sacramental Word, which gives Christ as gift, and in which he is the acting subject. The sacramental Word of Christ is the gospel, a Word which gives that about which it tells. And as gospel it finds its adequate form in the living Word, the oral and proclaimed Word in the church. If a written Word—e.g. the Bible Word—becomes gospel, it is only possible because it borrows in a sense the form of the living Word and is accepted by the reader as a Word in which from the pages of the Bible the risen Christ personally speaks to him. Therefore Luther says that the gospel is really not a written Word but an oral Word. But this living Word, which is the instrument of the Spirit in his work of reconciling Christ, is in its content identical with the written Word. For the risen Christ is himself identical with the historic Jesus. Therefore it may be said that the Spirit is hidden in the letter and that the oral sermon draws the gospel out of the Scriptures. The living Word in the church does not proclaim just anything, and it does not proclaim Christ as a part of our religious experience; but it proclaims the Scriptures' message about Christ. The Spirit cannot work without the Word, and it cannot make the real Jesus Christ present without the aid of the Bible's testimony about Christ, preached contemporarily as gospel, as a promise of the Christ of the Bible as gift. As gospel the Word is in a certain sense the inner Word. It cannot become a real gospel unless the Spirit in the inner man works together with the outward Word of the preacher and makes Christ truly present in the outward Word. And yet it is true that the inward Word of the Spirit cannot be separated from the outward Word of the gospel. The gospel is not an inward Word in the same sense as the natural law. It is not a Word which is created in the inner man, or which is written by God in the heart without the aid of something from without. But it is a Word which comes from without, just as the voice of the preacher reaches our ears from without. And when Luther speaks of the Word of the Spirit as an *inner* Word, it simply means that the outward Word, when the Spirit uses it, does not continue to be outward, that is not in the sense that the letter is a "mere outward," but that it really from without penetrates into the heart and there makes Christ truly present. The law is an outward Word, because it makes man rely on his own resources and it does not bring Christ into man's heart as a gift, but leaves Christ outside as an example, a model, or as a judge. But in another sense the law may be considered as an inward Word, when it is kept in mind that the content of the law does not go beyond the natural law, which is written in the heart of every man. The gospel, however, is an inward Word, because the Spirit by this Word brings Christ into the heart as the gift of God, as the one who does not merely in a demanding manner describe our life, but who in mercy gives us life. And simultaneously it may be called an outward Word because its content does not originate in the heart of any man, but it comes to everyone from without, as the sermons which proclaim it always reach our ears from the outside, and as the righteousness which it gives us always is the foreign and extraneous righteousness of Christ, not a righteousness which is found in our own nature.

The Word may be without the Spirit, but not as the Word of God; and the Spirit may be without the Word, but not as the revealing Spirit. Hereby we understand the tension which we found between the two series of thoughts which we described in Luther's view of the relationship between the Spirit and the Word. We have previously suggested that this tension cannot be solved by logic but only by Christ. Those suggestions have now been completely demonstrated. We understand that Luther on the one side so strongly emphasizes the sovereignty of the Spirit, and therefore the insufficiency of the outward Word. It is stated that the wind bloweth where it listeth. It is not in our power to bring it. The Word of God is therefore no guaranteed possession. It is in the hand of God and it must be sought from God prayerfully. The emphasis on the sovereignty of the Spirit and the insufficiency of the outward Word depends upon Luther's Christocentric concept of the Word. It is only as the carrier of the real presence of Christ that the Word is the Word of God. Apart from him it is a letter.

But the real presence of Christ is a miracle, the miracle which the Holy Spirit performs when he proclaims the resurrection of Jesus on earth by letting the risen Christ be truly present in the proclaimed Word. But a miracle can never be made into a guaranteed possession. If we attempt to eliminate this whole part of Luther's proclamation of the Word it is an indication of the fact that the realism in his discussion of Christ's real presence is not recognized, but that his presence in the Word is understood only as a purely ideal presence. For it is clear that it is unavoidable to make Christ's presence a guaranteed possession if his presence in the Word is viewed merely as a purely ideal presence. If, for example, his presence in the Word means to us only that the Word just speaks about him, that his "image" in the Word (understood as a historic source), appears before us and by its ethical sublimity or its religious originality influences our own moral and religious consciousness or that the right doctrine about his work in our behalf is clearly developed there to be either accepted or rejected by us, then the presence of Christ in the Word is no miracle. It is no miracle that the "image" of Jesus influences our moral and religious consciousness, or that we accept a doctrine which we find in Scripture. Both of these are very natural phenomena, which do not demand any strength from above. Even the presence of Socrates in the dialogues of Plato may influence our religious and moral consciousness, and we accept part of his teaching there as we please. If the presence of Christ in the Word shall be nothing else than the presence of his image or the presence of a correct doctrine about him then there naturally will be no space for a sovereign Spirit and his free work. In that case the Spirit becomes a synonym for warm feelings or a superfluous accompaniment to the natural influence which comes from the figure of Jesus or the correct doctrine about him. As long as it is understood that the presence of Christ in the Word is a real presence and therefore a divine miracle, it will also be clear that this real presence in the Word can never be secure for us, but can only be the object of prayer and expectation, and that where it is considered as secure and taken for granted we can no longer know what the real presence of Christ is.

But that the real presence of Christ can only be the object of our prayer and expectation does not mean that we are simply left to chance. It is not just a matter of chance that we receive what we pray for and expect. It is not an accident that the Spirit works through the outward Word, an incident that perhaps only takes place now and then and perhaps might not take place at all. The thought which we emphasized about the Spirit's *necessarily* following the outward Word is not to be construed as taking back that which was just said about the sovereignty of the Spirit and the insufficiency of the outward Word. It is to be understood as underscoring the fact that the outward Word even in its insufficiency *promises* the coming of the Spirit, and that he who believes this promise and prays about the Spirit will not be disappointed. The outward Word is the humanity of Christ himself as the symbol, the ladder of Jacob, that leads us to God. He who believes in this symbol in contrast to all free speculations will not go astray. In this connection we understand the important fact that no matter how strongly Luther emphasized the instrumental view of the relationship between the Spirit and the Word, he never directly identified the work of the outward Word with the work of the Spirit, but he always laid down an interval of time between the outward work of the Word and the coming of the Spirit. First the Word must be heard, and thereafter (*mox, sobald*) the Spirit will come. This interval of time signifies that the connection between the Spirit and the outward Word is not a necessary metaphysical connection but a connection between the promise and its fulfillment, between the prayer and the answer to prayer. This interval of time is necessary in order to make room for the motion of faith away from all *sensus proprius,* away from all self-righteousness to Christ. Here we recall what we previously said about faith as *arduissima res* and as conformity to Christ. If it really is Christ who is present in the Word then he is also only present as a reality of faith, hidden in the Word which can only be accepted by a faith which, in spite of all inward and outward experience, lays hold on the message of the Word. Such a faith is motion, a constantly continuing motion away from one's self, reason and experience and righteousness, to Christ in the Word, the alien righteousness. Where there is to be room for this motion the connection of the Spirit with the Word cannot be understood as an inner, insoluble, metaphysical unity which lets the Word work *ex opere operato*. For in such a view of the Word as the means of grace there is no room for prayer, for expectation, and for the motion of faith. Where the connection between Spirit and Word is understood as a metaphysical union, the work of the Spirit is guaranteed by the outward Word. It is such a concept that Luther makes impossible by laying down an interval of time between the work of the outward Word and the coming of the Spirit. It is in this interval of time that the prayer for the Spirit shall live, and the expectation of the promise of God, and the motion of faith away from all *sensus proprius* to *verbum promissionis*, away from *justitia propria* to *justitia aliena*. Luther has said nothing about the length of this interval of time. It takes just as long as is necessary to let go of *sensus* and lay hold on the promise. The *mox* and the *sobald* by which Luther signifies this interval of time simply expresses that the fulfillment is certain in the very moment that the promise is accepted, that the prayer is answered in the very moment the prayer is uttered—but also not a moment before. If the question is asked if we have not taken something back of what we have previously said about the sovereignty of the Spirit and the insufficiency of the outward Word, we answer this: from a logical point of view it may seem that way. But what has previously been said about the sovereignty of the Spirit and the insufficiency of the outward Word would only be taken back if what has been said about the fulfillment and the certainty of answer to prayer were rationally smoothed out to an obvious doctrine of apocatastasis or a synergism free of contradiction, where the responsibility for the ineffectiveness of the Word is placed in the free will of man. But such a rationalization does not take place in Luther. It is the problem of predestination we meet in the tension between the two series of thoughts in Luther's doctrine of the Spirit and the Word.

And it is a testimony to the unique coherence in Luther's thinking, that we meet the problem of predestination at just this point. But the problem of predestination does not permit any rationalization. It only refers faith to seek assurance in Christ. The relation is exactly the same in considering the Spirit and the Word. Luther has never, like the Thomistic doctrine of the sacraments or the orthodox doctrine of inspiration, made a rationally clear doctrine of the means of grace free of tension, by which the work of the Spirit can be calculated and guaranteed in advance. It is here we find the decisive distinction between Luther's and the Roman Catholic (and orthodox Lutheran!) concept of the means of grace. We shall later refer to this difference. Here we shall just point out that it is the realistic understanding of the Spirit's work as mediator of Christ's real presence which is at the basis of the peculiar dynamic in Luther's concept of the relationship between the Spirit and the Word. Because the Word is the outward manifestation of the sphere of revelation in which the living Christ, God hidden in the flesh, comes near to us, it is impossible to understand the grace of the Word as a new nature which because of the inner metaphysical connection of the Word with the Spirit naturally follows the Word. Therefore it is impossible to experience this work of the Spirit except in and with the motion of faith away from ourselves to Christ. This dynamic is conditioned on the fact that the work of the Spirit is to make the risen and living Christ present in the Word, *Christus ipse*. This dynamic makes every rational doctrine of the means of grace impossible. If such is wanted we must yield the realism of faith and substitute the living Christ with a figure which can be conceived of rationally. This can be done, e.g. by permitting the means of grace to grant a new nature. The gift of grace, *donum gratiae,* is then no longer the *fides Christi* in which the living Christ himself is retained as our alien righteousness, but it is an infused love, a new habit of mind or inspiration, by which it becomes possible for us to seek God with a new strength. The realism of faith is then substituted with a rational, metaphysical grace. Or we might substitute the living Christ with a "figure" of him or with a doctrine about him, i.e. with his idea. In such a case he is always present in the Word, that is, in an ideal sense. And when we are not interested in any other presence of Christ than the ideal, the work of the Spirit becomes superfluous. Here for the realism of faith is substituted a religious-ethical or a religious-intellectual spiritualism. Both of these viewpoints permit a rational doctrine of the means of grace. But they also mean that the realism of faith has been relinquished. A rational doctrine of the means of grace can be obtained at no cheaper price. Luther reveals the real greatness in his understanding of the Spirit and the Word by not letting himself be tempted to evolve any kind of a rational doctrine of the means of grace, but retaining the realism of faith with its unavoidable tension, and by causing the dynamic of this tension to meet us no matter from what direction we approach the theme of the Spirit and the Word and no matter how we formulate our questions about this theme.

In summary we can then state that Luther's thoughts about the Spirit and the Word sharpen and deepen our previous impressions of the realism of his concept of the work of the Spirit. Just as we have previously seen that the Spirit is the real and divine sphere in which Christ is truly present and in which only faith and love (and for that matter all empirical piety) can live, so we have now seen that this sphere has its outward manifestation in the Word. That it is this divine sphere of revelation which is manifested in the Word is evident, since the Word is not the certain carrier of the Spirit. Just as Christ is a mere idea outside the realism of the Spirit, and empirical piety without the realism of the Spirit is only flesh, so the Word apart from the realism of the Spirit is only a letter, a law that kills. Any kind of rational doctrine of the means of grace which metaphysically binds the Spirit in its manifestation is a break with realism of revelation in the Bible. It substitutes God's own sovereign presence in the Word with a metaphysical power proceeding from God, bound in the Word. It is for that matter of no significance whether this rationalized doctrine of the means of grace appears in the form of a Roman Catholic doctrine of the sacraments, an orthodox Lutheran doctrine of the verbal inspiration or modern Protestant historicism. In each one of the three the revelation is at the mercy of the one who *has* the means of grace. The distinction between an idealistic and a realistic concept of the Spirit as was seen in the beginning has here shown itself in a new perspective.

The Spirit and the Sacraments

In the previous presentation of the Spirit's work through the outward Word the sacraments seem almost to have disappeared from the horizon. We constantly spoke about the Word of the Scriptures made alive in *verbum vocale* while we merely touched upon the sacraments in passing. That the sacraments in some way belonged to the Word was suggested, but the relation between the Word and the sacrament was left undefined. The strong emphasis on *verbum vocale* almost seemed to make the sacraments more problematic. Is there really any room for the sacrament when the preached Word is considered the real means of grace? Is not rather the sacrament, in consequence of its character, related to that concept of grace which we have described as *caritas* idealism, while it has no organic place in the realistic and personal concept of the Spirit which we met in Luther? The idea of the Spirit as a source of the infused grace fits well into the idea of the sacrament as the canal through which the supernatural grace flows to man. But does it make sense to speak about the sacrament when the grace is Christ's alien righteousness which is offered us in the gospel and is grasped by faith which lays hold on the Word of the gospel? Does not Luther's emphasis on the Word as the basic means of grace mean that he breaks through the whole medieval sacramentalism to a higher and more personal form of religion in such a way that the sacrament is spiritualized and subordinated to the Word even though it is not really displaced by the Word? Thus the question has often been considered. This is really the classic, neo-Protestant view of Luther's relation to the medieval sacramental religion.

It is not necessary to prove further that Luther's rediscovery of the gospel led to a sharp rejection of the traditional doctrine of the sacraments. The many writings about the sacraments in the years between 1517 and 1521 prove that. In a certain sense the whole struggle about the indulgences and all the literature of that struggle are concerned with the traditional concept of the sacraments, concentrating especially on the sacrament of penance. But the break with the traditional sacramental doctrine does not necessarily mean that all sacramental understanding of Christianity and piety has been relinquished or that the concept of the sacrament has been spiritualized. It is too superficial to think that the whole contrast between the traditional doctrine of the sacraments and that of Luther can be solved in the formula of the "sacramental-magical" versus a "spiritual understanding of the divine." With this simplification of the problem it becomes impossible to explain Luther's later attitude in the struggle about the Lord's Supper. For the doctrine of the Lord's Supper which he opposed no doubt represented a more "spiritual" viewpoint than his own rather "magical" doctrine of the real presence. And all theories suggesting that Luther "fell back" into scholastic thinking are impossible. It should be added, moreover, that Luther in his fight with the enthusiasts always maintained a very distinct suspicion of all demands for a more "spiritual" religion. Where a more "spiritual" religion is placed over against sacramental religion we are far removed from Luther. In such tendencies he always, and correctly so, suspected the spirit of the enthusiasts. Spiritualizing tendencies are difficult to find in Luther. We shall speak more extensively about that later. The present suggestions are just made as a preliminary warning against a too easy simplification of the problem of Luther's relation to "sacramental religion." In other words we are at the outset very skeptical toward a concept which, in Luther's strong emphasis on *verbum vocale*, sees a prejudice toward "sacramental" piety in favor of a so-called "spiritual concept of the divine" (including also the sacraments). But with this skepticism we are compelled to study the question further. It is all the more necessary so that the presentation in the previous section shall not be misconstrued from a modern spiritualistic point of view.

However, it is not within the scope of this work to give an exhaustive presentation of Luther's doctrine of the sacraments, especially that of the young Luther. In the subsequent study we merely indicate the lines of thought which are important for the correct understanding of Luther's concept of the instruments of the Spirit, especially his view of the relationship between the Spirit and the Word.

The most obvious line in the young Luther's doctrine of the sacraments is the polemic against the scholastic teaching about the sacrament working *ex opere operato.* The most frequently occurring sentence in Luther's writings about the question of the sacraments (from the first extensive discussion of it in connection with the fight over indulgences in early 1518 until 1520 when the question must be regarded as completely explained with *De Captivitate*), the sentence which the papal bull *Exsurge Domine* also places first among the *Errores Martini Luther,* is as follows: *Haeretica sententia est, sed usitata, sacramenta Novae legis iustificantem gratiam illis dare, qui non ponunt obicem.*[17] Here we are obviously at the core of Luther's concept of the sacrament. It is positively expressed in the sentence which Luther characterized as *vulgatissimum et probatissimum dictum: Non sacramentum, sed fides sacramenti justificat.*[18] From the very beginning Luther strongly resists the scholastic teaching about the sacraments of the New Testament as *signa efficacia*, which, by virtue of the completion of the ritual act, contain and mediate the grace of God unless the recipient locks the door *(obicem ponit)* by an actual mortal sin. In this doctrine Luther finds a denial of the evangelical faith that justifies. If the sacrament is not received by faith, it must inevitably be understood as man's own *opus.* Before God there are only two possibilities: to accept by faith or to seek merit through works. If the sacrament therefore is not evangelically understood, i.e. understood as the work of God which can only be accepted by faith, it is already

---

17 Denzinger, *Enchiridion symbolorum*, Freiburg, 1932, No. 741, p. 275: *Haeretica sententia est, sed usitata, sacramenta Novae legis iustificantem gratiam illis dare, qui non ponunt obicem.* This passage is given in *W. A.,* VI, 608, 2 ff. (1520) as: *Haeretica est sententia, sed usitata, Sacramenta novae legis gratiam dare illis, qui non ponunt obicem.*

18 *W. A.,* LVII, Heb., 170, 1 ff.; I, 286, 18 ff.; 324, 16 ff.; 544, 40 ff.; 595, 6 ff.; 631, 7 ff. (1518); II, 15, 32 ff. (1518); 715, 35 ff. (1519); VI, 97, 26 ff.; 531, 20 ff.; 532, 28 ff.; 533, 12 ff. (1520).

understood as nomistic, i.e. as the work of man which shall win a merit from God.

From a superficial point of view it may seem as if the scholastic doctrine of the sacraments with great force favors the thought about the objectivity of and the gift of God in the sacrament. The *ex opere operato* doctrine in a certain sense completely emphasizes the work of God. The validity and the effect of the sacrament must not be made dependent on the officiant or the receiver. It depends solely on the divine Word which is the form of the sacrament. It is therefore described as *ex opere operato*. The sacraments of the Old Testament, however, operated *ex opere operantis*. Their validity and effect depended on the receiver's merit. But these sacraments are no doubt placed lower than those of the New Testament because they are not dependent on the divine Word but on something in the receiver.

Over against this, Luther's protest may appear as a type of synergism. When this protest emphasizes that the sacraments bring the grace only if accepted by faith, and that therefore in this respect there is no difference between the Old Testament and the New Testament sacraments, it may seem as if Luther does not dare to let the sacrament depend alone on the work of God, but instead lets its effectiveness depend upon a co-operation between the grace of God and faith of man.

However, this is only a superficial point of view. When Luther so strongly emphasizes faith as the necessary qualification without which the sacrament cannot bring grace, faith is not considered as man's work as different from that of God, but on the contrary as an indispensable part in the act of God. It is true that Luther has expressed himself a few times in such a way that his concept of faith might be understood as tending toward synergism. When he as clearly as possible attempts to formulate his understanding of the sacraments in opposition to the scholastic view, then, in order to emphasize the necessity of faith over against the *ex opere operato* idea, he may use the scholastic formula *ex opere operantis*. If this formula is isolated and taken in its exact scholastic meaning, it certainly says that faith is understood as a human effort which co-operates with the grace of God. However, this idea does not at all describe the view of Luther. And at other places he has expressed himself sufficiently clearly in order to prevent such a concept of faith.

When Luther stresses the necessity of faith, it is in order to emphasize the character of the sacrament as a divine act. Luther holds that the weakness of the scholastics on this point is one of the reasons that the Lord's Supper, for example, through the sacrificial idea of the mass, has degenerated to a meritorious *opus* instead of God's gift of grace. The decisive point in understanding the sacrament is not that God's grace is made the only decisive factor but how this sole decisive factor is construed. When God's grace is understood in such a way that the degree of its effect can be determined without strongly underscoring the necessity of faith, then it is no longer in the strictest sense grace. For faith is the only possible attitude in which grace is truly the grace of God. Faith is the unconditional surrender of man to God's sovereign grace. It may also be stated thus: faith is the only attitude that corresponds to the living Christ himself as God's gift and our alien righteousness. Where faith is not the correlative of grace, there the gift of grace is not understood as the living Christ himself. If we speak of a grace which can be mediated *ex opere operato* and of which the human correlative is not determined by something else or more than a *non ponere obicem,* then this grace is not God's sovereign grace, its gift is not the living Christ himself given us as our alien righteousness. Grace is then in one way or another understood as a divine power which is brought into the soul by the mediation of the sacrament and thereby lifts our nature up into the level of the supernatural so that the soul is empowered to live supernatural virtues of the supernatural life. That means that where faith is not emphasized as the correlative of grace, there grace is viewed in such a way that without contradiction it can be made to comply with the scheme of merit and permit itself to be viewed under the mark of the law. Grace is then understood as the means given by God by which to win salvation. The relation of Christ to this sacramental grace is that he by his vicarious suffering and death has gained the grace for us. The suffering and death of Christ are thereby put into the scheme of merit and understood by the spirit of the law. Because of the suffering of Christ in his human nature and the satisfaction thus earned, grace is infused. The sacraments flow from the wounds of Christ.

It is no wonder that the Lord's Supper on this background is thought of as propitiatory sacrifice. This is in line with the whole scholastic concept of grace and the sacraments. The idea of the sacrifice in the mass is really the most logical development of the medieval doctrine of the sacraments. On the one hand this doctrine contains the assurance of the objective power of the word of consecration. By virtue of the word of consecration the wine and the bread on the altar are changed into the Body and Blood of Jesus. And this Body and Blood as God's gift of grace assist in gaining the true merit from God. Is it any wonder that it first of all must be viewed as a propitiatory sacrifice? Atonement is the first condition for merit. It is the beginning of the piety of merit. But it is in reality not only sacrifice in the mass, but the whole sacramental system which becomes enclosed in the scheme of merit in the satisfaction theory. Baptism obliterates original sin. The sacrament of penance wipes out mortal sins committed after baptism, and the sacrifice in the mass takes away venial sins here and in purgatory, etc. In this way sacramental grace is understood as a power which expels sin, something that is fused into the soul in order to make us worthy to gain salvation in the right way. There is no indication in this doctrine of grace that the scheme of merit is broken, that the law is superseded by the gospel. On the contrary, the law governs, the scheme of merit is kept intact.

This is already found in the scholastic definition of the essence of the sacrament. The sacrament, according to the scholastic concept, consists of matter and form. The matter is the visible rite, the form is the consecrating Word. By using this Aristotelian matter-form device for the sacrament, the function of the Word is clearly defined as consecration. The scholastic view of sacramental grace in the merit system is already found in the concept of the sacramental Word as an essentially consecrating Word. The con-

secrating Word has as its function to guarantee that the sacramental grace is truly present in the sacrament, that the metaphysical connection between the outward sign and the inward
essence is a true reality.

Over against this traditional doctrine of the sacrament it was
Luther's task to understand the sacrament from the evangelical
point of view. Luther could not understand sacramental grace
as a means by which to gain merits. Sacramental grace should be
seen wholly from the gospel point of view.

It is important to note that the spiritualistic problem which is
found in the contrast between the sacrament as an expression for
a rite connected with material things, and the Word as an expression for a "spiritual" form of religion never meant anything to
Luther. From the moment he recognized this contrast in the scholastic teaching, Luther's opposition to the scholastic concept of the
sacraments is found in a totally different direction from the contrast between a sacramental and spiritualistic view of religion. It
may be quite natural for modern Protestantism (from whose view
the last few remnants of sacramental piety have long since disappeared) constantly, in the manner of Karl Holl, to describe
Luther's view of the sacraments as a spiritualizing of the medieval view by emphasizing the Word as the bearer of a "spiritual"
form of religion in contrast to the sacrament as a bearer of a lower
form of religion connected with the sacramental-magical. But
such a description can only confuse us by compelling us, if we
follow it to its logical conclusion, to lay down a sharp distinction
between the young and supposedly more "spiritual" Luther, and
the old Luther who in the struggle with the enthusiasts' theology
of the Spirit and doctrine of the sacraments has fallen back into
scholasticism and magic. How unobjective and unhistorical such
an interpretation is, needs no further elucidation. Luther has
never attacked scholasticism for being a form of theology which
connected worship with outward things. You will have to search
much in Luther to find even one passage where the Word as
bearer of a more spiritual form of religion is placed in opposition
to the sacrament or even emphasized at its expense. The modern

separation of Word-religion and sacrament-religion has no place in the writings of Luther in spite of his strong emphasis on the Word. This important contrast, which is so important to modern spiritualistic and nonsacramental Protestantism, has never mattered at all to Luther, at least not after his evangelical awakening. However, this contrast mattered very much for the enthusiasts whom Luther fought so passionately. It should also give some misgiving to those who want to differentiate between the Word and the sacrament as bearers of "spiritual" and "sacramental" piety, that Luther in the struggle with the enthusiasts always places the Word as *verbum externum* on the line with the sacraments in opposition to a "spiritual" concept of the Word as something "inner," something higher and better than just *externa res*. To Luther the Word itself is sacramental in the sense of something outward which, for that matter, might be designated material, nonspiritual. Luther does not think of the Word as bearer of an abstract content but as a bearer of God's concrete act of revelation, in other words, as sacrament.

The spiritualistic method of expressing this problem must never be injected into the discussion if we desire to understand Luther's opposition to the scholastic teaching of the sacraments. The decisive difference in Luther's understanding of the sacrament is not the difference between "things" and "spirit," but the difference between law and gospel, between *opus* and *fides*.

By the polemic against the doctrine of *ex opere operato* Luther first of all limits his concept of the sacraments from the scheme of merit. By demanding faith as a prerequisite for the work of sacramental grace Luther makes it impossible to conceive of this grace as a means in a scheme of merit. For faith is the attitude which always excludes every merit before God. But this limitation is of a negative character. It is more important that Luther positively defines the nature of the sacrament in such a way that the doctrine of *ex opere operato* is excluded in advance as incompatible with the nature of the sacrament. For it cannot be concluded that Luther is generally agreed with the scholastics in the understanding of the nature of the sacrament but disagrees only about what qualifications should be asked of the recipient. Such a view of the disagreement would lead to a misinterpretation of Luther in the direction of synergism, since his view in this interpretation merely seems to be a more strict demand on the co-operation of the recipient. No, just as we saw that the scholastic *ex opere operato* doctrine was the basis in defining the nature of the sacrament, that is, by using the Aristotelian matter-form formula by which the Word of the sacrament was interpreted in a one-sided manner as the consecrating Word, so it is true for Luther that his polemic against this *ex opere operato* doctrine is not fully finished before the definition of the nature of sacrament is such that this doctrine is excluded in advance. Here the concept of the Word of the sacrament is of special significance.

It is, doubtless, a significant fact that Luther did not define the nature of the sacrament in the Aristotelian matter-form formula. Here is already an indication of the fact that the Word of the sacrament is not first and foremost a consecrating Word. Now it is true that this formula was not used in the older medieval theology either. But the introduction of it later on simply meant a more precise definition of the view of the sacramental Word which previously had been generally accepted. When Luther is satisfied to speak about the Word and the visible means it means more than a return to an older and less metaphysical way of expression. This is really an indication that Luther's concept of the function of the sacramental Word has changed. This change consists in this, that the sacramental Word is no longer considered a special Word of consecration but as identical with the gospel itself.

This is expressed in the use of the concept *promissio,* a concept which is not unknown in the nominalistic tradition, but which in Luther takes on a wholly new and decisive significance in the understanding of the concept of the sacrament. In every sacrament there is a divine *promissio* expressed in the Word which accompanies the sacrament. This *promissio* is the decisive factor. It is what makes the sacrament a sacrament. To this *promissio* is added the outward means which serves as a visible confirmation of the fulfillment of the promise. But it is natural that the promise holds a primary position in relation to its confirmation. The Word may be without the visible means but the means can never work without the Word.[19]

When the important part of the sacrament is the divine promise, it is already clear that faith is necessary for the right reception of it. For promise and faith are correlated concepts. Where faith is mentioned there must always be a promise on which to lay hold, and where we speak of a promise faith is always demanded.[20] By virtue of understanding the word of the sacrament as *promissio* faith enters into the concept of the sacrament in the sense that it thus forms the real connection between the Word and the external element. For the external element is the confirmation of the promise. But only faith in the promise can receive the confirmation. Where there is no faith it is senseless to speak about confirmation of a promise. Where there is no faith the external element loses its special function.

Simultaneously with the fact that the view of the sacramental Word is changed from a Word of consecration to a promise, the concept of the element in the sacrament is greatly changed. It is no longer just a substance which is "formed" by the Word into an instrument to mediate grace viewed as a new nature *(habitus, inspiratio)*, but the symbol receives an independent significance as God's seal on the fulfillment of his promise. However, as the promise can only be received by faith, so also the symbol which confirms its fulfillment.

All this may almost appear a spiritualization of the concept of the sacrament and it may seem strictly contradictory to the assertion we just made that all spiritualizing tendencies are far from Luther. It is therefore necessary that we make yet a further explanation of the significance of the concept of the sacrament as consisting of the words of promise and a symbol of confirmation. There is no spiritualization at all in this concept of the sacrament. On the

---

[19] *W. A.*, VI, 518, 17 (1520); also VI, 363, 6 ff.; 694, 33 ff. (1520); I, 604, 35 ff. (1518).

[20] *W. A.*, VI, 88, 31 (1520); II, 13, 18 (1518). Also VI, 514, 13 ff. (1520) and LVI, 45, 15 ff. (1515-16).

contrary, it is this formulation which does away with all Luther's earlier tendencies toward a certain spiritualization. Yes, without exaggeration it may be said that back of this new formulation is hidden a recapturing of the New Testament and early Christian elements in the concept of the sacrament. This view, instead of leading to a displacement of sacramental piety in favor of a spiritualistic "religion of words," makes a view of Christianity with a strong sacramental concept so much more possible than the one of the Middle Ages.

Here it is first of all important to note that the emphasis on the promise means doing away with the isolation in which the medieval sacramental system threatened to place the individual sacrament. That was especially true in the case of baptism. In the sense that a mortal sin invalidates the grace of baptism so that it can only be recaptured by the sacrament of penance, baptism is placed in the shadow of penance. Baptism even has to yield its real significance in the continued life of the Christian to the sacrament of penance. Baptism seems to be just a temporary episode within the period of time before the first mortal sin. It is very evident that in the medieval empirical piety both the sacrifice of the mass and the sacrament of penance had a much greater significance than that of baptism and the Holy Communion. This is a very typical difference between the early Christian age and the Middle Ages in the concept of the sacrament. The idea of promise not only places each individual sacrament in the connection which constitutes the relation of the individual to his private sins but into the totality of the whole story of salvation. For the promise, which is attached to each sacrament, even though it has a special form given by the institution, is in this special form merely a deepening of the one sole identical promise, which God again and again since the fall of man has proclaimed in different situations accompanied by different signs (the rainbow, circumcision, etc.) until in the testament of Jesus, the Lord's Supper, and in baptism it has been finally and totally formulated, and in these it is accompanied by the irrevocable and certain signs.[21] Baptism and the Lord's Supper do not pre-

---

[21] *W. A.*, VI, 514, 1 (1520); 515, 5. Also VI, 356, 20 ff.; 358, 5 ff. (1520).

sent a special promise as is maintained by the Franciscan and nominalistic doctrines of the sacraments which may have certain similarities to Luther's thoughts about the special "order" or "covenant," that the inner grace always must follow the outward signs. Here we are concerned with the only and at all times identical promise, the promise about the living Christ. However, there is a difference between the Old and the New Testaments. The Old Testament promises temporal benefits, while the New Testament promises eternal benefits. This, however, does not mean that there is a difference between the content of the promise of the Old and the New Testaments. Christ is promised in both but in the Old Testament Christ is hidden under the "figure," the type of him, which constitutes the temporal content of the promise, while in the promise of the New Testament he is present as the incarnated Word. That the content of the promise under these two forms is the same is seen by the fact that Luther, in harmony with the Apostle Paul, holds that the Old Testament saints become justified by faith in the promise of the Old Testament. Luther does not accept any difference in principle between the Old and the New Testament sacraments. Where the Old Testament sacraments are accepted in the same faith which is demanded for the acceptance of the New Testament sacraments, there they already have the same effect and give the same justifying grace.[22]

The content of the promise of both baptism and the Lord's Supper is therefore Christ himself. The sacraments are by this connection with the universal promise of God placed in the center of the story of salvation. They get a much more central position than in the medieval teaching of the sacraments.

The difference may be formulated thus: the perspective of Lutheran sacramental doctrine is theocentric, the scholastic perspective is anthropocentric. By the concept of promise the individual sacraments are placed into the whole of God's order of salvation which spans the time between creation and the consummation. For the promise of God goes back to creation, and its fulfillment takes

---

[22] *W. A.*, VI, 356, 25 (1520); 357, 32; 385, 5. Also VI, 515, 5 ff.; IX, 447, 1 ff. (Poliander's codex, 1519-21).

place at the end of time. We shall later examine the significance of this for the eschatological points in the sacraments. The medieval teaching of the sacraments, however, is anthropocentric. It catalogues the individual sacraments systematically according to the value they have for the individual's ability to overcome his sin and thereby become able to do works of merit. They partly remove special groups of sins that may prevent merit, and they partly infuse the supernatural power necessary for a constant ascension of the ladder of merit.

By taking the concept of promise into the definition of the essence of the sacrament it becomes impossible to get the sacrament placed in the order of merit at all, for simultaneously the sacrament is brought into a comprehensive connection with the whole story of salvation. In other words, it is understood christologically. That which makes the sacrament a sacrament is the fact that it carries the promise of God himself, the selfsame promise about Christ as was spoken to Noah, Abraham, Moses, and David, etc. Therefore we must expect to meet in the sacrament none other than the living Christ as the gift of God. Luther states it in this way: Christ is the real sacrament; his incarnation is the real sign of confirmation of the promise about him. The Word of promise in the sacrament promises Christ and the sign confirms that God has kept his promise. When the Word of the sacrament in baptism promises salvation and in the Lord's Supper the forgiveness of sin then the meaning of these special words which are attached to the particular sacrament is no other than the living Christ himself. Therefore the Word of the sacrament, both in baptism and the Lord's Supper, is in harmony with the Word that is being preached, with respect to its content. The sermon is nothing else than the proclamation of the covenant of baptism and the testament which constitutes the Lord's Supper. Therefore the gospel must be preached whenever the Lord's Supper is celebrated.[23]

And now it is important to understand that this connection between the preaching of the gospel and the sacrament does not

---

23 *W. A.*, VI, 528, 8 (1520); 231, 16 (1520). Also I, 334, 3 ff.; 604, 35 ff. (1518); VI, 374, 1 ff.; 526, 1 ff. (1520).

mean a spiritualizing of the idea of the sacrament but a sacramentalization of the message. For the promise is heard in the sacrament not as unfulfilled but as already fulfilled in Christ. That is what the symbol in the sacrament declares. The thought we sometimes find in Luther, that the Word is more than the symbol because the symbol may be dispensed with but not the Word, has nothing at all to do with the relative indifference of spiritualism toward the outward symbol.[24] In the first place Luther is here referring to the traditional and medieval thoughts which were recognized by all, from Thomas to Biel, as sound church doctrine. In the second place it should be noted that Luther in other connections emphasized that the outward symbol is indispensable. When Luther refers to traditional thoughts about the possible occasional dispensability of the outward symbol, he does it in order to attack the opponents with their own weapons. By making such exceptions they have proved the concept that the essence in the sacrament is the promise of God. But the logical priority which belongs to the Word in its relation to the symbol, and which is proved by incidents of exception, *susceptio sacramenti ex voto,* does not mean that the outward symbol is of no importance, or that normally it might just as well or rather be eliminated. Luther never meant this any more than Thomas and Biel did. It has fallen to the lot of modern nonsacramental Protestantism to misunderstand Luther in this way. For to both Luther and scholasticism the incident of exception was not a possibility one could adopt as one pleased, but it was an emergency exception which proves the rule. But also, just because it was such an exception, Luther clearly emphasized the essence of the sacrament, the promise, with which one cannot dispense even in the greatest emergency. That the outward symbol in an emergency may disappear is not at all the same as to make it generally of no relative value. Only a defective knowledge of Roman Catholic teaching of the sacrament has made Protestant theologians interpret in this way certain expressions about the possible dispensability of the outward sign found in Luther's early writings about the sacraments. The fact that in an emergency the symbol may be

---

[24] *W. A.,* VI, 518, 17 (1520); also VI, 363, 6 ff.; I, 604, 37 ff. (1518).

dispensed with indicates that it is subordinate to the promise. But even in this subordination the symbol has a most important function. For it is the symbol which separates the sacrament from the sermon. In the content of the Word of promise they are identical.

But what then is the significance of the symbol? In what way does Luther's concept of the sacrament differ from that of the sermon when the sermon can be a part of the sacrament (the proclamation of the covenant of baptism and the testament of the Lord's Supper) and when the outward symbol of the sacrament may be dispensed with in an emergency? The answer must be: it is the symbol that makes the difference.

This makes it all the more necessary that we study thoroughly Luther's view of the symbol.

The concept of *signum* as the main word in the medieval doctrine of the sacrament has a very long history which we are not able to discuss here. Already in the early Middle Ages it was taken over from Augustine as an essential part of the definition of the sacrament. It proved itself very fitting for that purpose because it expressed the unity of the visible element and the invisible grace which is the peculiar aspect of the sacrament. Moreover the *signum*-concept gave expression to the similarity which is found between the visible element and the invisible work of grace, by which new ways were opened for a symbolical understanding of the outward rite.

This concept Luther accepts and retains. But simultaneously with the fact that the concept of the sacrament is changed by the new understanding of the Word of the sacrament as *promissio,* the *signum*-concept also gets a new aspect. The symbol is no longer understood as *signum efficax* in a scholastic sense, but as a symbol of confirmation of the promise which faith retains. *Signum* is understood as *sigillum,* as God's seal of his promise.[25] However, this does not do away with the symbolical aspect of the sign. As a sign of confirmation it constantly contains the power of the symbol-

---

25 *W. A.*, VI, 358, 35 (1520); also VI, 230, 23 ff. (1520); II, 697, 21 ff. (1519); IX, 448, 24 ff.; 460, 16 ff. (Poliander's codex, 1519-21); IV, 704, 35 ff. (1517). To the following interpretation of the significance of the symbol cf. *W. A.*, II, 729-34. 744-54.

ical. And it is precisely through this that the *signum* comes to work as a confirmation of the promise. "Symbol" in this connection does not mean a mere figurative expression but a real move of God into man's life. The symbol of the sacrament does not merely symbolize an ideal of imitation, but it "signifies" an act of God which cannot and will not be avoided. It should not be overlooked that words as *significare* and *bedeuten* do not have for Luther the modern idea of "the mere symbol." They both mean a pointing toward a reality. That the Word and the symbol in the sacrament *signify* something means that they point toward a present reality. It is because the symbol signifies (not just symbolizes) God's real move into man's life, that it serves as a confirmation of God's promise.

The significance of the symbol is clearly seen in Luther's doctrine of baptism. The symbol is the immersion in and the raising from the water. This symbol is not merely an allegorical picture of our death and resurrection with Christ in such a manner that we by *imitatio Christi* are permitted to realize this allegory in the form of humility and faith. Luther discards such an imitation-concept of the symbol of baptism. Immersing and raising does not "symbolize" a death and resurrection initiated by ourselves, but it signifies our true physical death and physical resurrection. This concept of the content of the symbol corresponds to the theocentric perspective which is given with *promissio*. That which is signified is not something we possess but something God completely possesses. The symbolism of baptism shows that God has placed his hand upon our life and truly makes it to conform with the death and resurrection of Christ in the way the symbol also shows it. The immersion of baptism means the real cross and not a self-chosen one made up of imitation-piety. All that God places upon us of real suffering of body and soul, particularly in daily life (and not in the mortifying practices of the life of the mystics and the monks!), culminating in physical death, is included in the symbol of baptism. The promise of baptism declares the complete salvation once and for all. In this sense it may be said that baptism makes man pure and blest (saved) once and for all. Hereby it is also stated that man is not saved by works. As a residue sin is not yet driven out. It is sin which God does not reckon to us because of the grace of baptism but it is no less real, and its real expulsion has only started in baptism and will not be done away with until the day of judgment. We recognize in these thoughts Luther's view on the relation between *gratia* and *donum*. God's total *gratia* is declared in baptism by the promise, while the gradually increasing *donum* is mediated by the symbol. Baptism is a covenant in which God promises to drive out all sin in us. The symbol of this is the act of baptism, the significance of which God endeavors to realize by his Spirit. The symbol of baptism and the realization of its significance by the constant work of God in us is a proof of the fact that the promise is constantly valid because God is constantly at work for its full realization. It must always be remembered that the symbol is in the hands of God. This is the all-decisive point. Luther here emphasizes—just as strongly as any time in the struggle with the enthusiasts—that it is God who is the acting subject in the sacrament. It is not the pastor who baptizes but God himself. It is not only the Word which is declared that is God's but the whole visible symbolic act has God as its subject. Therefore God sees to it that what the symbol signifies is realized. We could not speak of a genuine symbol and a genuine significance if it was not a reality which was signified. And this reality is God's work with us in fully realizing the promise.

The purely sacramental symbolic act is of course quickly over. But God is constantly working on the realization of its significance through his guidance of our destiny in life and in death. Therefore the symbol of baptism includes our whole life even to its resurrection. Because the symbol belongs to God the sacramental act of baptism as a symbol, and our own physical death and resurrection are unbreakably tied together as one unity of the process of salvation viewed eschatologically. Whatever there is between baptism and death is included in this unity, including the physical, yes, especially the physical. This is the genuine and therefore also the physical (as well as the spiritual) cross by which God realizes in us that death with Christ signified in baptism. The symbol in baptism gives our whole life an eschatological quality.

We are now able to understand in what sense the symbol is a confirmation of the promise. The content of the promise is Christ as God's gift to us, or, what is the synonym of that: salvation, the forgiveness of sins. By the symbol and the fulfillment of its significance in us through God's guidance of our life under the symbol of baptism till its culmination in the physical death and resurrection, God confirms that this promise is valid and that it is fulfilled and in the process of constant fulfillment in us. It is by truly putting the old man in us to death and by raising the new man that God fulfills the promise in us and truly gives us salvation in Christ.

In this connection it may well be said that the sacrament, in a very different sense from that of preaching, is pointed directly to the individual. But this must not be understood from the point of view of the individual to mean that the sacrament is degraded to be a means of special interest for the individual's private religiosity. That the sacrament, because of the symbol added to the promise in a different manner, yes, we may be tempted to say in a more palpable manner, than the preached message, directly applies the promise to the individual, depends upon the fact that the symbol gives an eschatological quality to the whole life of the individual *by incorporating him into the people of God*. The symbol of baptism becomes personal only by the fact that it takes the individual's whole existence and places it in God's historico-eschatological saving action of his people by which he puts them to death and makes them alive again in Christ. This saving eschatological act of God is always an act that creates the church and upholds it. For the church is the people who are the fruit of God's saving eschatological act down through history. Through this we have the connection between the Old Testament and the New Testament sacraments. This is why baptism always is the symbol of the fact that the individual belongs to the people of God, the church of God.

Baptism thus becomes the basic sacrament which includes the whole life, including the preached message and the other sacraments. The Lord's Supper is a remembrance of the covenant of baptism or as an old saying puts it: it is the traveling provisions on the way to which the symbol of baptism changes our life—the way with Christ through death to eternal life. The Lord's Supper is a bridge, a door, a ship, which leads from this life over to the life to come. Baptism and the Lord's Supper thus belong closely together. Baptism leads us into a new life here in the world while the Lord's Supper leads us through death to life eternal. The Lord's Supper is also viewed eschatologically. Luther underscores anew the basically eschatological tone in the story of the institution of the Lord's Supper, a tone kept vivid in the early church, but almost forgotten in medieval sacramental piety. The symbol of the Lord's Supper can only be understood against the background of baptism. While baptism brings our life under the symbol of death and resurrection and thereby condemns our whole old man to death and promises resurrection in Christ, the Lord's Supper comes to us with the Body and Blood of Jesus as the bread of life to use on this way of death.

The symbol of the Lord's Supper is more difficult to see in this period of Luther's writings. This is because of a certain oscillation between two concepts of the symbol of the Lord's Supper. In the earliest writings the Augustinian views dominate. The symbol here is seemingly now the bread and wine, and then the Body and Blood of Jesus. Its significance is the communion between the communicant and Christ with all his saints. Just as the many grains become one bread so the many become one body in Christ. The real unity with Christ and his saints is the significance of the symbol. The symbol is the bread and wine (the Body and Blood of Jesus) or perhaps better stated: the act of communion itself in which the one bread (which is the Body and Blood of Christ) is eaten by the many. In the writings from 1520, the symbol is clearly understood as the truly present Body and Blood of Jesus, and its significance is the forgiveness of sin (and eternal life) as the treasure which Jesus, by giving his Body and Blood for us, has obtained for us and willed to us in the Lord's Supper. This change in the presentation is because of the fact that the development of the *promissio*-concept, the whole presentation of the content of the Lord's Supper, was concentrated about the concept of the testament. This brought about a change in the understanding of the symbol and its significance which now is seen from this point of view. This was verified by an exegesis of the words of the testament, that is, of the words of institution and not, as previously, by a symbolical interpretation of the rite of the sacrament itself. However, too much stress must not be placed on this difference of presentation. The difference is of a formal nature. No essential difference in the concept of the Lord's Supper is found in the writings of 1519 and 1520. It is fully justified to add the thoughts from *De captivitate* and *Sermo de testamento Christi* to the content of the sermons of 1519. We do not have views here which exclude one another. Basically there is no real difference between the idea of the work of the Lord's Supper as *communio* and as the forgiveness of sins (and eternal life). Both expressions presuppose the truly present Christ and signify the effects of his presence. When the Lord's Supper is thus seen in its connection with baptism and thereby in its saving eschatological connection, the inner unity of the two views will be obvious. We saw that baptism, because it placed the individual in God's saving eschatological act, made the individual a member of the church. It is to the baptized that the Lord's Supper, the bread of life, is given. The Lord's Supper is given as sustenance to the people who by baptism have become one with Christ. Inasmuch as the Lord's Supper is confirmation and a strengthening of the grace of baptism, it is also a sacrament preserving the church. Therefore it must also become a strengthening of the unity of God's people. For when the Lord's Supper gives us Christ as food and drink, it gives us him who, as the fulfillment of God's promise, is the unity of God's saving eschatological act. No one can receive him unless he becomes one with all God's people.[26] Emphasizing this side of the significance of the Lord's Supper can in no wise be said to be opposed to the testament of Jesus. For the words of institution are directed to a congregation, not to the individual, and they ask for an operation which preserves the church, i.e. the food of the new covenant. When on the other hand it is stated that the fruit of the Lord's

---

[26] *W. A.*, II, 692, 30 (1519); 743, 20. Also IX, 445, 11 ff. (Poliander's codex, 1519-21).

Supper is forgiveness of sin and eternal life, the last word (eternal life) indicates that the forgiveness of sin is not to be understood in the ordinary scholastic sense, but is a general expression for the whole new life in Christ (compare the third article of the creed, the forgiveness of sin and the eternal life). The forgiveness of sin is thus basically the same as communion with Christ and all his saints. This is seen most clearly in a comparison between the methods in which the two formulations in the respective connections are further developed. They are explained thus that as far as content is concerned they become identical. *Both expressions signify the unity with Christ in the struggle against sin, death, and the devil.*[27]

The symbol of the Lord's Supper is the physical eating and drinking of the Body and Blood of Christ under bread and wine. Its significance is the deliverance from sin and death and devil in true unity with Christ. And this symbol is, as in baptism, a confirmation of God's promise, of his testament. By giving us the symbol and by realizing its significance in us God confirms the fulfillment for us of his promise, his testament. For as far as the Lord's Supper is concerned it is true that it is God who both gives the symbol and realizes its significance. But the symbols of baptism and the Lord's Supper must be seen in their mutual connection. It is to the baptized—to them who by baptism have entered the way that with Christ leads to death and through death to resurrection—that the Lord's Supper is offered. Not until the Lord's Supper is seen in this relation to baptism does it become natural to call the Lord's Supper *viaticum*. But here we also find a paradoxical connection between the two sacramental symbols. Baptism leads us into a new life here on earth. It is the sacrament of regeneration. Its symbol is first of all attached to death, the physical death, and then through death to life. The Lord's Supper, however, is the sacrament of death, it is the bridge to the life to come. But its symbol is first of all attached to life because it is the sacrament that nourishes, the bread of life which through the forgiveness of sins gives new life. The symbol of the Lord's Supper is

---

27 *W. A.*, II, 748, 14 (1519); 749, 1 ff. Also VI, 376, 17 (1520).

attached to death all through life. Baptism attaches death to the living in order to lead them through death into life. The Lord's Supper gives life to the dying so that through life they may be led into death. And in this paradoxical mutual connection the symbol of baptism and the Lord's Supper is a confirmation of the validity of God's promise to us.

On this way, and only on this way which is marked by the symbol of baptism and the Lord's Supper, do we find penitence and preaching of the Word. Penitence is always a return to baptism. Luther at this point argues against speaking of baptism as a second life raft after the shipwreck. If the covenant of baptism were no longer valid, no penitence would be possible. Or it would only be possible as a human effort under the symbol of the law. True penitence, evangelical penitence is a remembrance of the covenant of baptism. Penitence always takes place in the symbol of baptism.

The preaching of the gospel is, in somewhat the same manner as penitence, a remembrance of and a proclamation of the covenant of baptism. Or (which is the same thing) it is a proclamation of the testament in the Lord's Supper. Penitence and the preaching of the gospel presuppose baptism and the Lord's Supper. In other words, penitence and preaching of the gospel belong only in the congregation's work through baptism and the Supper. When penitence and preaching are understood on the basis of this connection with baptism and the Lord's Supper as words that belong only in the church together with baptism and the Supper, it would be easy to state Luther's view in the well-known words of Grundtvig: only by "the washing and the table" do we have the Word of God. Penitence and preaching therefore have no special symbol. Their symbol is always that of baptism and the Lord's Supper.

Penitence and preaching are sacramental words. They are sacramental because they announce the fulfillment of the promise. They truly give the Christ of whom the promise speaks. Therefore they are also constantly connected with the symbols which God has given in the fulfillment of the promise, i.e. the symbol of baptism and the Supper. It is only by these symbols that penitence and preaching take place.

As we previously stated, it is now clear that the connection between the preaching of the gospel and the sacrament does not mean a spiritualizing of the concept of the sacrament, but the sacramentalizing of the preaching. And it also becomes clear what we meant by saying that the Lutheran doctrine of the sacraments signified a recapture of the lost New Testament and early Christian ideas of the understanding of the sacrament—ideas which certainly do not lead to an abolition of sacramental piety in favor of a "spiritualistic religion of words." On the contrary, it makes possible a much more definite sacramental view of Christianity than that which is represented by the Middle Ages.

The word "sacramental" may, of course, be understood in more than one way. It may be understood in the narrow sense and simply mean the two sacraments, baptism and the Lord's Supper. And it may be understood in the broader sense as a designation of a fundamental religious view, which seeks to find God, not in pure spiritual ideas, but in the small outward things of the world which are used by God as means of manifesting himself in the visible and physical world. Luther's concept of the Christian faith may in both cases be described as sacramental—even over against that of the Middle Ages. If we compare medieval sacramental teaching with that of Luther we soon discover that the two main sacraments, baptism and the Supper, have a far more central position in Luther's thinking than in the thinking of the Middle Ages. In the latter, baptism was pushed aside by penance and the Supper by the mass. The result is that the ancient Christian and eschatological idea in the concept of the sacrament, which was lost during the Middle Ages, is brought back again by Luther. For Luther both baptism and the Supper are eschatological signs. Our life receives its eschatological quality from baptism and the Supper. This means that the sacraments are placed in the center of a universal, historico-eschatological concept in contrast to the narrow, anthropocentric, sacramental system of scholasticism. With respect to these characteristics of the sacramental teaching of Luther it is not wrong to characterize his view of the Christian faith as being more genuinely sacramental, in the more narrow sense of the word, than that of the Middle Ages. For with Luther the biblical sacraments, baptism and the Supper, occupy a more central position than they do in medieval piety. The early Christian eschatological element is thus regained.

But also when the word "sacramental" is used in the wider sense, it is true that Luther's understanding of the Christian faith is more genuinely sacramental than that of the Middle Ages. For what is essential in the sacramental view of God's presence and work, as it is presented in the Bible itself, is the fact that God himself, or the risen Christ, descends to man and is present here by the humble, outward, material sign. It is characteristic of the view of Christianity current in the Middle Ages—especially near the end of the Middle Ages—that in spite of the doctrine of transubstantiation, in spite of the worship of the sacrament, and in spite of the great spider web of sacramental ideas, there was an increasing elimination of God from the things that are lowly and present. One need only think of the popular worship of Mary and the saints which is so characteristic of the Middle Ages and of the more intellectually proud mysticism. Both are the result of an antisacramental tendency and both are very characteristic of the Christian life of the Middle Ages. This antisacramental attitude transmits itself to the sacrament with the result that the sacrament, instead of being understood as God's gracious descent to things lowly, becomes the means for man's lifting himself higher up. The method by which the sacraments in the Middle Ages are fitted into the scheme of merit is in itself truly antisacramental. But in the understanding of the individual sacraments it may also be seen how the genuine sacramental is curtailed in medieval theology.

The most striking example of this is the Eucharist. While the early Christian celebration of the Eucharist contained a living consciousness of the personal and gracious presence of Christ in his congregation, the remnants of the great Eucharistic service of the ancient church are in the Roman mass completely absorbed in the cult of the sacrifice of the mass, which in its true tendency is decidedly antisacramental. Luther has not characterized the medieval piety in which he was brought up by the picture of Christ as the stern judge because it is in contrast to the piety that has its source in the sacrifice of the mass but because it is a very striking characteristic of this piety. It is true that the Body and Blood are present on the altar. But they are not there primarily as the means by which God descends to us—for in that case the communion and not the sacrifice of the mass should be the most prominent view of the Supper. This is not the case in medieval piety where the communion is pushed aside by the sacrifice in the mass. It is primarily as the substance of a sacrifice of atonement—therefore transubstantiation!—that it is brought before God who is *far away*. This view is essentially antisacramental. The sacrifice in the mass places the Supper on a level with the veneration of the saints and the relics—even though it is the most pious of all exercises of merit.

In this connection it is seen how little the idea of Roman Catholic "sacramental magic" is justified. This expression is very unfortunate and should be eliminated from Protestant dogmatics, where it only causes confusion. Roman theologians rightly reject the accusation that they think "magically" about the sacraments. Grace, according to Romanism, is not a certain power, which may be injected into man in spite of his personal attitude to God. Such a view is definitely labeled by the odious word "magic." But back of the accusation of "sacramental magic" was the legitimate observation that in place of the genuine thought of sacramentalism about God's true and Christ's personal presence under the visible sign, has been substituted, in the scholastic theology, the thought of something that is not the real presence of God but an energy given by God which by the sacrament is infused into human nature and which helps it to strive upward toward God who is far away. It is significant for the medieval (and the whole Roman Catholic) concept of the sacraments that it is the idea of *gratia infusa* which is connected metaphysically with the sacrament. That which is present in the sacrament is a power coming out from God rather than God and the risen Christ himself. When this power is placed in the system of merit as a means for man's lifting himself to God, it in reality strengthens an antisacramental view of God and Christ. (All sacramental magic is antisacramental!) The same observation may be made with respect to the idea of the church. The ancient sacramental idea of the church, the church as the body of Christ, is changed by the rise of the papal and hierarchical system in an antisacramental direction. Here again the immediate presence of God and Christ in and through the office of the Word and the sacrament is replaced by the indirect divine work of God by virtue of an organization instituted by God. Here, as in the view of the sacrament, that which is made and wrought by God (or Christ) is made to substitute for God or Christ himself.

The departure from the eschatological concept of the sacrament is connected with this antisacramental tendency which has its source in the anthropocentric perspective that permeates the whole Roman sacramental teaching and that is based on its *eros* character, on the priority which is given the system of merit and law. The genuinely biblical, sacramental view is always based on the eschatological. When it is God himself, or the risen Christ, who is hidden under the visible sign, we find an unsolved tension. For God himself—or Christ—may well be revealed through the sign but, because it is under a sign that he is revealed, he is also hidden. He is *Deus in carne absconditus.* Only in this hidden state in the flesh does God reveal himself in this age. In the world to come he will reveal himself as he is, no longer hidden by the visible sign. That which produces eschatological tension in this genuinely biblical, sacramental view is the unity of the strictly personal idea of God and the sacramental form of revelation. If the idea of God is not considered from a strictly personal point of view, a sacramental form of revelation does not contain this form of tension. If the concept of God is idealistic, Platonic, or Aristotelian; if God is considered as the transcendent source of the ideas that are mirrored in visible things (or are realized in them), there is, of course, a certain tension between the absolutely transcendent concept of God and the realization of the ideas in concrete things. But *this* tension is not of an eschatological character. It is only the tension between the beginning and the end of the process in which man is on his way into the source of all things. The tension of Platonism between the two worlds or that of Aristotelianism between *causa prima* and *causae secunda* is not the tension between this world of sin and the coming world of God, but the tension between the outward and the inward in this one world of metaphysics. The sacramental view becomes the introductory stage in a metaphysical process of understanding which concludes with a mystical view of the source of all things. But a sacramental view which is resolved in metaphysics and not in eschatology is not a genuinely biblical view. When mysticism takes the place of the Bible it indicates that the strictly personal idea of God is crowded out by the metaphysical concept of God. The connection between sacramental piety and mysticism is a decidedly typical characteristic of medieval piety. The whole "ecclesiastical" tendency of medieval mysticism represents this connection which makes sacramental piety the beginning of a process which culminates in mystic contemplation. This leads to two developments: God is not truly present in the sacrament, but only a power coming from God to help us onward toward God; and God is therefore not the present God, who is hidden only by outward things and whose real revelation takes a place in the world to come, but he is the transcendent cause back of everything. God should therefore be sought in a timeless sphere outside of the present. This, however, does not mean that eschatology has disappeared from medieval Christianity for, on the contrary, it has some very definite eschatological ideas. But the part that mysticism (and the accompanying metaphysics) has in the total view permits eschatology to be influenced by mysticism. The state of salvation in medieval theology is understood as the true contemplation of God. The eschatological goal is completely marked by mysticism and metaphysics.

If we study Luther's view, as we have seen it in the writings about the sacraments from the years of the struggle about indulgences, against the background of these characteristics of the medieval sacramental doctrine, we find a far more genuine and biblical, sacramental concept. It is here first and foremost decisive that God in Christ is personally present in the Word and the sacrament. God himself in the living Christ is not superseded by a power coming from God. It is important to note that it is this view of the real presence of the living Christ which is the basis for a correlation between *promissio* and *signum*. That God in Christ is personally present is seen by qualifying the sacramental Word as *promissio*. In a personal sense God appears in the word of promise which can only be accepted by faith. Every impersonal concept of the relationship between man and God in the sacrament is here excluded. The correlation of *promissio-fides* bars the way for all tendencies in that direction. But when God's personal message in the sacrament is *promissio* and not *lex*, it means that God not only will appear personally but that in this personal appearance he will come near to us and give himself to us in Christ. That this promise is fulfilled the sign confirms. The sign is the humanity of Christ in which God now is present with us in a hidden manner. The signs of baptism and the Supper are also a part of this humanity. Christ is hidden in both of these signs but he is present as the one who has received our life into himself and given it its eschatological quality. In the sign of baptism and its significance which is realized by God himself, our life with its death and resurrection is placed in real unity with the death and resurrection of Christ and thus is reborn to live eternally. In the sign of the Supper and the realization of its meaning by God, our whole life is placed under the power of the living Christ to conquer sin and death because the body and blood of Jesus given for our sins are under the bread and wine, given to us as nourishment for the forgiveness of sin and eternal life. These two signs unite us with the eschatological people of God. They are signs which establish and sustain the church.

In Luther's teaching of the sacraments we meet a genuine biblical sacramentalism characterized by the fact that God himself in Christ is personally present under the visible sign. Therefore God's *promissio* is connected with every sacrament. And in order for us to realize that the personally present Christ truly *is given* to us so that our whole life receives an eschatological quality, the sign is connected with the *promissio* of the sacrament.

The basic sacrament is Christ himself. He unites God's *promissio* and *signum*. Christ is the promised Messiah of the Old Testament. God fulfills in him his promise to dwell in us. The sign that indicates that this promise is fulfilled is the humanity of Christ. Under the cover of the humanity of Christ God is secretly present fulfilling the promise. The preaching in the church and the Word of the sacrament constitute the message of this sole, at all times identical, promise of God, but the message is of a *fulfilled promise.* Therefore this message is accompanied by the sign. But after the incarnation of Jesus this sign is always the same. It is the humanity of Jesus. The signs of baptism and the Supper are therefore only a part of the humanity of Jesus. They are that part of his humanity in which, after his resurrection and ascension, he is present among us. But both the promise and the sign can only be received by faith. Only he who by faith receives the promise can receive the confirmation of the promise in the sign. He who does not reckon with any promise—and only by faith can we reckon with the promise—can, of course, not get the promise realized. To the unbeliever who does not trust in the promise the sign is changed to a human *opus,* and thereby it becomes law and makes for condemnation instead of salvation. In this sense the sign is to Luther always *signum efficax.* It always effects salvation or condemnation. It is never neutral.

Luther holds that the Word and the sacrament are inseparably united. But it is impossible to understand their mutual relationship by placing them side by side as two different and almost competing means of grace as is often done by modern Protestantism where the sacrament is ignored. For the Word is itself a part of the sacrament, and the Word of the sacrament is identical with the Word which is preached. To Luther there is no modern "problem" in the mutual relationship between the preached message and the sacrament. The preached message and the sacrament both belong to the same historico-eschatological totality. There is no other Word than that which is preached to men who are living in the efficacy of their baptism and their use of the Supper. There is no sacrament without a promise. And the promise must be proclaimed in order to be believed. The preached message together with the confession of sin assumes sacramental character by this dependence on the sacramental signs. This does not mean that the preaching of the Word as the basic means of grace and the strong emphasis on *verbum vocale* signify a regression of the sacrament. Such a hostile attitude toward the sacrament in the emphasis on "the Word," is something which modern man has attributed to Luther's strong emphasis on the Word because of modern man's own hostile attitude to the sacrament. There is no degradation of the sacrament in Luther's strong emphasis on the Word because the Word and the sacrament are not understood by Luther as competing with one another. The fact is that the strong emphasis on *verbum vocale* simply stresses the value of the sacrament. Preaching is a part of the right use of the sacrament. Therefore the strong emphasis on the *verbum vocale* adds new honor and dignity to the sacrament.

It is the genuine sacramental and eschatological view of revelation which causes the Word to be so inseparably united with the sacrament and the sacrament with the Word. Where this genuine view of the sacrament is curtailed, the word and the sacrament will be divided and their unity becomes a problem. This is what happens in the scholastic doctrine of grace, where sacramental grace is not viewed as the personal presence of Christ, but as a supernatural power from God in the soul. Then the Word becomes merely a word of consecration, which is to guarantee the presence of grace in the sign of the sacrament, and the proclamation of the Word is so little needed that in the Roman mass, for example, it may be recited almost inaudibly. The preached message is thus separated from the sacrament and may easily disappear completely or it may become the preaching of the law (*imitatio*-preaching). The preached message seems to be superfluous. It has become a problem.

Something similar also takes place in modern Protestantism where the presence of Christ in the Word is not thought of realistically but from the idealistic point of view. The presence of Christ in the Word then simply means his historic image as it influences our religious and moral consciousness, or—in the more orthodox form—the right teaching of the Scriptures about the atoning work of Christ, where Christ is present in the sense that he is the content of this doctrine. Faith, which is man's subjective reaction to this impression (or this teaching), does not seem to need any sacrament. For it is *all* given in the Word, and the sacrament seems to become a cumbersome addition. Its purpose can then only be psychologically explained ("it speaks with greater force to the individual," it gives a more objective point of support, etc.). The sacrament becomes superfluous. It too has become a problem. Luther does not view preaching and the sacrament as a problem. They are both based in God's total work of salvation: promise, incarnation, baptism, preaching, the Supper, and the fulfillment. How should we be received into this totality except by promise and sign? And how should there be promise without preaching, and sign without a sacrament?

It has been necessary to study Luther's concept of the sacraments so thoroughly, even though it may seem to be a digression from our real theme, because the sacraments are often misunderstood because of spiritualizing. And such a misunderstanding would place all we have said previously about the Word and the Spirit in a completely false light. We have now seen that a spiritualistic interpretation of Luther's sacramental concept cannot be maintained. It must be considered a distortion of Luther based on modern spiritualistic suppositions. Luther's own view is absolutely sacramental. In the sense that it stresses the presence of God in Christ by Word and sacrament it is even more sacramental than the medieval concept of Christianity. The Word and the sacrament are in Luther united in one sacramental concept. It is on this background that the previous section about the Spirit and the Word must be understood. What we said there about the Spirit's relation to the Word applies also to the sacrament, because the Word is a part of the sacrament, and the sacrament is never without the Word. We have previously stated that it is faith which unites the promise and the sign because it is only through faith that the sign can be confirmed. Recalling what we learned about the relation between the Spirit and the Word and the Spirit and experience, we may then also state that it is the Holy Spirit which unites the promise and the sign. It is the Spirit that causes Christ to be truly present in the Word and that makes it a gospel which kindles faith and supports it. Therefore it is only by the Holy Spirit that the promise and the sign are fused into the unity by which we are put into a relationship to the living Christ. The sacrament as the living unity of *promissio* and *signum* received by faith, is created by the work of the Spirit. Without the work of the Spirit this unity is destroyed. The Word becomes law, the sign becomes work, and faith disappears completely. This applies to all that was said previously about the sovereignty of the Spirit and the insufficiency of the outward Word, and it applies also to the sacrament. Just as the written or preached Word without the Spirit is *littera*, in like manner the Word of the sacrament without the Spirit is *littera*, and its sign is only a human *opus*.

But this is not the only thing we have learned by the study of Luther's concept of the sacrament and his view of the relation between the Spirit and his means of work. On two other points we have received a deeper insight as to what was said previously about the Spirit and the Word.

It now becomes clearer why it is not an empty gesture to hope and pray to meet the Spirit in the outward Word, since the promise accompanies such hope and prayer. The sign of baptism gives our whole life an eschatological quality and places it in the totality of the saving act of God. We begin to die in the moment of baptism and the whole Christian life is by the sign of baptism a constant dying and resurrection to new life. In that sense baptism is our regeneration. But this conformity to Christ, which is the significance of the sign of baptism, God realizes in us through the *Holy Spirit*. It is therefore said that we are regenerated by water and the Spirit. In baptism we receive the Spirit in rich measure, that is, God in baptism makes a new pact with us in which he begins to make us new people. The sign of this covenant is the outward ritual of baptism. Just as long as we live under the sign of baptism, and we do this until our death and resurrection, God works in us to make us conform to Christ in his death and resurrection. In all this the Holy Spirit works even when we are not able to see it and understand it, for, as we noticed in the introductory sections, it is only the Holy Spirit which creates true conformity with Christ and faith in him. The inner conflict in which the Holy Spirit seems entirely lost to us is, as we have seen before, the place where the Spirit is most active to make us conform to Christ. In the covenant of baptism the Holy Spirit has come richly upon us. This does not mean that we ourselves can see where and when he acts. That the Spirit in the Word makes Christ truly present for us and thereby makes the Word gospel, is not the same as the psychological phenomenon that a sermon becomes very "real" to us or creates within us "warm" feelings. (Sometimes God is very active in a sermon that bores us, and the devil may be very active in the sermon that calls forth our tears.) In the groanings of inner conflict the Spirit works for us through the Word also, even though we are not able to feel that it is a living word or to see that it is a gospel, but on the other hand consider everything dead, and all words as an accusing law. And yet it is a fact that in the very moment the groaning of the Spirit breaks through and finds the way to God, Christ is near in his Word as a gift of God, even though he is hidden to our reason and our feelings. Our assurance that the Spirit will not separate itself from the Word is based on the covenant of baptism. By this covenant we are placed in the totality of the saving act of God. And this saving act is never passive. Therefore we know by the promise of baptism and its sign that the Spirit has come upon us richly and that God is doing his work no matter how it progresses. Under the sign of baptism we are being conformed with Christ in death and resurrection. Therefore inner conflict is also a part of God's work in us, and when we have to wait on the Spirit—sometimes a long time—it is also an indication of the fact that we have received the Spirit in rich measure. The abundance of the Spirit is indicated by the fact that we are not able to comprehend more than one iota of him. He is hidden in the Word and in faith and not in our feelings. Our expectation of the Spirit's work is therefore not without a definite foundation. It rests on God's covenant with us in baptism and the sign of the covenant that he has begun to put to death our old man and raise a new man, and that he will perfect that which he has begun.

The second point in Luther's view of the mutual relationship of the Spirit and the Word which has become clear by studying his sacramental concept is the idea of Christ's real presence in the Word. Several times we have used the formula, Christ's real presence or Christ's presence as a redeeming reality, in order to describe the work of the Spirit in the Word. Having learned to know Luther's concept of the sacraments we can see that this formula cannot be understood too realistically. Christ is truly present in his *humanity*. This humanity is *now* the outward reality of the signs of the Word and the sacrament. Christ is truly present with us only when the Word and the signs give our whole life an eschatological quality. Christ's real presence is therefore not merely outside of us but within us, not in the sense of the mystics but in the sense of the eschatological understanding of the sacrament. Christ is not near as our *object*—as the object for our understanding, or our love, or our mystical experience. He is not near as a means to satisfy our hunger for bliss or reach for moral perfection. Christ is only near as the one who embraces our whole existence and places it within the totality of God's saving act, where all our own efforts have been put aside and where God alone guides all toward his eternal goal. Christ's real presence does not mean merely that his image appears in the Word about him (in that way Socrates may be present in the dialogues of Plato). And it does not mean that Christ is present as the content of a definite doctrine. It does mean that in the sign of baptism his humanity embraces and makes our own existence conform to him and, in the sign of the Supper, places our whole existence under his power to conquer over sin and death. Christ's real presence is not a momentary religious experience, but a total eschatological, historical act of salvation influencing our whole life. To say that Christ by the Spirit is really present in the preached Word means that the living and risen Christ, who in the sign of baptism has united our death and resurrection with his death and resurrection by the preached Word as well as by confession and the Supper, continues the work that he began in the moment of baptism by putting to death our old man and by raising a new man. It is this task, started in baptism and perfected in the resurrection, at which God works when he lets the *verbum vocale* speak to us. That Christ is truly present in the Word means that the Word is in him and that he himself speaks the Word and works through it. The connection between him and the Word is made by the Spirit alone. That the Word is gospel and gives Christ to us is simply another way of saying that it gives us to Christ so that he becomes the one who directs us, not we the ones who use him. This last expression is perhaps a little more striking than the first one. To express the matter in this way—that the Word is in Christ (not Christ in the Word), that the gospel gives us to Christ (not Christ to us)—has the significance of underscoring the fact that we are not anthropocentric in our perspective when we speak about the Spirit's work. The statement that Christ is present in the Word may be interpreted anthropocentrically, that means that Christ is understood as that which the heart *demands*, as the satisfaction of an individual religious urge. Such an anthropocentric concept of Christ has been found both in orthodox and pietistic circles. But it is *not* Lutheran. And the gospel *may* be understood anthropocentrically as the Word which gives us the desired "peace" (in the sense of religious harmony). Such an understanding of the word "gospel" has been found rather often. But it was not Luther's view. In Luther's teaching of the sacrament it is seen that Christ is not present as the one who satisfies the desire of the moment but as the one who takes our whole life into his sphere of work toward the eternal goal, whether this leads through life or death, through inner conflict or peace. He is present in the Word as the one in whose hand the Word has been placed, and only in this manner! In Luther's teaching of the sacrament it is seen that the gospel is not a Word that merely brings rest and peace, but a Word which gives us and our whole life into the hands of the living Christ. Only as such is the Word really a glad tiding, and only as the Word about him into whose hand we are given, does the gospel give us Christ as a gift.

When we then speak of the work of the Spirit in the Word and the sacraments, it means that the Spirit in the Word and sacrament makes us confront the *living One* before whom we are not masters, and whom we cannot use as a means, not even as a means by which to win salvation. For the living One is always the one who predestinates. And where we do not meet him, there the Spirit is not present. There we are alone with our own death and change the Word to *ratio* and the sign to *opus*. We can understand that this concept of the Word and the sacrament does not permit any rational doctrine of the means of grace, as does the scholastic doctrine of *gratia infusa* or the orthodox doctrine of verbal inspiration. Such a rational doctrine of the means of grace is only possible where the living One has been forgotten, and where predestination has been denied and the Spirit is minimized. We cannot by the aid of Luther present a doctrine by which the work of the Word and the sacrament can be interpreted in a rational manner. Such a doctrine would ignore the *living One*. And it is the living One we meet when we approach the Word and the sacrament. How the Spirit works and what Christ does, he decides in his free and sovereign way. But that it is he who works, who lives, and who decides in a free and sovereign way—this is the gospel. Where we are the ones who live and work and decide, there we have the law but no gospel.

In harmony with the method used so far we conclude this section and thereby this chapter about the means of the Spirit with a review of the insight we have gained. Luther's realistic concept of the Spirit as the sphere of revelation in which the living Christ alone can be near us, and in which faith and love alone can exist, because there alone it has connection with the living Christ, has received its concrete definition, whereas before we only spoke about it in general terms.

Our understanding of the sphere of revelation is not merely a figurative paraphrasing of a psychological relation to a historic concept of Jesus, but it is to be considered in an almost crudely realistic manner. This we learn in Luther's view of the Word and the sacrament as the means of the Spirit. The sphere of revelation is not to be found within the category of idealism. It is not to be found in the self-contemplation of mysticism. It cannot be traced in the realm of speculation. The "spirituality" we reach by these methods is the abstract spirituality of ideas. As a contrast to all this false spirituality, the Spirit of God creates his own manifestation in the humanity of Christ. This humanity is the sign through which God is revealed. And this humanity of Christ which is our own nature we may approach through the Word and the sacrament, not understood as visible illustrations of an invisible idea, but as concrete means for the work of the risen Christ in us and by us.

But it is the Spirit which is manifested in the Word and the sacrament. Therefore it is not possible to make the Word and the sacrament human properties. The Word and the sacrament do not guarantee the presence of the Spirit. They do not carry the Spirit. It is, however, the Spirit that carries the Word and the sacrament. It is the Spirit that makes the Word the gospel of God and the sacrament God's sign of confirmation.

It is not to be deplored that Lutheran theology has not succeeded in formulating a rational doctrine about the Word since the orthodox theory of verbal inspiration was relinquished—a doctrine by which the difference between the true Lutheran view of the Word and the Roman Catholic concept of the sacraments could be clearly demonstrated. It was no loss to Lutheran theology that the inspiration theory disappeared, and its reappearance will only mean a return to orthodoxy away from Luther's living witness about the Spirit. There is a factual basis for the strange hiatus in the thinking which characterized true evangelical theology when forced to face this direct question: "Yes, but where is the Word of God *precisely* stated?" The very lack of precision here is a meritorious characteristic of evangelical theology. Nor *shall* evangelical theology become a teaching of the Word which can with rational clarity compete with the Roman Catholic doctrine of the sacrament—or, in truth, compete with the monumental orthodox doctrine of verbal inspiration. Evangelical theology does not intend to delimit itself from Catholicism with the same rigid clarity as Catholicism is able to use in delimiting itself from Protestantism. The day evangelical theology can do that it has failed in its mission—even toward Catholicism.

The special connection existing between the Spirit and his means cannot be rationally defined as the relation between a transcendent cause and an imminent effect. None of the categories used by *ratio* is able to contain the connection between the Spirit and his means. If it was possible to define this connection in a rational manner, it would mean that the work of the Spirit was placed within the sphere of the law. *Ratio* and *lex* belong together. That which *ratio* may decide, *lex* is able to do. Where there is a rational teaching of the means of grace, there grace is made into means serving the piety of the law. The rational category used—such as the category of cause—is the strong hold by which we lay hold on grace to use it in the service of the law.

In Luther it is grace that uses man in the service of God, not man who uses grace in his own service. Therefore the idea of conformity is insolubly united with his concept of faith. *Conformitas Christi* and *fides Christi* are identical. It was only late Lutheranism that began to speak about a faith that was separated from the real conformity with Christ in his death and resurrection.

When man is to be used by grace he cannot be master as he is when under the law he uses grace for himself. When man is to be used by grace, God must remain the absolutely sovereign Lord and man his creation. This is shown in Luther's doctrine of the means of grace by the characteristic hiatus which we find again and again—the break of continuity which gets into the Lutheran distinction between the outward and the inward Word, between the Word as *littera* and *spiritus*, between the dead letter and the living gospel, between the Word of promise and the sign of confirmation. Because of this break in his relation to the means of grace, man always stands with all guarantee removed, expectant, his prayers directed to God's promise of mercy. We expressed it thus that Luther's concept of the Word and the sacrament was genuinely sacramental, because by Word and sacrament it brought man into relation with the *living One*. Under the law man lives and uses grace as an instrument for his own endeavor. Therefore grace may be enclosed by the categories of *ratio*. Under the gospel grace (that is, Christ himself) lives and calls the dead man to life, so that he may be used by the living God.

In the definition of the sacrament as a unity of *promissio* and *signum* the teaching of the gospel became very prominent. *Promissio* means the unity with God's saving act in history, and *signum* means the unity with God's eschatological fulfillment of this history. In this *promissio* and in this *signum* man is taken completely out of the realm of the law where he works for his own salvation with all means possible and he is placed in God's all-embracing, eschatological, saving act.

Our previous description of the Spirit as the sphere of revelation takes on a concrete content through all this. We have used the word "sphere" to set forth the contrast to every rational and legal concept of the Spirit's relation to his means of grace. By every rational and legalistic description of this relation, the Spirit's work is made a means which may be used by us in fulfilling the law. By describing the Spirit as a sphere it is indicated that the Spirit—or his works—cannot be dominated by us. On the contrary, we are dominated by the Spirit and his work. Within the sphere of the Spirit, Christ is present, the Word is gospel, the sacrament is the unity of promise and confirmation, and we ourselves by the prayer of faith are constantly moving toward Christ as our alien righteousness. From him we reach out to our neighbor in works of love. But the relation between this "sphere" and that which it contains cannot be described rationally. In the very moment we make the Spirit a part of our rational description, we place ourselves outside his sphere and attempt instead to use the operation of the Spirit within the sphere of our own legal piety. We cannot speak rationally about the connection between the sphere of the Spirit and that which is found within his limits (the living Christ, the gospel, the sacrament, faith and love). It can only be proclaimed. It is not possible to describe the Spirit's connection with his means, it is only possible through preaching to promise it.

Since we have come to know Luther's teaching about the Word and the sacraments it is possible to see why this is so. It is because the Spirit as the sphere of revelation is understood in a strictly personal sense. The Spirit as the sphere of revelation is the *living One*. The word "sphere" may be misleading because it may suggest something impersonal, a divine medium of some kind, different from God's own person. Such a misunderstanding of the previously presented sections is now prevented. The Spirit as the sphere of revelation is the living God personally. Therefore he is manifested in the Word of promise and in the sign of confirmation. The Spirit is one with the personal God who is the father of Jesus Christ and acting in history. In the Word of promise and in the sign of confirmation God reveals himself as the one who directs his creation toward the goal he has set for it in Jesus Christ. Between the Word of promise and the sign of confirmation God embraces all of history from the creation to its fulfillment. It is the all-embracing eschatological act of salvation in which we are placed by the Word and the sacrament. And in this work with us we meet God as Lord, that is, as a *person*. It is this personal and sovereign work of God with us in Jesus Christ which, when it becomes our sphere of life, we know as the Holy Spirit. If we are outside of this all-embracing eschatological act of God's salvation we are outside the sphere of the Spirit. In that case the promise, Jesus Christ himself, the sacrament, the Christian life in faith and love, all become merely law, something of which we hear, but of which we are not a part, wherefore we are urged to work ourselves into it in one way or another. It is the curse of the law to be outside when we should be inside but are not able to enter. But if we are within God's all-embracing eschatological act of salvation, we are within the sphere of the Spirit, and then God has drawn us into his own reality as his sphere of life. Then the promise, Jesus Christ, the sacrament, the Christian life in faith and love, are not something of which we merely hear, but something of which we are placed in the very center, something that happens to us. Inside or outside, this is the decisive difference. No rational theology can build a bridge over this gap. The Spirit alone realizes it, in the *experience*.

Where this gap cannot be seen, the difference between the law and the gospel is not known, i.e. one is still in the realm of the law. The Luther research which holds that the idea of the Holy

Spirit may be dispensed with as remains of tradition which we either seek to eliminate, as does Rudolf Otto, or quietly to overlook, as does most modern study of Luther, has hardly started to learn the rudiments of the difficult art of differentiating between the law and the gospel. If Luther's doctrine of justification by faith alone is presented in such a way that the idea of the Holy Spirit may be excluded it simply means that the whole thing has been changed into law. In the very moment that the gospel message becomes a kind of ideology, it has become law. The difference between the law and the gospel is *never* a difference between two ideologies, an evangelical theology and a legalistic one, but it is *always* the difference between *all* ideology on the one hand (even the most beautiful and evangelical ideology) and God's reality on the other. When this is admitted it will be seen that Luther could not speak about the gospel, about faith, about grace without speaking about the Holy Spirit. This concept is not one which happened to be left over from tradition—everything depends upon it. If the Holy Spirit is not included in the understanding of Luther's thoughts then all has been changed into Lutheran ideology, which is just as different from Luther's living witness of Christ and the Spirit as are the five letters b-r-e-a-d from the nourishing actual bread for the man who is dying of starvation.

The decisive gap is that between the inside and the outside of the real sphere of revelation of the Spirit. If the Spirit was understood in an impersonal way, only the law remained. The sphere was then a distant domain which we had to reach by our own strength. The fact, however, as we have seen especially in the last chapter, is that the Spirit as the sphere of life of the revelation or the gospel is not such an impersonally conceived medium, but it is the living and acting God himself who comes to us and draws us into himself as our sphere of life. The contrast to the view which we previously named *"caritas* idealism" and which is represented by medieval theology is here complete. In *caritas* idealism we see man working his way to the eternal, passive God. In Luther's realistic witness of the Spirit we see the active and struggling God on the way to man who is dead in his sins. In *caritas* idealism a rational doctrine of the means of grace guarantees the effectiveness of grace, and yet this guarantee does not reach beyond the curse of the law. In Luther's realistic witness of the Spirit there is no guarantee at all, but a doctrine of the means of grace which, in the place of guarantee, shows us a great hiatus. But by this hiatus there has been made room for the *living One* who cannot be reconciled to any guarantee. Therefore, because there is room for the witness about the living God we are placed under the blessing of the gospel. Of course, this must not be understood to mean that Luther should have secured a place for the living God by a theological maneuver, and then at the same time have smuggled that guarantee in through the back door. The hiatus in Luther's theology means that there is a place for the *testimony* about the living God, not that we have enclosed him and brought him into the system. The hiatus in Luther's theology means that there is room for constant preaching, for the proclamation. In the proclamation we expect the gracious coming of the Spirit. And we expect it because the Spirit is a person, the active God himself. Where the coming of the Spirit has been previously calculated in the system instead of expected in the preaching, there we do not speak about the Spirit as God's own living person, but only as the transcendent cause of the grace we have obtained through the system.

We now take one backward glance. The Holy Spirit is to Luther a present reality, not a transcendent causality. As a present reality the Spirit is the sphere into which Jesus Christ comes out of the grave of history and ideality, or pure idea, and is truly present and in which we are therefore driven by his presence into the constant prayer of faith and into acts of love toward our neighbor. As a really present sphere of life the Spirit manifests itself concretely in the outward sign of Christ's humanity, in the Word and the sacrament. Such a reality manifested in the Word and the sacrament, however, is not thought of as an impersonally considered divine medium, but is the living and acting God himself who draws us into his all-embracing, eschatological, saving act.

In the last chapter we have seen how decisive it is for Luther's view of the Holy Spirit that the Spirit is understood as God himself in his own person, and that the work of the Spirit is therefore one with the father's eschatological saving act in Christ, by which he leads his creation toward the goal he has set for it. In other words, Luther's concept of the Holy Spirit is trinitarian in principle. We have thus reached the question which we shall discuss in the last chapter of the first part of our thesis, namely the idea of the Holy Spirit in connection with Luther's doctrine of the Trinity.

Chapter III

THE PERSON OF THE HOLY SPIRIT

Luther and the Traditional Doctrine of the Trinity

In the two previous chapters we have studied Luther's view of the Spirit's work and his means of performing this work. We now proceed to study his understanding of the Spirit as a person, that is, we begin to study Luther's doctrine of the Trinity.

If in the treatment of Luther's view of the work of the Spirit we learned that to a great extent he used the traditional terminology, we shall see that this applies much more to his doctrine of the Trinity. It is especially difficult in the young Luther to find any deviations from the orthodox doctrine of the Trinity which we know from Augustine and scholasticism. Where Luther's lecturing and preaching gave him an opportunity, he treated the traditional doctrine of the Trinity sympathetically and as something not open to question. This does not mean that Luther feared or opposed such orthodox lines of thought. A number of German Luther scholars have believed that they had to designate these thoughts as "an academic exercise of the intellect, a scholastic attempt to resolve the old basic problem of trinity and unity,"[1] or as some less fortunate "mental fabrication."[2] Luther thinks of the Trinity as a mystery worthy of worship and he does not hesitate to make several speculative interpretations of Scripture supporting the traditional doctrine of the Trinity. It is true that Luther, in harmony with

---

[1] Rudolf Otto, p. 9: . . . *eine Übung des Geistes, ein schulmässiger Versuch, die alte Meisterfrage nach drei und eins zu lösen.*

[2] Johannes von Walter, *Die Theologie Luthers,* p. 133; *Gedankengespinste.*

his general condemnation of all rational speculations which attempt to seek the divine majesty outside of God's revelation, warns against the trinitarian speculations of the scholastics, that is, against such as are not based on Scripture. The warning, however, is not against the subject as such, but only against a false and unscriptural treatment of the subject. Luther finds the whole substance of the orthodox doctrine of the Trinity in Scripture. Therefore, because the doctrine of the Trinity is the doctrine of Scripture, it is not harmful but necessary to speak about these things. The doctrine of the Trinity is the content of the prologue of John. This prologue is gospel—superb yet clear and simple. It is, however, important in such great themes to hold onto the Word of Scripture and to avoid self-willed speculations.

The young Luther's most explicit and coherent treatment of the doctrine of the Trinity is found in the Christmas sermon of 1514 (*W. A.*, I, 20, 1 ff.). Here we find Luther following traditional dogmatic lines.[3] However, there are some points in this sermon that deserve attention. Luther introduces new analogies to the problem of the Trinity besides those of Augustine. And the most noteworthy is the fact that the one-sided psychological orientation of the Augustinian analogies here encounters an opposite tendency. Besides *creatura intellectualis* and *creatura rationalis* (angels and men) Luther thinks of *creatura sensualis* (animals) and *creatura animalis* (plants) and *creatura inanimalis* (lifeless things) as examples of analogies of the Trinity. In all these creatures there is a motion which is real and yet at the same time it does not change the true nature of the particular plant. Thus there is also in God an eternal motion which in no way changes the nature of God. The Father is *res mobilis*, the Son is *motus rei*, and the Spirit is *quies motus*. Because the analogies from the nonpsychological realms are included and placed side by side with the psychological analogies, it is more emphasized than in Augustine that the analogy from psychology only presents a figurative similarity with God's unsearchable majesty. Augustine also strongly emphasizes

---

[3] Julius Kostlin, I, pp. 70-74. Johannes von Walter, *op. cit.*, p. 133 ff. Erich Seeberg, *Luthers Theologie*, II, p. 48 ff.

the insufficiency of the analogy, but yet he holds that the soul, which is God's image, is much closer to the spiritual nature of God than the visible world which only presents weak *vestigia* of the triune essence of God. It may be that Luther's presentation already at this early stage has a greater distrust of the unimpaired ability of the soul to reflect the spiritual nature of God than we find in Augustine. It is surmised that the doctrine of the Trinity is already getting another position than it had in scholasticism. In scholasticism the doctrine of the Trinity and anthropology are united in a manner that makes the inner essence of the human soul a reflection of the essence of God. Already in the sermon of 1514, we notice that Luther is beginning to deviate from this view, which also was very contrary to his concept of sin which held that the inner soul was touched by the fall. And when the concept *motus*, which also later plays a part in Luther's presentation of the doctrine of the Trinity, gets into the foreground, it seems to prove that the Trinity doctrine is no longer orientated on the basis of God's passive nature as reflected in man's process of understanding, but on the basis of God's activity in revelation as it is seen in the history of revelation.[4] This is also indicated by the fact that from the beginning Luther connects the Word, Logos, the Son, with Genesis 1:3, where the Word is God's creative Word. In the sermon of 1514 we discover the beginning of the exegesis about the Trinity which in Luther takes the place of the speculation of the scholastics. The doctrine of the Trinity is thereby brought into closest connection with the history of revelation. This does not mean that the so-called economic Trinity has supplanted the immanent Trinity. Luther certainly holds that the doctrine of the Trinity is a *real* Trinity doctrine, that is, it does not only treat a triple manner of God's revealing act, but a triad in God's eternal nature. Luther holds that the triad of the revealing act is only possible because God's eternal nature—aside from his revelation—is a Trinity. But—and this is the special view of Luther—this eternal Trinity we meet only in his revelation. Therefore it is impossible to speak about God's triune nature as reflected speculatively and

---

[4] E. Vogelsang, *Die Anfänge von Luthers Christologie*, p. 160 ff.; pp. 165-168.

independently of Scripture in man's *mens*. We must abide by the testimony of Scripture. The reference to Scripture in 1514 means more to Luther than all the psychological and physiological analogies.

What does this mean in Luther's concept of the nature of the Holy Spirit—that he so firmly accepts this doctrine of the Trinity?

First of all, it means that Luther never doubts that the Spirit is God himself personally and not a mere divine manifestation of power. In *Eine kurtze Form*, the catechetical presentation of this period, the explanation of the third article of faith is introduced with the confession of the Holy Spirit as "true God with the Father and Son."[5] But this confession is not caused merely by Luther's respect for tradition. The confession as to the divinity of the Spirit has its background in the realistic understanding of the work of the Spirit. The experience of the Spirit's work as *consolator* and interpellator, who in the death and darkness of inner conflict gains for us life by interceding for us in groanings that cannot be uttered, and who makes the living Christ so present that the activity of faith and love directly issues from his presence, does not permit a less definite concept of the person of the Holy Spirit. *Nun ist von den zwei personen der glaub mit sprüchen der schrifft gegründet und befestigt, die dritt steet Matthei 28, 'Geet hyn und taufft in dem namen des vaters, des suns und des heyligen geysts' Da gibt er die gotheit auch dem heyligen geyst, dann ich darff nit trawen oder glauben dann allain got, dann ich mus einen haben, der da mechtig ist uber todt, helle und teüffel und uber alle creaturen, das er inen gebieten kün, das sie mir nit schaden. Nun got beschleüst hie, das man auch in dem heyligen geyst glawben und trawen sol, so muss er auch got sein.*[6] Man in inner conflict is completely in the power of death, hell, and the devil. No one is able to intercede there, and no one else can conquer but Christ who has the power over death, hell, and the devil and who is able to say, "Depart from me." And the Holy Spirit, who in *Eine kurtze Form* is presented as the one who creates life here in time and also on the last day,

---

5 . . . *warhafftiger got mit dem Vatter und Sun.*
6 *W. A.*, XII, 587, 19 (*Prædiken Trin.*, 1522).

can be no one else than the *warhafftiger got*, by whom the Father by Christ and in Christ accomplishes all and creates life.

However, one should not, as it has happened so often, understand Luther's adherence to the traditional Trinity doctrine as merely an accustomed way of thinking. The zeal with which Luther is searching for a Trinity doctrine based on the Scriptures shows that the doctrine to him is more than a mere tradition. The fact is that in scholasticism the Trinity doctrine, in spite of a careful preservation of the traditional terminology, had lost connection with its source in the struggles of the ancient church. Luther places it anew into its original connection, by which it assumes new life. Scholastic theology retained all its traditional confession of the eternal divinity of the Son and the Spirit. But because of the synergistic doctrine of salvation it gave man's free will a significance which was really a limitation of the domain of the work of both the Son and the Spirit. The realistic understanding of the Spirit's work had to yield where a principal continuity between man's uninjured religio-ethical essence and the eternal life should be maintained. This does not come in the form of Pelagianism, but perhaps in the form of a strong anti-Pelagianistic and Augustinian Thomism, and yet it comes in such a way that the gratuitous grace meets us and fulfills the ideal urge of man. In harmony with this the doctrine of the Trinity had the function of proving the divine likeness of God in man, and then, in an inverted sense, of throwing light upon the character of the divine Trinity by the psychological self-understanding of man. The living connection between the secret of the immanent Trinity and God's act of revelation was broken, and it was substituted by the speculation over the relation between man's *mens* and God's eternal spirituality. Luther, however, gives new life to the original meaning of the Trinity doctrine in his understanding of the total impotency of man over against the powers of perdition. Luther's proof of the divinity of the Spirit and the Son, *denn ich mus einen haben, der da mechtig ist uber todt, hell und teüffel und uber alle creaturen, das er inen gebieten kün, das sie mir nit schaden,*[7] corresponds well with Athanasius'

---

[7] See footnote 6.

proof of *omoousios*. It is the impossibility of man's redeeming himself which proves that God the redeemer truly is God in the sense of the incomprehensible meaning of that word. Therefore the doctrine of the Trinity in Athanasius and Luther is a living one while in scholasticism it has become a fossilized tradition, or rather, a tradition which has been given new life, but in a very different connection than the one in which it originally lived.

That the traditional Trinity formulas are living and not mere rudimentary, routine thinking on the part of Luther is not only seen in his persistent work to give them a complete and solid scriptural basis and thus to connect them solidly with the history of revelation, but it is also seen in Luther's use of these formulas. The glorification of the divine majesty of the Son and the Spirit in the doctrine of the Trinity is not a metaphysical appendix which may be quietly separated from Luther's ethico-religious message. This has been maintained by referring to a much misused word by Melanchthon that it is better to worship than to explore the mysteries of God. But this doctrine retains direct connection with the center of Luther's concept of Christianity. This connection is seen in Luther's exposition of *Gloria patri* in the second lecture on the Psalms: *Verum ut ad usitata nos accomodemus, placeat interim, quod Patri potentia et virtus, Filio sapientia et consilium, Spirituisancto bonitas et charitas tribuator, atque his notionibus apprehendantur, ut qui psallit gloriam patri, suam simul offerat vanissimam gloriam, confessus suam infirmitatem et impotentiam, nec optet fortis et potens esse nisi in deo patre. Dum psallit gloriam filio, abominetur suam sapientiam et consilium mactatisque his bestiis offerat, confessus suam insipientiam et stultitiam, nec optet sapiens prudensque haberi nec apud se nec apud homines nisi in deo suo filio. Dum psallit gloriam spirituisancto, ponat fiduciam iustitiae et bonitatis suae, peccata confessus, optetque ex deo spirituisancto iustus et bonus fieri mactetque opinionem bestialem suae iustitiae. Ita fit, ut omnia deo, nobis nihil relinquamus nisi confusionem et confessionem malorum et nihili et miseriae nostrorum. Ita iustificati sumus, reddentes unucuique quod suum est.*[8]

---

[8] *W. A.*, V, 198, 31 ff.; also IV, 206, 26 ff. (1513-15).

The connection between a trinitarian faith in God and *theologia crucis* is seen here. If the divinity of the Son and the Spirit is not preached without limitation, the *humilitas* theology becomes imitation-piety and the most refined form of self-righteousness. Imitation-piety really contains an attack on the doctrine of the Trinity inasmuch as it limits the domain of the divine work of the Son and the Spirit and thereby also robs them of their divine honor. All piety which is not *theologia crucis* is an attack on the trinitarian faith in God.

We must not minimize Luther's confession of the Trinity doctrine of the ancient church, which he staunchly maintained in his first writings and continued to do till his death. If we minimize this confession we thereby change everything Luther says about Christ and about faith. We have previously seen that the realistic understanding of the work of the Spirit is that which decisively separates Luther from the medieval *caritas* idealism with its *imitatio* piety. But this only applies when the Holy Spirit is understood as God himself without any limitations. If, as in the neo-Protestant theology and its offshoots, the idea of the Spirit is considered closely related to the idealistic idea of the continuity between man's highest spiritual nature and the center of existence, then the connection between the confession of the divinity of the Spirit and the condemnation of our own *opinio bestialis justitiae* disappears. For in this case a part of man's high nature is reserved, the valuation of which will not be characterized as *bestialis opinio*. And if one approaches the interpretation of Luther with this idea of the Spirit it is no wonder that we get embarrassed with Luther's message about the work of the Spirit and his divine personality, and that we would rather have the first reduced to a superfluous idea accompanying an easily understood, psychological process, and the other reduced to little more than a rudimentary routine of thinking.

We have then seen that the realism in Luther's concept of the Spirit's work and the radical basis in his *theologia crucis*, which is the other side of this realism, demands the confession of the divinity of the Spirit in the sense used in the ancient church. The Spirit—who with unutterable groanings intercedes for the soul in inner conflict, and who makes Christ a truly present reality in this conflict, and who through the constant motion of faith and love draws him into God's all-embracing, eschatological act of salvation—is no one else than God himself. Luther's adherence to the traditional doctrine of the Trinity is therefore not based on a mere pious reverence for an honorable tradition, but it is based on the fact that Luther's understanding of God's revelation is in harmony with the real intention of the Trinity doctrine of the ancient church.

Something else, however, besides confessing the eternal divinity of the Son and the Spirit, belongs to the traditional Trinity doctrine to which Luther adheres. This doctrine separates the orthodox interpretation of the Christian message of Christianity not only from the denial of the divinity of the Son and the Spirit, but also from the denial of the person's special personality (modalism). Luther energetically emphasizes this element of the Trinity doctrine in his trinitarian exegesis of the first verses of the prologue of John and the first chapter of Genesis.[9]

Is antimodalism of any real significance in Luther's concept of the Spirit and his work, or is that part of the Trinity doctrine perhaps a bit of routine thinking?

It is not unusual to hear that Luther not only had no interest in the antimodalistic definitions of the traditional Trinity doctrine but that his own idea of Christ and the Spirit with the strong emphasis on the unity of God must be much like that of modalism. Even Karl Holl in his study of Luther makes himself a spokesman for such a view. When Holl, erroneously however, attempts to find modalistic tendencies in Luther, it is no doubt because his own view of Christianity is of a modalistic type. In Holl's study, *Der Neubau der Sittlichkeit,* there is this statement: "Where both (prayer and the Word) are used faithfully, Luther does not doubt that the warm feeling for God and the inner joy because of good-

---

9 For example, *W. A.,* X, 1, I, 183. 13 ff.; 191, 11 ff. (1522).

ness grow steadily, both of which he designates directly as the Holy Spirit or as the Christ in man."[10] According to Holl, Luther had no scruples in placing signs of equality between the Christian's new life (in the sense of the "warm feeling for God and the inner joy because of goodness") and the Holy Spirit, and also between the Holy Spirit understood as such and Christ in man. A similar concept is found in Reinhold Seeberg. Seeberg, however, being an outstanding authority on the history of dogma, recognizes the impossibility of ascribing to Luther a conscious modalistic concept. He is rightly opposed to Holl's assertion that Luther represents a pronounced modalism. It is all the more strange that, in its close relation to Karl Holl's concept of Luther, Seeberg's interpretation of Luther's thoughts gets a modalistic character. To Seeberg as well as to Holl, as we have stated so often, the chief point in Luther's doctrine of justification is the view of grace as a sanctifying power which gradually changes man from sinner to righteous. This transforming grace is an indwelling of Christ's spiritual power in the soul and not only a union of the human will with Christ's will. The total religious and ethical development in man caused by grace is his righteousness. But *this* righteousness is effective before God only because it may be designated as Christ's righteousness. Seeberg wants to understand Luther's expression "Christ's righteousness" as a spiritual influence which comes from Christ and which gradually overcomes original sin. Seen from above this process is the royal rule of Christ, which truly coincides with the work of the Spirit. However, Seeberg rightly emphasizes that Luther's Trinity doctrine is not only a habitual repetition of ancient church formulas, but an expression for the theology of his faith. And much more clearly than Holl does he clarify the significance of the orthodox differentiation between the individual persons and their different offices. But the identification of the empirical ethical and religious development with the indwelling Christ and with the Holy Spirit is, however, entirely in line with

---

10 *Wo beides* (prayer and the Word) *treu genützt wurde, da zweifelte Luther nicht, würde das warme Gefühl für Gott und die innere Freude am Guten stetig wachsen, die er ohne Bedenken als den Heiligen Geist oder als den Christus im Menschen bezeichnete.*

Holl's statement: "the warm feeling for God and the inner joy because of goodness" equals the Holy Ghost, which equals Christ in man. Thus while he opposes a pronounced modalism in Luther, Seeberg ascribes to him a modalism anyway.

If the Holl and Seeberg concept were correct it would mean that Luther, contrary to his own theory, represented in practice a definite modalism. For the identification of empirical piety with the Spirit and of the Spirit with Christ in us means that the individual's personal existence is abolished, and that the names, Father, Son, and Spirit may be used at random. We have, however, shown that the identification of empirical piety with Christ in us cannot be harmonized with Luther's concept of *fides Christi*. Such an identification means a modalistic mixture of the personal existence of the Father and the Son of which Luther never was guilty. True and real piety is something wrought by God. It is God's "creature" which rightly belongs to the Father, but as creature this piety can never be identified with *Christus ipse*. In the same way it is impossible for Luther—as Holl permits him to do, and even *ohne Bedenken!*—to make any marks of similarity between Christ in us and the Holy Spirit. If Christ and the Spirit are not separated, it becomes impossible to distinguish between Christ of the law and Christ of the gospel, between Christ as an idea and Christ as a redeeming reality. For it is the Spirit alone which makes the all-decisive difference. Where, as in Holl, the Spirit and Christ in us are easily permitted to appear as synonymous it is an indication that only Christ of the law is considered, the idea of Christ. Holl's whole interpretation of Luther is really an imitation-interpretation. The religion of Luther is interpreted as the absolute *Sollen* ("Thou shalt"), that is, it is viewed from the point of view of the law *(Gewissensreligion)*. Therefore it is also very characteristic of Holl's view of Luther that, without noticing that Luther understands the first commandment from a Christ-centered point of view, he lets this commandment substitute for Christ in inner conflict. And Holl seems to think that we there have Luther's "religion" in its purest form. But this really means that Holl's Christ is only the historic figure of Christ, and that his purpose is to call forth the warm feeling for God and the inner joy because of goodness, a function which may be replaced in inner conflict by the first commandment. Holl believes most strongly that the religious impression, whether it is brought about by Christ or by the first commandment, has the character of the *Unbedingtes Sollen* (the unqualified "Thou shalt"). It is therefore hardly accidental that Holl's great work on Luther by-passes Luther's doctrine of the sacraments. Every time Holl speaks about Luther's view of the sacraments it is in order to show how far Luther is from true sacramental piety. That Luther struggled passionately for the doctrine of the real presence and that he fought with no less passion against the "sacramentalists" and against the papists may not be learned from Holl's book on Luther. It is easy to understand why this is so. On the basis of Holl's definition of Luther's "religion," we never get to a point where it is possible to gain any interest for Luther's sacramental thought. But that also means that the contrast between the law and the gospel which was so important to Luther is strangely obscured. If Holl had seen how decisive this contrast was to Luther, his description of Luther's religion would hardly have been so Kantian, and the great theme of Christ's significance for Luther's faith would hardly have been referred to the footnotes. The Spirit would not have been identified with *das Gefühl der göttlichen Gnade* (the feeling of divine grace).

In contrast to these modern attempts either directly to trace modalistic tendencies in Luther or, in spite of Luther's own strong insistence on the traditional Trinity doctrine, to give his thought about Christ and the Holy Spirit a modalistic sense, the previous presentation about the Spirit's work and means has shown that the ancient Trinity doctrine—the antimodalistic doctrine—is the only true answer to the question of Luther's concept of the person of the Spirit. According to Luther the Spirit is God himself. It is nonetheless important to him to distinguish clearly between the personal being of the Spirit and of the Father and of the Son. Only when the Spirit is distinguished clearly from the Father and the Son is it possible to preach Christ's real redeeming presence as *fides Christi*. When the personal being of the Spirit is more or less dissolved in the being of the Father and the Son the relation to Christ becomes possible only as a relation to his historic figure, to the idea of him, or to a power of Christ grasped in a *mystic* experience. That is, the historic Christ remains in the grave. A relation to the risen and living Christ is possible only through the Spirit in a realistic sense and not understood as a mere expression for warm feelings. In contrast to neo-Protestantism, which only knows of a human relation to the figure of Jesus or his idea, Luther agrees with the New Testament and the ancient church in his understanding of the work of the Spirit. But his thought cannot be identified with the orthodox view for which the historic Christ in the first place becomes the content of the correct doctrine of an objective, *in foro coeli,* completed satisfying work.

Luther's attitude to the traditional Trinity doctrine is characterized by a strong conservatism. But it is a conservatism which is rooted in a profound understanding of the Christian message. Luther's doctrine of the Trinity, with its realistic understanding of the presence of both the Spirit and Christ through faith, differs widely from the isolation of the same doctrine in scholasticism, whose whole idealistic structure, in spite of the preservation of the great apparatus of the Trinity doctrine, is foreign to the purpose of the original Trinity doctrine. The Trinity doctrine received new life in Luther. It may even be said that in Luther the Trinity doctrine has received a depth which goes beyond that of the ancient church. Luther not only accepts the old dogma but he fills it with a new content and re-creates it productively.

The Spirit as a Creative Spirit

If in conclusion we now want to summarize into one expression all of Luther's concept of the Holy Spirit, which we have shown gradually in the account of Luther's view of the Spirit's work, his means, and his person, we can only do it by the old name of the Spirit which the Bible and the liturgy of the church have sanctified: *Spiritus creator,* the creative Spirit.

As is indicated by this description, the work of the Spirit is a miracle. We have seen how the experience of inner conflict permits no other understanding of the Spirit's work. In inner conflict man is completely in the power of death. Nothing of his own righteousness is effective. The groaning of the Spirit toward God is a real raising from death, a new creation. When the gospel says that no one can enter the kingdom of God without the new birth of water and the Spirit it simply means that the old man must be destroyed totally. The old man must become as the earth which was waste and void before the first creation so that God the Holy Spirit can create the new man out of nothing. Very often the word from Romans 8:26 about the Holy Spirit as comforter and interceder in inner conflict is used in connection with Genesis 1:1 where the Spirit moved upon the waters at the first creation. And by the creative Word the Spirit brings life and light into the darkness of the deep.[11] This is an allegorical interpretation but it is not *mere* allegorizing. It is the same Spirit and the same work described in both cases. There is in reality no difference between the first and the second creation because in both cases it is actually a creation out of nothing.

But the message about the Holy Spirit as the creative Spirit which moves upon man in the depths of darkness and hell in order to create light out of darkness and life out of nothing is in harmony with the summarized formulation of the witness about the Spirit which Luther has given in *Eine kurze Form der zehen Gebote, eine kurze Form des Glaubens, eine kurze Form des Vaterunsers* of 1520: *ynn und tzu dem vatter duch Christum und seyn leben, leyden, sterben und alles was von yhm gesagt ist, niemant kummen noch ettwas derselben erlangen mag on des heyligen geysts werck, mit wilchem der vatter und der sun mich und alle die seynen ruret, wecket, ruffet, tzeucht, durch und ynn Christo lebendig, heylig und geystlich macht und alsso zum vatter bringt, dan er ist das, da mit der vatter durch Christus und ynn Christo alles wirckt und lebendig macht.*[12]

All other activities in connection with Scripture and the dog-

---

[11] *W. A.*, I, 565, 23 ff. (1518); V, 87 ff.; 203 ff.; 385 ff.; 553, 4 ff. (1519-21). LVI, 378, 2 ff. (1515-16); IX, 330, 20 ff. (Poliander's codex, 1519-21).

[12] *W. A.*, VII, 218, 26.

matic tradition which Luther may ascribe to the Holy Spirit, such as *consolatio, sanctificatio, illuminatio,* are ascribed to the Holy Spirit as *spiritus creator.*

The first part is described in our study of the Spirit's work in inner conflict: the Spirit is interpellator and consoler. But this comfort of the Spirit is identical with his creative and life-giving work. The Spirit knows no other form for comfort than the one in which man is brought through death into life. The Spirit does not comfort by stopping inner conflict midway but by raising to new life the man who is overcome by death. Thus sanctification is simply another expression for the creative work of the Spirit. That which is sanctified is that which is separated from profane use and dedicated to a holy and divine use. Especially when death and hell surround man in inner conflict is he set aside, separated, and consecrated to God. This consecration is the work of the Spirit. The consecration, the separation from the world, and the dedication to God take place through death and resurrection, through God's *opus alienum* and *opus proprium.*

Most interesting is Luther's understanding of the concept *illuminatio.* Luther does not mean that man is lifted up into the supernatural sphere where it becomes possible for us to know God in his own inner essence. The scholastic idea of *illuminatio* is foreign to Luther. The enlightenment of the Spirit means knowledge of the will of God. This is possible only by the fact that our own will in being conformed to Christ is put to death and the will of God is raised in its place. The enlightenment is not an enlightenment about God's inner nature, but about God's will for us. Its content is the right *fides Christi* and *conformitas Christi.* This is possible only in and with the work in which the Spirit makes Christ present to us and makes us conform to him in faith. Enlightenment is not a special operation of the Spirit outside of the mediative work of Christ by the Spirit. It is not a direct or an immediate inspiration in the soul but is identical with the work by which the Spirit makes Christ a present reality and in the motion of faith and love, the work by which he makes us conform to Christ in his death and resurrection. The enlightenment is the knowledge of the will of

God created by this reality which is found in the truly present Christ.

Already in the first lecture on the Psalms we discover the thought, which later became very important in the development of Luther's concept of the church in contrast to the Roman Catholic clericalism, namely, that all who have the Spirit of God, according to I Corinthians 2:11-15, are "spiritual" so that they are able to judge all things. The Holy Spirit is the illuminator who makes it possible for every believer to judge spiritual things. After the Leipzig disputation which started the development away from the hierarchical church concept this thought becomes more prominent in Luther. An example of this is seen in *De captivitate babylonica* of 1520, and in the church postils of 1522. This enlightenment, however, is only gained by the experience of the Holy Spirit putting to death and making alive. All heresies and all ungodly dogmas come into being through men who do not want to accept God's *operatio* but will rather be *magistri operosi* than *discipuli passibiles*. The false teaching consists in this, that we make our own idea applicable to heavenly things and that we speak about God with the same ease and unconcernedness as the shoemaker speaks about his leather. We are void of the Spirit of God, which alone searches the depths of God. No one can think properly about God and about himself unless the Spirit of God is in him. The principle of false teaching is *sensus,* the experience which relies only on that which can be observed in the visible world. But this *sensus*-experience is not a neutral, ethical and religious source of knowledge. It is one of the pronounced consequences of man's proud and ungodly nature, his *caro,* and it is therefore in the same opposition to the true knowledge of God as the *incurvitas in se ipso* of pride is to faith and self-condemnation when they submit to the witness of the Holy Spirit. *Sensus* means the experience and reason of man as they manifest themselves outside the sphere of the Spirit, and that means under dominion of the law. When man is not able to know God with the enlightenment of the Holy Spirit it is not because the object of the knowledge is beyond the boundaries of natural knowledge so that it is *supra naturam*. This hindrance God has removed by becoming man and thereby getting inside the limitation of reason in the "sign" of Christ's humanity. Luther's knowledge of God is not, as in scholasticism, the knowledge of God's inner essence but the knowledge of God in his revelation, of *Deus incarnatus*. The knowledge of God is therefore not *supra naturam* in the same sense in which scholasticism uses this concept. The enlightenment does not mean that our knowledge is lifted up in the supernatural plan so that it is enabled to lay hold on God's own supernatural being. The hindrance to our knowledge of God (and of his will) is the fact that God, revealed in "flesh" (Christ), is placed in absolute opposition to our human *sensus* and *ratio*. Christ, God revealed in the flesh, is the revelation of a will which is contrary to our own will. Therefore the enlightenment by the Holy Spirit does not mean that our *sensus*-experience and *ratio*-speculation are merely supplied by the supernatural sources so that grace lifts them up in the true plan of the knowledge of God. The enlightenment consists in this, that the *sensus*-experience and *ratio*-speculation are completely destroyed, smashed, removed, in order to make room for faith and the experience of faith. In the first lecture on the Psalms this contrast is between carnal and spiritual knowledge according to the "Neoplatonic" formula: *sensus* in contrast to *intellectus*. The object of *intellectus* is *Deus in carne absconditus*. But *intellectus* is determined in the Bible—other than in philosophy—from its object and not from the soul's capacity, the function of which it is. Therefore the true *intellectus* becomes one with *sapientia crucis Christi*, a *sapientia abscondita in mysterio* (I Cor. 2:7). This *sapientia* in the form of *sapientia crucis Christi* also contains self-condemnation. "Therefore is *spiritualia* not acquired by direct communication of the divine truth but can only be received through the knowledge of one's own total lack of divine truth, that is, through the consciousness of sin."[13]

In the lecture on Romans this contrast between *sensus* and *intellectus* is deepened to a contrast between *sapientia (prudentia) carnis* and *sapientia (prudentia) spiritus*. *Prudentia carnis* seeks its own in all things, also in God. It makes man his own *objectum*

---

13 N. Nøjgaard, p. 84.

finale et ultimum, that is, an idol. This *sapientia carnis* is that which dominates all natural knowledge of God and all theology which is not enlightened by the Spirit of God. It dominates *lumen naturae* which is prevalent in all idolatry both inside and outside of Christendom. This knowledge is not able to comprehend the work of God which is hidden in its contrast. But it is necessary, if God should reveal himself to us in Christ's humanity, that his action be hidden in his paradox, cross, death, and punishment of hell, both in the archetype of his action as well as in its copy— all the saints. The real *prudentia spiritus* in contrast to *prudentia carnis* seeks only that which belongs to God, also when he is *Deus negative* and our *adversarius.* If therefore the carnal man is to be enlightened by the Spirit of God it cannot be done by "simple communication," for all carnal knowledge must be put to death so that a spiritual knowledge can be put in its place. Only in and by the old man's death and the new man's resurrection does the enlightenment of the Spirit take place—is our *sensus* transformed. The enlightenment is the *transformatio sensus* itself, which is one with God's mortifying and life-giving work by the Spirit. The true knowledge of God is only gained in the conformity with Christ and faith in Christ which is the work of the Spirit. In this conformity God condemns when he releases, puts to death when he makes alive, and sends to hell when he gives eternal bliss. In the unity of his *opus alienum* and his *opus proprium* God is in us the *spiritus creator* who gives us his life by taking ours, who gives us his holiness by making us sinners, and who also gives us his enlightenment by making us blind.

This view of the Spirit naturally makes Luther argue strongly against the Catholic thought of a "natural" faith, a *fides acquisita.* Such a faith is no real faith. It is rather the opposite, *quasi non cotide ad sensum experiantur, quid prosit christiana doctrina iis, qui non trahuntur intus a deo.*[14] No, a true knowledge of God comes in a very different way: *Viva, immo vita et res est, si spiritus doceat: scit, loquitur, operatur omnia in omnibus quem deus*

---

14 *W. A.,* II, 566, 39.

docuerit, non secus certe quam dum creat hominem e novo.[15] *Non secus certe quam dum creat hominem e novo.* That is the way theological epistemology has it. Even enlightenment is an act of creation. And it is not an act of creation to be placed beside the other work of the Spirit. The enlightenment takes place in and with the new creative work of the Spirit when he makes Christ present and when he makes us conform to him. Therefore Luther also says about the right training of theologians: *Vivendo, immo moriendo et damnando fit theologus, non intelligendo, legendo aut speculando.*[16]

Spiritus creator is thus a name which expresses the type of the Spirit's work in its different forms. *Spiritus gratiae* and *spiritus precum* are always *spiritus creator* whether we think of the spirit as *spiritus precum,* who in inner conflict intercedes for us with unutterable groanings and in the motion of faith draws us to Christ, or whether we see him as *spiritus gratiae,* who places us in the reality of Christ so that we are one with Christ and are used by Christ as his instruments in works of love. And all the time this work means that as the living One descends into our death he there, by his own living presence, creates something out of nothing. Anything which the Spirit does in us and with us is a creation out of nothing.

This special view of the nature of the Spirit's work which is found in the name *creator* signifies the contrast to *caritas* idealism for which the Spirit only becomes *perfector naturae*. In *caritas* idealism we are thinking of a man who is truly adjusted (beamed) toward God. In spite of sin and death his principal longing for goodness need only be sublimated by the Spirit or lifted up into the supernatural plan to find its real object, God. It need only be strengthened and guided further on the way to God. In this system the Spirit may perhaps be the transcendent cause but he is not the present creator. The transcendent cause is kept in the distance while its influence co-operates with man's longing for goodness and he thus perfects the already quickened man. *Caritas* idealism

---

15 *W. A.,* II, 567, 2.
16 *W. A.,* V, 163, 28.

shows us that which is alive in man on the way toward God—that which is supported on the way by the Spirit, and which lets infused grace remove all hindrances and help it over all obstacles in the way. Man himself is on the way but God, toward whom he is going, is himself the eternally passive, the one who is eternally self-sufficient in self-knowledge and in self-love. The reward at the end of the course is to have a part in God's eternal self-knowledge and self-love. In his teaching about the creative Spirit Luther thinks of a man who is dead, whose inward struggle is unquenchable *concupiscentia* and self-seeking. And there is no ideal striving, no *amor boni*, which is not infected by *concupiscentia*. This ideal longing is of the flesh as long as man is outside the sphere of the creative Spirit, that is, as long as he is selfish. To such a man dead in sin the Spirit descends and makes all God's reality present in the midst of his death. The Spirit is the presence of the living God himself in his all-embracing, eschatological act, with man in Christ Jesus as the new sphere of life in the midst of our death. Because this act takes place in the midst of our death the reality of God puts on a strange garb. It appears as unutterable groanings in the midst of the fury of death and hell. It brings us Christ as the master over death and hell, not in his heavenly glory, but in the hidden reality of faith, opposed to all *sensus* and all *ratio*—a reality which only faith can grasp, which is *arduissima res*, a reality which is hidden in the lowly sign of the Word and the sacrament, a reality which, when it becomes our own life's reality, is not a glorious story of a saint but faith's constantly taking refuge in an alien righteousness and love's coming to alleviate the distress of the neighbor in life's daily work. This is always done under the burden of the cross. But in this strange garb, which no one would surmise to be God's reality because it resembles the very opposite, God's whole reality is found in the midst of all our distress. It is a creation out of nothing. The message about the creative Spirit shows us God on the way to distant man, who is lost in sin and death, in order constantly to create new life out of nothing, life out of death. Therefore God must show himself in a manner which is in contrast to every metaphysical concept of God. Whatever metaphysics may attribute to

God—such as his remoteness, his "blessedness," his immovability, his impassibility—is constantly disavowed by the creative Spirit who is present in the midst of the fury of death and hell where God, if he is "good," *can* not be present (except in all his gifts or his influence). There he struggles and suffers with lost man and he conquers in a way in which the blessed, impassive, eternally self-sufficient "God" cannot struggle at all and suffer. Thus the preaching of the creative Spirit makes impossible every synthesis of the idea of God in metaphysics and the Bible. The magnificent structure of Thomas falls apart, when it is struck by the word of this testimony.

In the name *spiritus creator* we not only find the nature of the work of the Spirit creating something of nothing in contrast to idealistic ideas about the perfecting of the most noble in man. This name also expresses clearly who the Spirit is. The Spirit is the third person of the Triune God. Therefore the work of the Spirit cannot be isolated from the work of the Father and the Son. The work of the Trinity is outwardly indivisible. The Triune God has really only one work to accomplish just as he himself is only one true God. That is his eternally life-creating and life-saving work. And this is the one work into which he as the creative spirit draws us, away from the destruction of sin, death, and hell.

Luther always speaks about creation in terms of the Trinity. The first creation was done by God through his eternal Word. When God by his Word had made creation out of nothing he saw by his Spirit that it was very good. Then he took it into his heart by the Spirit in the Word by which it was created and he caused it to exist constantly in the Word by the Spirit. Thus Luther from the outset used the trinitarian terms when he spoke about creation. The Father is the origin and constant source.

The Son is the Word by which that which is created is brought forth from nothing. The Spirit is the sanctifying and preserving love of God by which he takes creation into himself and preserves it in the Word.

Luther's idea of creation is always considered from the trinitarian point of view. The Holy Spirit is given the work of the sanctifying love of God to preserve and sustain his whole creation.

To a postpietistic theology, which is used to limiting the thought about the Holy Spirit to the sphere of the religious life, this may seem strange. And it is possible to put these thoughts in Luther aside as something unessential. However, they *are* found in Luther and at different times in his life when he happens to study the story of the creation exegetically.

That such thoughts about the Spirit's cosmic work are found in Luther should not cause any surprise. For Luther is here considering biblical thoughts. "Thou hidest thy face, they are troubled: thou takest away their breath, they die, and return to their dust. Thou sendest forth thy Spirit, they are created: and thou renewest the face of the earth. The glory of the Lord shall endure forever: the Lord shall rejoice in his works" Psalm 104:29-31. The Bible and Luther, who lived in the Bible's cosmology, do not know a world existing independently of the Triune God. To biblical—and Lutheran—Christianity the visible world is a creation by the Spirit of God, the same Spirit who gives us new birth in baptism, who comforts us in inner conflict so that by the Holy Spirit we constantly live and breathe (physically!), so that we break the bread and drink the wine which gladden the heart of man. Yes, in the Holy Spirit we use God's good gifts for our enjoyment and we do not think only of repenting and going to church. We moderns, on the contrary, live in a world whose nature is thought of as a machine which is propelled by itself. Man is understood as a sovereign ruler who only needs God when he has to die or when he might possibly have to repent, which to modern man (and in this case, for an exception, man is biblical in his thinking) is almost as bad as to die. ("Repentance" in the Bible means to die!)

It is a question if we have truly understood Luther's concept of the Holy Spirit, if we view his trinitarian concept of creation as theological trifling. The difficulty of modern Protestant theologians in considering Luther seriously on this point is based on the fact that the tradition of several generations of theological or non-theological tradition has given us the idea that the Trinity doctrine is a subtle speculation and that it has made a Sabellian and adoptionist view a natural point of departure. Here Luther was different. He maintained that trinitarian thinking and biblical Christianity were one and the same thing. Our danger is not that we may overemphasize these thoughts in Luther but that we may forget them completely.

Instead of minimizing Luther's trinitarian concept and the office of the Holy Spirit as the sustainer of creation we shall try to be as serious as Luther was. That Luther speaks in trinitarian terms about creation means first of all that creation and redemption to him are part of the same all-embracing act of God. We have previously had the opportunity to stress the theocentric perspective in Luther's doctrine about the Spirit. It is this perspective in Luther's trinitarian doctrine which is applied to creation and redemption. In speaking about the work of the Holy Spirit in creation Luther underscores that he does not have a narrow anthropocentric view of the Spirit based on man's religious need. The work of the Holy Spirit is not postulated from "below," from the religious man's need of the assistance of the Spirit, but from "above," from God's eternal plan for his creation. When Luther in his exegesis of the first chapter of Genesis takes time to discuss that the Spirit also has a work to do outside of man's religious existence and when he does not find such a reference as insignificant and uninteresting as his modern interpreters do, it is a powerful reminder to the religious man that God's world is greater than his, and that the thinking of the Bible is from the point of view of God's world and not from the world of religious man. On the contrary, when a number of modern Luther scholars dislike finding such nonspiritual thoughts in Luther, it is a sign that they are thinking from "below." The children of God who in the revealed Word have been permitted to look from "above" do not need to be jealous because God also is interested in his other creation. For he is keeping the best for them anyway.

We take this hint seriously and assume that the Spirit's work, as we have heard about it so far within the category of piety, is a part of a greater whole. The work of the Spirit in the pious world is a part of God's all-embracing, life-creating, and life-saving work. Therefore the believer when he reads the first chapter of the Bible must be satisfied to hear that it is the same Holy Spirit who by unutterable groanings in the darkness and death of inner conflict calls us to life, who makes the risen Christ a present reality, and who places us by him in the sphere of faith and love. When he reads the first chapter of the Bible the believer must be content to hear that this Spirit also has a work to do with God's other creation, with the grass in the field, with the birds under the heavens, and with all that exists.

Just as the creation is a work of the Triune God so also is redemption. Creation and redemption in reality are only two stages in the same work. We are reminded of this when the Spirit is called Creator. In the act of redemption it is also the Father who is the source and the fountain of that which is brought about. God acts only by his Word in redemption. Just as God in the creation called everything forth by his Word out of nothing, so in redemption he calls his lost children out of the destruction of sin, death, and the devil. This took place when the Word became flesh and when it by life, death, and resurrection conquered over sin, death, and the devil by placing itself completely under its tyranny. But just as in the first creation the creature could not exist except that God by his Spirit loved it and in his Word took it into himself anew, in like manner the sinners redeemed by Christ cannot stand but will fall back into the destruction of sin, death, and the devil if God does not by his Spirit look to them in love and sustain them and take them into himself anew in Christ. The finished work of redemption is not something man himself is able to appropriate and retain. It can only be given by the Spirit. The creative work of the Spirit is to bring men in Christ to the Father. Thus Luther speaks in trinitarian terms about redemption.

Without this trinitarian background the words of Luther about the Holy Spirit and his work cannot be rightly understood. This background means that Luther's doctrine about the Spirit is placed in the all-embracing, theocentric perspective without which it must inevitably be falsified psychologically and nomistically. Viewed from the trinitarian background creation and redemption are stages of one act of God. The Spirit's work in redemption may have another place in the economy of God than his work in creation. Yet they both belong to the same economy. In the word "creator" we summarize both of these phases of the Spirit's work. In both cases it means that God himself stoops down to his creation and becomes its sphere of life. But in the economy of creation we are concerned with the whole creation of God which is made out of absolutely nothing. In the economy of redemption we are concerned only with that part of the creation of God which *fell* away, and therefore must be torn anew from the fury of sin, death, and the devil's intention to destroy the work of God. The economy of creation covers all that exists while the economy of redemption is extended to all the elect.

This brings before us the tension between the universal economy of creation and the particular economy of redemption, a problem which becomes all the more complicated because it is not only all creation which confronts man; it is the created but unredeemed man which stands before the created, redeemed, and *elect* man. This problem of predestination we shall not study further in this thesis. However, no one can constantly study Luther's teaching about the Spirit without meeting the problem of predestination in his theology. It is an eternal protest against a smooth rationalistic system in which the living God is enclosed and made a means for legalistic piety. The problem of predestination, which corresponds to what we have previously named "hiatus" in Luther's theology, may therefore also be said to be a clear expression of the *evangelical* character of Luther's theology, because the living message of the glad tidings of God's own Word alone is able to fill the hiatus in the system and release the tension of predestination. However, where this tension is rationalized and the hiatus in the system is filled out abstractively it means that God and his free action are restricted and placed among human possibilities, that is, they are placed within the system of the law. This smooth system always belongs to the law. The separation (the *diastasis*) between the economy of creation and redemption does not therefore mean that we have rescinded what we said of creation and redemption as one act of God. But it means that the testimony about the unity of creation and redemption in God is a *testimony*, not a rational fact, and therefore the hiatus must be found in this testimony. In the very moment we express the testimony about the unity of creation and redemption we point to the separation between creation and redemption *in us*. It means that we have not rationalized the problem of predestination and that the system has not removed the possibility of a living kerygma—that the rationalism of the law has not done away with the wonder of the gospel.

Viewed from "above" creation and redemption are one continuous act of God. This is expressed in the doctrine of the Trinity. Seen from "below" the secret of predestination is placed between the economy of creation and redemption. This is expressed in the teaching about the insufficiency of the outward Word and the sovereign freedom of the Spirit. Both points of view belong to Luther's concept of the Holy Spirit. Only in their unity are we able to see what we understand by *spiritus creator*.

In conclusion we shall summarize briefly the main points of Luther's view of the Holy Spirit as we have seen them in the first part of our work.

The Holy Spirit is the Triune God personally present in our distress as *spiritus creator*. The background for the work of the Spirit is therefore always the lost condition of man under the tyranny of sin, death, and the devil just as it is most clearly seen in the situation of inner conflict. In inner conflict the Spirit appears as the present reality in contrast to every idealistic dimming of the Spirit's reality into the remoteness of a transcendental causality.

As a present reality the Spirit manifests itself in the humanity of Christ. The Spirit is the real divine sphere in which Christ comes out of the remoteness of history and becomes a living, present reality or, as Luther likes to state it: experience.

Therefore the means of the Spirit are the Word and the sacraments which are the concrete forms among us of Christ's humanity. Within the sphere of the Spirit, the Word is gospel and the sacrament is the eschatological sign of confirmation.

Within the sphere of the Spirit, our life is embodied by Word and sacrament in the totality of God's saving, eschatological act.

It means that faith—our taking the living Christ as our alien righteousness—is our constant refuge. The constant work in favor of our neighbor is our love in which the living Christ himself is working in and through man who in faith has come to him for his alien righteousness.

Within the sphere of the Spirit this constant rhythm in the motion of faith toward, and the motion of love from, the living Christ is a progress toward the eternal life. It is a growth of righteousness and an expulsion of sin. For within the Spirit's sphere our faith and love are embodied in the totality of the saving, eschatological act of the Triune God whose aim is the final destruction of sin, death, and the devil. The powers of the age to come are an experienced reality in us through the Spirit. The Spirit is an eschatological experience.

These thoughts express the reality of the Spirit. The risen Christ is truly present by the Spirit in the Word and the sacrament, and our faith and love are truly embodied in God's saving, eschatological act. But it is the Spirit's reality of which we have spoken. That is, this reality is absolutely different from all other reality which may be felt by *sensus* and perceived by *ratio*. The truly present Christ is the Christ of faith, not of feeling or perception. He is our alien righteousness, not a felt mental power. God into whose eschatological, saving act we are received is *Deus in carne absconditus.* Our faith and love as a progress in sanctification are hidden and are never identical with the known psychological progress of empirical piety. The progress—and its aim in fulfillment—is an object of *hope*, something which awaits us. It is not an object of substantiation. This concealment in the reality of the Spirit is because the Spirit is *spiritus creator* who creates life out of the dead. All our own, also our *sensus* and our *ratio*, must die where the Spirit is working. Therefore God must hide himself in his contrast when he is to be real to us.

In this concealment the Spirit is not bound to his means. He is completely free in his mastery of the means. Therefore on the one hand it is said: the Spirit is the real, divine sphere in which Christ comes out of the remoteness of history and the realm of pure ideas and becomes living, present reality—becomes experience. On the other hand, it must immediately be added that outside of the sphere of the Spirit Jesus Christ is *only* history, *only* ideality, *only* a mystic experience, which in all cases mean not *Christus ipse*, not experience. Therefore on the one hand it is stated that the means of the Spirit are the Word and the sacrament. Within the sphere of the Spirit the Word is gospel and the sacrament is an eschatological sign of confirmation. But on the other hand it must at once be added that outside the sphere of the Spirit the Word is *only* law and the sacrament *only opus operatum*, and that certainly means that they are not means of grace. Therefore it is said that our life by Word and sacrament is received into the totality of God's saving, eschatological act. Our faith is a constant taking refuge in the living Christ. Our love is his work for our neighbor done by us as his instruments. But it must at once be added that outside the sphere of the Spirit our faith is an impotent *fides acquisita*, and our love only the work of the law by which we aim to please God. That certainly does not mean a righteousness for God. Therefore it is said that within the sphere of the Spirit the constant rhythm of the motion of faith toward Christ and the motion of love from Christ is a progress toward eternal life, a growth of righteousness, and an expulsion of sin. For our faith and love are by the Spirit received into the totality of God's saving, eschatological act, the aim of which is the final destruction of sin, death, and the devil. But on the other hand it must at once be added that outside the sphere of the Spirit there is no progress. Even though our real progress by psychological observation may be ever so prominent it is altogether flesh and therefore in the grip of death and the wrath of God. That certainly does not mean the power of the coming age.

This "on the other hand" signifies the Spirit's sovereignty in his reality. That the Spirit is real and present does not mean that we may have the Spirit or his gifts in our possession, but on the other hand that the Spirit and his gifts take possession of us. There is therefore in Luther's teaching about the Spirit and the Spirit's means the "hiatus" toward which this "on the other and" always points. The means of the Spirit are no guarantee of the Spirit's reality, which permits us to use the Spirit and his gifts. But the Spirit as the sovereign Lord wants to be expected, implored, promised, and proclaimed.

This tense connection of reality and sovereignty, which is the peculiar characteristic in Luther's testimony about the Spirit, has its background in Luther's doctrine of the Trinity in which the unlimited divinity of the Spirit is maintained. Both views are maintained in the name *spiritus creator*. The Spirit is *creator* and as such it is really present in the midst of our death and damnation. But the Spirit is also *spiritus*, one with the Father and the Son in divine majesty and in the eternal, unbroken act of God in creation and redemption. This unity of reality and sovereignty filled with tension covers the mystery of predestination, which is proof of the fact that we are concerned with the *living* God. By retaining this tension in the understanding of the relation between *gratia* and *donum*, between Word and Spirit, between Spirit and faith, by not smoothing out the tension logically, Luther's testimony of the Spirit establishes its evangelical character. It is not a closed system which makes God man's servant within the law, but it keeps open the place for the concrete kerygma which in the service of the Spirit shall make man God's servant in the gospel. For the gospel is not as the law a system dominated by man, but a message expected from God. The work of God under the law is attached to the system closed by *ratio*. Man is here the living one, the Lord, and God is the servant in relation to man. But God is simultaneously the remote one. For in the system of the law and reason, only the gift of God and the work of God can be captured, not God himself. In the gospel God is free and sovereign, and man must be content to wait for the good tidings and pray about it. But in this sovereignty of God he is himself truly present. For where man is no longer master there is room for God's creative work, and there God is always present himself as creator and redeemer. And there God *serves* and gives his life as a ransom for many, not through the carnal desire of man, but with his own love as master.

The tension between the views of the Spirit's reality and sovereignty can only be concretely solved in the experience of the

Spirit's reality. Only by waiting on the Spirit will you be able to satisfy him. And Luther has several things to say about where the work of the Spirit may be expected. It is in the deepest distress and greatest poverty in inner conflict. Therefore the times in the history of the church which are poorest of Spirit are those which are richest in the power and piety of man.

Luther has no real "doctrine" of the Spirit in the sense of a rational theory which cannot be questioned. On the contrary we have seen that it is something essential in Luther's testimony about the Spirit that it contained a "hiatus." Luther has only a testimony about the Spirit, so strong and living that it has been proclaimed only a few times in this way since the days of the early church.

We have several times compared Luther's testimony about the Spirit with other ways of understanding the Spirit's work. It was thus natural to emphasize specially the medieval *caritas* idealism because it so clearly gives an example of the piety which is under the law in spite of all talk of grace, and where the Spirit only becomes an expression of the supernatural causality of religious life. And yet we have not advanced *caritas* idealism as a historic quantity (we have therefore not interested ourselves in its different shades, Augustinianism, Thomism, Nominalism, etc.) but as a type of piety which is diametrically opposed to Luther's view. It is therefore not surprising that we found the main lines of this *caritas* idealism also in pietism and in the understanding of Christianity based on Holl's Luther research. This is because there are really only two ways of understanding the Spirit: the realistic view of the gospel and the idealistic view of legalistic piety. Every view of Luther which is unable to find a natural place for Luther's testimony about the Spirit discloses that it belongs to a piety which is of the legalistic type.

The book of Rudolf Otto which was mentioned in the introduction and often quoted later with respect to Luther's view of the Holy Spirit may be taken as a typical example of the Luther research which viewed Luther from the viewpoint of a piety attached to the law, *in casu* the Ritschlian interpretation of Christianity. He came to the conclusion that it is very possible to present

Luther's Reformation concept of Christianity without touching on his view of the Holy Spirit. He even holds that such a presentation, which depended only on "psychological motivation" of the Word and faith, was to be preferred to a presentation which found anything important in the rather superfluous view of the Spirit as a helper.

We have come to a conclusion which must be characterized as diametrically opposed to that of Rudolf Otto. Without the idea of the Holy Spirit all Luther's thoughts about Christ, about justification, about Word and sacrament, about faith and love, are changed to a great ideology under the law. For only the real presence of the Spirit places the boundary between a Christ-idea and *Christus ipse*, between gospel and law, between *littera* and *spiritus*, between sacrament and *sacrificium*, between faith and religion, between love and morality. Only the real presence of the Spirit leads from the domain of the law into that of the gospel.

We believe that our presentation is a more correct and a more faithful presentation of Luther's own thought than that of Rudolf Otto. We also believe that we in our presentation have placed Luther in a more correct historico-dogmatic perspective than that in which he has been placed by much modern Luther research. That is, we have placed him together with the strong pneumatic realism of the early church in contrast to all idealistic and nomistic understanding of both ancient and modern Christianity and not as a forerunner or an ally of the psychological and spiritual-moralistic spiritualism of a modern age. In this basic part of our work we have placed Luther in close connection with biblical pneumatological realism. In the following we shall delve into the sharp contrast to all spiritualism which is a consequence of biblical realism and which we could only hastily indicate in this basic part of the work.

Part Two

LUTHER'S TESTIMONY ABOUT THE SPIRIT IN HIS CONTROVERSY WITH THE ENTHUSIASTS

Chapter IV

THE CONTINUITY IN LUTHER'S TESTIMONY
ABOUT THE SPIRIT

The Experience of Inner Conflict

It is well known how Luther after his return from the Wartburg and in the following period had to fight on two fronts. He had to continue his struggle with the Roman Church. He also had to take up the struggle with the new enthusiast movements which contended that they wanted to finish the work of the Reformation. They maintained that the Reformer himself had not finished the work.

In this new encounter with the enthusiasts the struggle concerned itself with the understanding of the Spirit. The Spirit and spirituality were the slogan of this new movement. In this struggle Luther strongly emphasized that the Spirit is never found independent of the outward means through which he works, that is, the Word and the sacraments. Does this mean that Luther's stronger emphasis on the Spirit's outward means has changed his view on the Spirit? Does this stronger emphasis mean that the impression we got in our basic work of Luther's view of the Holy Spirit and his work now must be radically changed? Does this stronger emphasis on the Spirit's outward instruments mean that Luther has been forced to "the right" and that, as in the scholastic theology which he opposed, he now makes himself a spokesman for a rational doctrine of the means of grace? Would this mean not only that we are bound to the outward signs, the Word and the sacraments, but that the Spirit also is bound by them?

If Luther's polemic and sharp testimony about the Spirit is to be rightly understood, it is important that these questions be answered first. Luther's thoughts about the Spirit are often presented in such a way that only the polemic statements against the enthusiasts are mentioned. However, this makes us view Luther's understanding of the Spirit in too narrow a perspective. It is natural that Luther's testimony is not heard in all its strength by simply studying his polemic against the enthusiasts. The polemic which emphasizes but a single part of Luther's view of the Spirit's work has its background in Luther's total concept of the Spirit, and it must be interpreted on this background and not detached from it.

In order to avoid this limitation of the horizon to the polemic we have built the whole basic part of our work on sources drawn only from the period before the struggle with the enthusiasts. If this method is to be satisfactory we must be able to show that Luther's view of the Spirit as it was presented on the basis of the early sources is the same view which Luther presents during the struggle with the enthusiasts. Of course, it must not appear as an unfair condition when we ask that the polemic statements be understood in connection with and on the background of the previously described total picture of Luther's understanding of the Holy Spirit.

Therefore we introduce the second part of our work by a number of references to sources from the years after 1522 to show that the total view of the Spirit and his work which was sketched in the first part is still Luther's. Simultaneously we look for possible shades of views which might have been introduced with respect to the details in this total view.

In Chapter I, section 1, we saw how significant is the experience of inner conflict for the understanding of the Spirit's work. Romans 8:26 became the chief source for the young Luther in understanding the Spirit's work. This same reference to inner conflict with Romans 8:26 as a testimony of the creative work of the Spirit follows Luther through the years. It is not only a part of a pre-Reformation *theologia crucis.*[1] The similarity with the early writings of Luther is very great. However, it must be noted that Luther more than ever underscores that the groanings of the Spirit which cannot be uttered are directed toward Christ. The contrast between the idealistic speculation of scholasticism and the realism of the experience of inner conflict is also emphasized in passing. The scholastics only interest themselves in what the Spirit is doing in heaven. But the important thing is what he is doing in us. The papists think they can have the Spirit without ever having been in inner conflict. But that is because they think of the Holy Spirit speculatively. The Holy Spirit, however, is he who is present and who helps us in our weakness. When we are strong the Spirit has fulfilled his work. In weakness, however, as when the Israelites stood before the Red Sea with the army of Pharaoh behind them, the Spirit is not present speculatively, but in reality, as the saving groanings for help.

The experience of inner conflict indicates the tyranny of the law in the conscience.[2] And since it is the work of the Spirit to bring the individual from the domain of the law into that of the gospel, from the idea into reality, it is no wonder that the experience of inner conflict assumes decisive significance in the understanding of the Spirit's work. By the power of the law man is completely in the hands of death and Satan. Therefore the Spirit's work must be seen most clearly here. The superiority of the gospel over the law is indicated by the fact that in inner conflict it can yield

---

[1] References to Romans 8:26 in the Weimar edition: XIV, 679, 3 ff., 8 ff. (1525); XI, 112, 34 ff. (Rörer, 1523); XIV, 606, 12 ff. (Rörer, 1523-24); XVI, 269, 4 ff. (Rörer, 1525); XXXI, 2, 249, 31 ff.; 404, 16 ff.; 541, 16 ff. (Lauterbach, 1527-30); XXVIII, 56, 31 ff. (Rörer, 1528); XL, 1, 581, 1 ff.; 582, 7 ff.; 584, 6 ff.; 586, 1 ff.; 591, 8 ff.; 592, 4 ff. (Rörer, 1531); XL, 2, 338, 5 ff.; 359, 11 ff.; 395, 13 ff.; XXXVI, 560, 11 ff. (Rörer, 1532); XLVI, 164, 2 ff.; 166, 10 ff. (Rörer, 1538); XLII, 662, 1 ff.; XLIII, 175, 19 ff.; 519, 11 ff.; XLIV, 82, 1 ff.; 575, 40 ff. (*Genesiskommentaren,* 1535-45). General references to the disturbing and consoling work of the Holy Spirit: L, 626, 22 ff. (1539); XVII, 1, 259, 22 ff.; 260, 1 ff.; 33 ff.; 269, 37 ff. (Rörer, 1525); XX, 399, 16 ff. (Rörer, 1526); XXXI, 2, 84, 35 ff.; 475, 11 ff. (Lauterbach, 1527-30); XXXI, 1, 94, 2 ff.; 99, 10 ff.; 146, 13-154, 7; 159, 3-160, 10; 327, 10 ff. (Veit Dietrich, 1530); XLV, 560-67; 614, 25 ff.; 725, 31; 727, 32 (Cruciger, 1537); XLII, 275, 2 ff.; XLIII, 118, 20 ff.; XLIV, 580, 13 ff. (*Genesiskommentaren,* 1535-45).

[2] *W. A.,* XL, 1, 531, 3; also XVII, 1, 259, 26-260, 2; 422, 11 ff. (Rörer, 1525); XX, 399, 31 ff. (Rörer, 1526); XL, 1, 582, 2 ff. (Rörer, 1531); XL, 2, 359, 10 ff. (Rörer, 1532).

itself so completely to the tyranny of the law that nothing is left but the groaning for Christ. But in this extremely reduced form of a mere sigh without words for Christ, the gospel is the victor over the law. Inner conflict may be said to be the battleground where the decisive final struggle between the law and the gospel, death and life, Satan and the Holy Spirit is fought. Therefore the place where we may learn to know the Holy Spirit is in the school of inner conflict.

As in the early writings, Luther continues to describe this school of the Spirit in inner conflict as experience. Without the experience of inner conflict the difference between the mere word and reality is covered. But *wens zum treffen khombt* (when it comes to the encounter) the faith which was a mere word dwindles into nothing and only the experienced faith wrought by the Holy Spirit is able to stand.[3] Therefore it is experience which places the distinction between the mere *fides historica* and the genuine faith. This experience is the witness of the Holy Spirit in the heart, which makes everything that the Spirit mentions into something truly *felt*.[4] The experience makes man *certain* in his faith. But the "feeling" here mentioned is not an *intus sentire*. It does not consist of psychological self-observation. It is the witness of the Holy Spirit. This is proved by the fact that it is given by the Word and sacrament and not by an inner experience.

Experience makes the distinction between *fides historica* and experienced faith, that is, between idea and reality and therefore also between law and gospel. In the experience of inner conflict it is seen how the Spirit guides us from the tyranny of the law into the freedom of the gospel. Therefore to distinguish between law and gospel is no dialectic art, but it is only possible in the experience realized by the Spirit. It is easy enough logically *(formali*

---

[3] *W. A.*, XX, 395, 27 (Rörer, 1526): '*Diligere*' *ist ein verstendlich wort et tamen nemo intelligit, nisi spiritus sanctus aperiat. Bene audivimus, loquimur, sed wens zum treffen khombt, so sein die wort verschwunden.* Also XX, 420, 1; 395, 16 ff.; 399, 16-38; XLV, 598, 17 ff. (Cruciger, 1537).

[4] *W. A.*, XVIII, 605, 32 (1525). Also XI, 109, 3 ff. (Rörer, 1523); XV, 556, 5 ff.; 564, 27 ff. (Rörer, 1524); XVII, 1, 262, 2 ff. (Rörer, 1525); XXXI, 2, 674, 13 ff. (Rörer, 1530-31); XL, 1, 574, 13 ff.; 577, 8 ff. (Rörer, 1531); XLI, 418, 24 ff. (Rörer, 1535); XLI, 565, 29 ff.; 601, 20 ff. (Rörer, 1536); XLV, 22, 6 ff. (Rörer, 1537 ff.).

causa) to distinguish between law and gospel as the demanding and the giving word. But in practice *(materiali causa)* when the question is: what is demanded of me in the individual moment, it is not easy to differentiate. Then the gospel easily becomes a law. For everything is law and demand outside the reality of the Holy Spirit. The real distinction between law and gospel is not made in theology, but in the experience of the Holy Spirit himself.

In this manner—also in the older Luther—the experience of inner conflict continues to be the point of departure for the realistic understanding of the Spirit. Luther holds that this connection between inner conflict and the Spirit's work is confirmed by the language of the Bible itself. The Hebrew word for Spirit, *ruach*, Luther paraphrases into "courage." The Spirit is present as our new courage in the despair of inner conflict.[5]

The Spirit and the Real Presence of Christ

In the experience of inner conflict we have noticed how the Spirit (the gospel) conquers by seeming to be overcome. By clothing himself in the humble appearance of a wordless sigh the Spirit puts the tyranny of the law and Satan to nought. Here there is a parallel between the Spirit's work and the redeeming work of Christ. Christ himself conquered once over all the powers of destruction by suffering inner conflict, the pangs of hell, and death. Yes, the Spirit's work is really only a continuation of the struggle Christ once fought with the powers of hell. In this sense it also applies to Luther after 1522, that the Spirit's work in inner conflict and otherwise consists in making the risen Christ present as a redeeming reality. The Spirit, who in the distress of inner conflict calls forth the unutterable sigh to the Father and Christ, who carries the strictly reduced form of the victorious gospel, is the sphere in which Christ, contrary to the mere idea of the law about him or the picture of him, is truly present as God's gift to us.[6]

---

5 *W. A.*, XV, 554, 4 (Rörer, 1524). Also XIV, 445, 1 ff. (1537); XVII, 1, 270, 1 ff.; 280, 1 ff. (Rörer, 1525); XVII, 1, 435, 17 ff. (Tryk, 1525); XXVIII, 45, 28 ff. (Rörer, 1528); XLV, 540, 3 ff., 568, 13 ff.; 587, 1 ff. (Cruciger, 1537).

6 *W. A.*, XL, 1, 585, 6 (Rörer, 1531); XLV, 586, 36 ff. (Cruciger, 1537); XXXIII, 226, 4; 227, 8 ff.; 232, 9 ff.; 234, 1 ff.; 235, 2 ff.; 32 ff.; 236, 41 ff.; XL, 1, 546, 5 (Rörer, 1531).

But in the understanding of the Spirit as a mediator of Christ's real presence there is a characteristic shade of difference between the younger and the older Luther. In the first part of our work we saw how the young Luther brought the principle of conformity so strongly to the foreground in the understanding of the real presence of Christ mediated by the Spirit. But *fides Christi* in the young Luther was identical with *conformitas Christi*. The young Luther did not know of any form for Christ's real presence where he did not make us conform to himself. Even the fact that in faith in Christ we are made to conform to the death and resurrection of Christ was the result of the reality of Christ's presence. Christ's real presence also contained, as we saw it, an *imputatio commutativa* between Christ and the sinner. But this imputation was inextricably attached to the real fellowship with Christ whose other side was called *conformitas Christi*. Or more concisely expressed: *imputatio commutativa,* which states that faith's new life in its taking refuge in Christ is identical with conformity to the risen Christ, is named inner conflict, self-condemnation, cross, repentance. The reality of fellowship in Christ through faith is stated by the fact that this fellowship is always real conformity to Christ in the cross, inner conflict and death and in his resurrection, priesthood, and kingdom (faith and love). That does not mean that this terminology of conformity completely disappears in the older Luther. But it is developed differently. Superficially speaking it may seem as if it has in some way been substituted with the thought of the living Christ who struggles against the powers of destruction.

Does this slight difference mean a real shift in Luther's thought?

This could only be the case if the thought of conformity should be understood on the basis of the *imitatio* ideal. In this case we would find a development from a pre-Reformation to a genuine evangelical point of view. And then it might be said that the thought of conformity had been substituted by the dualistic motive.

We have, however, established in the first part that the young Luther's thought of conformity must be kept separate from every form of *imitatio* piety. We have also seen that the terminology of conformity does not disappear completely from the older Luther's preaching and theology. The situation is therefore rather that the thought of conformity and the thought of Christ present by faith struggling against the powers of destruction are two ways of stating the same thing. The thought of conformity, evangelically understood, means that Christ conquers over the power of the law and the devil and the wrath of God in the conscience in inner conflict. For we know that Luther considered Christ's own inner conflict as a victory over the tempting forces. He conquers over them by yielding to them. This is the victory of which we have a part by being conformed to Christ. No longer thinking of inner conflict as a sign of the wrath of God but as a part of being conformed to Christ and therefore as a witness of the grace of God, man in inner conflict turns back the attack of the law, the devil, and the wrath of God. It is the victory of Christ which is thus transmitted to the believer. The unutterable groaning of the Spirit in inner conflict is the sign that he who is tempted is already conformed to Christ, who himself conquered in inner conflict by the same groaning. This groaning indicates that Christ himself is present by the Spirit to overcome the powers of inner conflict. The unity of the thought of conformity and the dualistic thought of struggle is based on the fact that every evangelically understood conformity always makes man completely passive and Christ active. Every evangelical dualism always understands Christ as the one who paradoxically conquers through suffering and death.

In every evangelical understanding of the thought of conformity Christ is seen in a dualistic perspective as the one who, by his voluntary suffering and death, conquers against all reason and who, by actively making his believers conform to his suffering and death, transmits this victory to them. In every evangelical elaboration of the dualistic motive of struggle the type of the struggle and of the victory is paradoxically understood, that is, a victory through voluntary suffering, defeat, and death. The evangelical idea of conformity is in its essence "conformable." If the thought of conformity is not understood dualistically, we get into a nomistic, *imitatio* idea. If dualism is not understood "conformably," it will degenerate into a pelagianizing mythology.

We can therefore see that the thought of conformity in the older Luther has not been lost even though its terminology is not as prominent as before. It is still very much present in the dualistic form of expression.

This can be observed in the manner the older Luther connects the Spirit with the work of the law in inner conflict.

Our presentation of the Spirit's work in the experience of inner conflict so far has contained a certain vagueness which we could not have clarified except by using the material of the older Luther. In our account of Luther's thoughts about experience we have seen that it is the Spirit which makes the distinction between idea and reality in experience and therefore also between the law and the gospel. Without the reality of the Spirit the Word is only law, the sacrament is *opus operatum,* and man's piety is only slavery of the law. Within the reality of the Spirit, however, the Word of God is gospel, the sacrament is the unity of God's promise and sign of confirmation, and piety is a life proceeding from the redeeming reality of Christ. By the work of the Spirit in inner conflict the miraculous transition from the one kingdom to the other takes place; from that of the law to that of the gospel, from the letter to the Spirit, from bondage to liberty, from death to life.

However, it should be noted that it is the *law* that brings man into inner conflict and thus makes him conform to Christ in his conflict, suffering, and cross. Inner conflict starts when the law makes itself master in the conscience and there permits God's destructive wrath to break forth with all its power. It is through this conflict wrought by the *law* that we become one with the suffering Christ. For this conflict, suffering, and death are a substitutionary submission to the same tyranny of the law, death, devil, and wrath. But then it may seem as if the negative aspect of conformity, the becoming one with Christ in his humility and death, belongs to the realm of the law, while only the positive aspect of conformity, the becoming one with Christ in his glorification and resurrection, belongs to the realm of the Spirit. Does this really mean that the experience of inner conflict becomes a struggle of repentance, which must be experienced under the mastery of the law, before the Spirit can enter with his quickening gospel?

Such a view takes us right into the midst of *imitatio* piety, which we have constantly contended that Luther never held. If the experience of inner conflict, despair, belongs to the realm of law alone, then it is fundamentally a struggle of repentance which must and can be demanded of man on the assumption that he must bring it about himself in order that grace may become effective. Then it is not the collapse of legalistic piety but its culmination.

This is the concept of the mortification-piety of mysticism and of certain forms of pietistic preaching of repentance. *Accusatio sui* in mysticism is the culmination of man's preparation for the experience of fellowship with God. It corresponds to *facere quod in se est* of scholasticism. In the *ordo salutis* of a certain type of pietistic preaching of repentance the knowledge of sin obtained in the struggle of repentance may be made the necessary condition for the reception of grace. When, however, the mastery of the *law* in the conscience brings forth inner conflict which makes us conform with the humble Christ, and the realm of the law is the contrast of the realm of the Spirit in such a way that the Spirit brings us from the realm of the law, bondage, letter, and death over into the realm of the gospel, Spirit, liberty, and life, it seems inevitable that conformity with Christ in his humility and death should be seen under the perspective of the law. The contrast, which we have constantly postulated between the medieval, nomistic, *imitatio* piety and Luther's evangelical idea of conformity, seems then to vanish completely. We have said that Luther's view of the conformity with Christ in inner conflict in opposition to medieval, imitation-piety is understood as a work of the Spirit and not as a human activity stimulated by the law. It is therefore not correct to say that the experience of the wrath of God in inner conflict as the concrete content of conformity, is based on the mastery in the conscience of the law, whose realm is fundamentally outside the realm of the Spirit.

It seems as if we must maintain that conformity is wrought by the Spirit. But in this case it does not become the conformity with Christ in the experience of the tyranny of the law in the conscience because the law is outside the realm of the Spirit. But if conformity does not embrace inner conflict under the tyranny of the law, what right have we to speak of conformity with the humble Christ? It will then only be possible to speak of a partial conformity. It is also possible to understand conformity with Christ in his humility as the result of the law and then reserve the work of the Spirit for conformity with Christ in his glorification. But in this case the conformity with Christ in his humility must be understood fundamentally as *imitatio*. Then it cannot be avoided that this conformity is understood as a human preparation for grace, a *facere quod in se est*. The Luther research, which by the strong emphasis on the idea of conformity in the young Luther wants to see a pre-Reformation remnant, then seems more correct in contrast to our assertion that the view of both the younger and the older Luther is essentially the same.

How shall we do away with this contradiction?

We first note that in the manner of expression itself, and in the older Luther as well, there is a seeming contradiction on this point. On the one hand we are told that the Spirit has nothing to do with the law. The law does not give the Spirit nor does it lead into the kingdom of God. The Holy Spirit is not a "man of the law," but the law's repealer who frees us from the law. The law can at most prepare a proper material for the Spirit. Corresponding to that it may be said that it is the Spirit that produces the proper knowledge of sin. The Holy Spirit itself leads us into the hell and death of inner conflict. And it must be said that it is by the ministry of the Word, by the preaching of the gospel, that the Holy Spirit convicts the world of sin.[7] On the other hand there are the many assertions that it is the law which in inner conflict rules over the conscience, and that it is the real task of the law to reveal sin.

---

[7] *W. A.*, XVIII, 139, 20 (1525). Also XVII, 1, 244, 5 ff. (Rörer, 1525); XXXI, 2, 268, 14 ff.; 396, 9 ff. (Lauterbach, 1527-30); XXXI, 1, 339, 28 ff. (Veit Dietrich, 1530); XXXIX, 2, 275, 1 ff. (*Promotionsdisp.* Theodor Fabricius and Stanislaus Rapagelanus, 1544).

Now it is the law which reveals sin, and then again it is the Holy Spirit itself who by the preaching of the gospel performs his office of chastising. Now it is the Holy Spirit who leads us into the hell and death of inner conflict, and then again it is the law which puts us to death in the conflict, the law which is not itself able to give the Spirit but which can only make it a proper material. Is it possible to harmonize these two groups of statements?

We get the answer in a third group of statements where Luther definitely considers the difficulty we have indicated here. In *Deuteronomion Mosi cum annotationibus,* 1525, Luther says about the law's work in revealing sin, that it is revealed when the law is preached and heard by the Spirit. This corresponds with what Luther says in the Smalcald Articles in the section about the sin-revealing work of the law, when he uses John 16:8 as the proof text. The law which is preached and heard by the Spirit has not the same effect as the law which is merely heard through human power. The difference between the two uses of the law—for it is that difference we here recognize and which is generally formulalated in the doctrine of the double use of the law—Luther also describes as the difference between Moses with his face veiled or unveiled. No one can endure to see Moses with unveiled face. That Moses only leads to despair. The disciples of Moses with the veiled face are those who live a decent life outwardly and who believe they thus earn salvation. They are the proud ones.

When the law is effective without the Spirit (the first use of the law), it does not work knowledge of sin. The law in its civic use shall place a barrier against outward evil. Yet its inward influence is not a knowledge of sin to salvation but to either hardness of heart or hypocrisy and false holiness. The second and real use of the law, that of revealing sin, does not take place without the cooperation of the Holy Spirit. If the law is heard without the Spirit it remains mere human words, and its power is not made known. When it is said elsewhere that it is the Spirit itself that leads into inner conflict and reveals sin, it does not contradict the fact that it also is the *law* which performs this work. For it is by the law that the Spirit performs its office of chastisement. And it is the Spirit alone who can do it.

But when it is stated simultaneously that the Spirit does not emphasize the law but repeals it, and that the law does not give the Spirit, what then is the relation between the Spirit and the law in its real or spiritual use in inner conflict?

Luther gives a very noteworthy answer to this question. The Holy Spirit may be present in two ways, either unveiled in his majesty as *autor legis* or enveloped in his gifts as *donum*. In the first form the Spirit punishes sin by the law and leads us into the death and hell of inner conflict. In the other form he quickens and sanctifies us.[8] As *autor legis* the Spirit is the presence of God without Christ. As *donum* the Spirit is the presence of God in Christ. Therefore all speculation, mysticism, and enthusiasm which know of a relation to God outside the incarnate God are associated with the unveiled God, but no one can associate with God in his unveiled majesty without dying. God in his majesty always causes death. We shall be able to talk about seeing God in his majesty only in the world to come.

We are now able to see that there are no contradictions between the two previously quoted groups of statements. When it is said that the law reveals sin, it is not contradictory to the statement that it is the Spirit who does this work. For in itself the law cannot reveal sin. In its *usus civilis* the law reveals no sin and it does not lead into inner conflict. It is only in its spiritual use, when the Holy Spirit is present in the word of the law as *deus nudus,* that it becomes the tyrant which brings man into the hell and death of inner conflict. When in some of the statements it was said that the Spirit performed the sin-revealing work by the preaching of the gospel, these statements, if they are to be seen in connection with the total view of Luther, can mean nothing else than that the law always in its spiritual use is preached together with the gospel. The gospel cannot be preached as gospel except in connection with the

---

8 *W. A.,* XXXIX, 1, 370, 12 (*1. disp. ctr. Antinom., 1537*); XXXIX, 1, 484, 12 (*2. disp. ctr. Antinom., 1538*); also XXXIX, 1, 217, 9 ff.; 244, 17; 245, 1 ff. (*Promotionsdisp.,* Palladius and Tileman, 1537).

law in its spiritual use. The gospel is the message of deliverance to them that are under the tyranny of the law. When the gospel brings this message it affirms the judgment of the law on man and thus it reveals sin. When Luther says that the Spirit by the preaching of the gospel reveals sin, the word "gospel" is not understood in the narrow sense as a contrast of the gospel to the law. It is understood in the wider sense of the preached gospel in its inextricable connection with the law in its spiritual use. Then in the strictest sense it is not in the gospel (understood as a contrast to the law) that the Spirit is near as the sin-revealing and slaying *Deus nudus*. In the gospel (in a narrow sense) the Spirit is always present only as *donum*, which makes Christ the gift of God a present, redeeming reality.

When it is said that the law is completely outside the reality of the Spirit and that in contrast to the gospel it cannot give the Spirit, then there is no contradiction in saying that it is by the law that the Spirit leads us into inner conflict and reveals the power of sin and prepares us for Christ. For in the first case it is the law itself which is considered, the law as a principle of life. As a life principle the law can only add to sin either, as in the case of coarse and licentious people, by calling forth a desire to do that which is forbidden and an aversion to that which is bidden or, as in the case of the false saints, by making man confident in his own virtue and piety and thus making him proud and unbelieving. As a life principle the law is entirely outside the reality of the Spirit and it cannot give the Spirit. However, when it is said that the law reveals sin and thus performs the work of the Spirit we are not speaking about the law itself, the law as a life principle, but about the law as a revelation of God's unveiled majesty. And in this sense the law is not outside the reality of the Spirit but it is God's own Word as the instrument of the Spirit. As a revealer of God in his majesty, however, the law cannot give the Spirit. For the Spirit as a gift is given only in and by the gospel. But as a revealer of God in his majesty the law prepares the material to be endowed with the Spirit as a gift. For only they who have become frightened and despairing through the majesty of God have any desire to receive the Spirit as a gift.

The contradiction in the concept of the idea of conformity disappears in the same way when we observe the duality in the appearance of the Spirit. When we maintained that the conformity with Christ in his humility was because of the mastery of the law in the conscience, it did not mean that the conformity belongs to the realm of the law and to the Spirit, that conformity becomes a preparation for grace stimulated by the law, an imitation directed by the law. For the realm of the law is that realm where the law is master as a life principle. When—as in the *imitatio* piety of mysticism—inner conflict itself is taken into that realm and made the culmination of the preparation for grace which man *demands,* we are not speaking of a real conflict, but the conflict has become a spiritual exercise, a work of the law. *Resignatio ad infernum* is therefore not the experience of a real hell, but a spiritual exercise in an imagined hell.

When we constantly have said that everything outside the reality of the Spirit, Christ himself, the gospel, the sacrament, and faith becomes a law, we have thought of the law as a principle of life. We have thought of the law as a master in the realm where the free will in obedience to the law establishes man's own righteousness. In this sense *imitatio* piety makes mortification into law. When Luther, however, speaks of the law as a means to reveal sin and to make us conform to the humble Christ in his conflict, he does not think of the law as such, the law as a life principle, but of the law as a revelation of *Deus nudus.* In this function the law is no longer master in its own realm. On the contrary, it is by the Spirit made a servant for the task of preparing man for Christ.

That which so definitely separates Luther from both medieval, *imitatio* piety and from the conversion preaching of the revival movements is his understanding of the spiritual use of the law. The spiritual use of the law is entirely in the service of the Holy Spirit, in the service of the gospel. The *imitatio* piety—and really also the conversion piety of the revival—does not know any real difference between the first and the second use of the law. The knowledge of sin is in both instances a work of the law, something which is demanded. In the case of the revivals it is best seen by the fact that the struggle of penitence becomes a period in a psychological development which leads to sanctification, which again is considered within the scheme of the law. The second use of the law is therefore not understood as something fundamentally different from the first. It does not signify the complete collapse of the piety of the law, but rather its culmination. For the struggle of penitence is understood as the necessary corridor toward the right way of living under the law. Even the objective doctrine of atonement may, as we have often suggested, be placed in such a fundamental, nomistic piety. For the appropriation of this doctrine in "faith" may be made into a part of the demanded struggle of penitence, into the positive part of this struggle which corresponds to the negative part in knowledge of sin, and together with this positive part it may thus become a mere required corridor toward a nomistically considered sanctification.

The second use or the spiritual use of the law in Luther means the final bankruptcy of all piety of the law. Inner conflict to Luther is not a corridor in a psychological development. If we understand inner conflict in this way we have no idea at all how radical Luther is in his view of inner conflict. Inner conflict to Luther is truly the end, death, destruction. No way leads further on the other side of inner conflict. It is not a negative element in a synthesis. It is the true, irrevocable, and terrible end of the way of legalistic pietism, the end of which those who so happily travel on that way have no idea at all. In the spiritual use of the law God in his majesty is manifest in the word of the law. The true presence of the Spirit, when the law is his instrument, means that *Deus nudus* is face to face with the sinner. From this encounter no one can go farther. It cannot simply be understood as a part in a psychological development or as a negative role in a synthesis. This encounter means death. It is the hell of inner conflict and the death of the sinner. The path which proceeds from here is called resurrection.

But the main thing in Luther's concept of the work of the Spirit in inner conflict is the fact that the Spirit, who in the second use of the law is truly present in the conscience as *Deus nudus,* is the *same* Spirit who in the *same* conflict sends the unutterable groanings to the Father and to Christ and thus leads us into the kingdom of the gospel. The Spirit who causes conflict by the law and gives comfort by the gospel is absolutely identical. This is seen by the fact that the prevailing tension between the two forms of the Spirit shall be resolved in the world to come. The spiritual use of the law does not in a strict sense belong to the realm of the law, but to the realm of the gospel. In the spiritual use of the law the law is no longer an independent power but is subordinated to the gospel and placed at its disposal. In the unity of the Spirit as *Deus nudus* and as *donum* the dynamics of Luther's view of God is found. Wrath and grace are united in one and the same God but in such a way that wrath is subordinated to grace. The tension between grace and wrath in Luther's concept of God is not of a dialectic type. It is not that grace could not be conceived of without wrath or vice versa. The tension is of an eschatological nature. Wrath is used in the service of grace and therefore it shall in the world to come be completely absorbed by grace. We cannot in this world see the Spirit in his majesty without dying. Therefore we must be satisfied to see the Spirit veiled by the signs. But in the world to come we shall see this majesty in his identity with the Spirit, which in the veiled appearance led us away from wrath to the kingdom of Christ. This eschatological release of the tension between wrath and grace, between law and gospel, belongs to the concept of the work of the Spirit. It shows that God reveals himself as the God of the law not to destroy man finally and let him remain in hell but in order to lead him through death to life, through hell to heaven. This unity of the Spirit's work in the second use of the law and in the gospel is familiar to us from the first part of this discussion where we described the unity of God's *opus alienum* and *opus proprium.* The second use of the law is God's *opus alienum* and the gospel his *opus proprium.*

However, if *Deus nudus* is detached from *Deus incarnatus,* which happens when inner conflict develops into despair, then *Deus nudus* is a devilish caricature of God and the law a power of destruction. It is the constant aim of the devil thus to separate the second use of the law from the gospel, *Deus nudus* from *Deus incarnatus*. On this point there is a constant struggle between God and the devil.[9] It is in this struggle that Christ conquered on the cross. And it is the same struggle and victory which take place in us when the Spirit as *Deus nudus* is conquered by the Spirit as *donum*. The Spirit is one in God. The Spirit who in the law leads us into inner conflict and the Spirit who in the gospel leads us out of the conflict is one and the same Spirit. Jesus Christ who cried out in the conflict on the cross and Christ who now sits on the throne of glory is one Lord. But that which is a unity in God the devil tries to separate for us so that we are alone with the Spirit in his majesty, alone with the dead Christ, alone with the condemning law—without any *donum,* without any risen Christ and without any gospel.

But the Spirit conquers over this separation. Where the Spirit in inner conflict completes his work, *opus alienum* and *opus proprium* are one and the same work. The spiritual use of the law and the gospel is one saving word of God, the tempted and conquering, the crucified and the risen Christ, *one* living Lord.

Thus it is seen that Luther's teaching about the spiritual use of the law simultaneously paraphrases the idea of conformity and the dualistic motive and thus shows us the connection between them and shows it in a way which we have not been able to see so clearly before. The spiritual use of the law in connection with the gospel paraphrases the idea of conformity. By the spiritual use of the law we are led into conflict, hell, and death, not that we should be lost in this, but that through it we might be led forward to the gospel with its life, salvation, and peace. This is the conformity with Christ in his death and resurrection. The spiritual use of the law simultaneously paraphrases the dualistic motive. That the law, instead of being a life principle, is used by the Spirit to prepare man for Christ and that the law spiritually understood is no longer permitted to maintain the devil's independence as he wants it but

---

[9] *W. A.*, XX, 605, 9 (Rörer, 1527); I, 227, 13 (1538); also XXVIII, 101, 1 ff. (Rörer, 1528); XL, 1, 75, 9-79, 7 (Rörer, 1531).

instead is torn from the devil and placed under the gospel as its servant to prepare the way, is simply another expression for Christ's constant struggle with and defeat of the devil and the law which are powers of destruction. We can therefore see in the doctrine about the spiritual use of the law how the lines from the idea of conformity, as we know them from the young Luther, and the dualistic motive, as it especially appears in the older Luther, contract into one. We consider it reasonable to suppose that the total view in both the younger and the older Luther is essentially the same in spite of all minor differences which we have no wish at all to minimize, even though they are of no value in our aim with this work. The young Luther's view about the unity of God's *opus alienum* and *opus proprium* in the conformity of inner conflict with Christ is essentially identical with the older Luther's statement about the connection between the law's second use and the gospel. And this statement about the connection between the law's second use and the gospel again is essentially identical with the thought of Christ's constant and repeated victory over the devil and the law which are the powers of destruction. When the young Luther says that the law spiritually understood is the same as the gospel, nothing else is said than what the older Luther states thus: the law helps so that grace might come to us.

The comparison with the older Luther gives a more clear understanding of the Spirit's work as a mediator of Christ's real presence. By the Spirit's presence as a majesty in the law the presence of the humble Christ is mediated, who in inner conflict and death struggles against the powers of destruction. In penitence we are truly made to conform with him. Since the law is only one, the law in its spiritual use and the gospel's message are *one* concrete Word of God. God's *opus alienum* through the law and the wrath, and God's *opus proprium* through the gospel and grace are one concrete act of God. The humble and glorified Christ mediated by the Spirit is *one* living Lord. The real Lutheran dynamics of the view of God is found in this concept of the Spirit's work. It excludes every possibility of conceiving penitence as a human preparation for grace. It is exactly the same view of the Spirit's Christ-mediating work we meet in the young Luther. The Spirit *thus* makes Christ present so that our own life is conformed to Christ in penitence and faith. But this view of the Christ-mediating work of the Spirit has become more richly colored by the thought of conformity which now also is expressed in the dualistic motive's accounts of struggle, and in the dialectic between the spiritual use of the law and the gospel. The tense unity of the idea of conformity between the humble and the exalted Christ, between penitence and faith, has received its corresponding part in the view of a double work of the Spirit: as *Deus nudus* in the Word of the law, by which the Spirit makes the humble Christ truly present through the conformity with him in inner conflict and penitence, and as *donum* in the Word of the gospel, by which the Spirit makes the risen Christ truly present with him through the conformity of faith and love. Luther's view of the Spirit as mediator of Christ's real presence is a many-colored but clear and well-arranged presentation. Its center is the thought of the crucified and risen Lord as the unity of God's *opus alienum* and *opus proprium*. In order to unite us with him in his humility the Spirit appears to us in the Word of the law as *Deus nudus*, and by this he leads us into the hell and death of inner conflict. In order to unify us with him in his power and glory of resurrection the same Spirit comes to us as *donum* and, veiled in the Words of the gospel, gives us the risen Christ as gift, as our alien righteousness, and as the One who acts through our works in favor of our neighbor. But thus he leads us out of hell and death in inner conflict and into life and salvation with the risen Christ. The center in Luther's total concept of Christianity is found in the thoughts we have sketched in this section. Luther's total understanding of Christianity is found in his thought about the Spirit, who makes Christ the all-decisive factor in our life. He is decisive in our conflicts and death, and in our restoration and life. Here we have also seen how decisive the meaning of the concept of the Holy Spirit is to an understanding of Luther's thought patterns. Only the Holy Spirit's own living person unites the spiritual use of the law with the gospel, *opus alienum* with *opus proprium*, the crucified with the risen One. Without the Spirit's own living person this unity falls apart. This happens when the devil gets his way. Without the idea of the living personal presence of the Holy Spirit there is no meaning in Luther's view of the dialectic between the law and the gospel, between penitence and faith, between the conformity with the crucified and the conformity with the risen One. Or the meaning is this, that the connection is made with us now, so that the passing from one to the other of the parts in this series is understood as a psychological development, as the passing from one stage to another in an *ordo salutis* understood as a psychological process, and thereby a part of the law, a definite type of piety which is placed upon men as a yoke of the law. It is possible already in the oldest Lutheranism to see faintly a development away from Luther's spiritual realism toward this rational nomism. It was not very long that they were able to retain Luther's dynamic realism.

The Spirit and Empirical Piety

The view described in the first part of the relation between the work of the Holy Spirit and empirical piety has already been partly confirmed in the previous presentation. The ambiguity of real piety became very clear when seen in the light of *De servo arbitrio* about the two struggling kingdoms. The third possibility of neutrality is not present. If we are not led by the Spirit into the kingdom of Christ then we are *eo ipso* in the kingdom of Satan, and then one's whole empirical piety is nothing other than condemned works of the law. Man is flesh, and in the flesh there is nothing which is not judged.[10] The righteousness which counts before God is not man's real piety but Christ's alien righteousness.[11] The new man which is born anew by water and the Spirit is that man who

---

[10] *W. A.*, XVIII, 739, 11; 743, 27; 765, 30; 775, 1; also XVIII, 766, 4 ff.; 774, 29 ff.; XVII, 1, 125, 1 ff.; 137, 1 ff.; 245, 2 ff. (Rörer, 1525); XX, 650, 7 ff.; 750, 11 ff. (Rörer, 1527); XXVI, 352, 1 ff. (1528); XXX, 1, 45, 26 ff. (Rörer, 1528); XXXIX, 1, 378, 8 ff. (*1. disp. ctr. Antinom.*, 1537).

[11] *W. A.*, XVIII, 767, 14. Also 777, 26 ff.; 778, 38 ff.; XL, 1, 47, 1 ff.; 283, 7 ff. (Rörer, 1531); XXXIX, 2, 289, 16 ff. (*Promotionsdisp.*, Georg Major and Joh. Faber, 1544); 237, 23 ff. (*Promotionsdisp.*, Hier. Nopp and Fr. Bachofen, 1543); XVII, 1, 245-246, 10 (Rörer, 1525); XX, 637, 5 ff.; 644, 10 ff. (Rörer, 1527); XXXI, 1, 167, 7 ff. (1530); XXXI, 2, 71, 5 ff.; 439, 3 ff. (Lauterbach, 1527-30); XLVI, 44, 23 ff. (Cruciger, 1537); XLI, 64, 7; 66, 27 ff. (Rörer, 1537); XLVI, 376, 13 ff. (Rörer, 1538).

in faith takes refuge in Christ. It is not the converted man in his empirical piety.

But simultaneously the older Luther also speaks just as strongly as the younger Luther about a progress in sanctification, a constant struggle against sin, as an increasing cleansing and expulsion of sin. The growth of this sanctification is the Spirit's work. The man who by faith in Christ is Spirit, is simultaneously flesh by virtue of his self. And that is as *totus homo*. The old man, the flesh, is not merely the "lower" part of man (the real self minus the empirical piety); but it is man in his totality. The struggle in man is therefore not a struggle between a higher and lower part of man's nature, but between man's real self and the Spirit of God. Therefore, that which the struggle is against is our total real self, and that which fights it is the Spirit. Thus the two apparent contradictory sentences from I John are both true: "Whosoever is born of God doth not commit sin; for his seed remaineth in him: and he cannot sin, because he is born of God" (I John 3:9). "If we say that we have no sin, we deceive ourselves, and the truth is not in us" (I John 1:8). There will always be a real self for the Spirit to fight no matter how pious it might otherwise be. Christ's alien righteousness, to which faith clings, may of course cover all the remaining sin, so that it is no longer attributed to one. But it does not destroy the remaining sin as a reality. The sin as a reality is remaining. Justification therefore means that war is declared upon the remaining sin. The beginning of its expulsion starts in justification. But this expulsion of sin is only in its beginning in this life. Only in the resurrection will it be completely finished.[12]

It is the Spirit which expels sin by the Word about the forgiveness of sin, not man's increasing empirical piety. Expulsion of sin is therefore not as a matter of course identical with a psychologically noticeable and therefore unmistakable increase of empirical piety. On the contrary, the sin which is to be expelled comprises the total man. It presupposes a real sinner when we speak of sanctification, that is a total sinner, not one who by virtue of a visibly

---

[12] *W. A.*, XXX, 1, 190, 23 (Large Catechism); 190, 37; also from the commentary on Genesis: XLIV, 473, 35; 508, 21 ff.; 769, 7 ff.; 776, 10 ff.

increasing empirical piety is just partly a sinner. The expulsion of sin is that destruction of the power of sin which is a result of the fact that we as total sinners are brought into Christ's kingdom. As it is clearly stated in the explanation to Luther's *Small Catechism*, the expulsion of sin is this, that the Spirit daily works penitence through the law and faith through the gospel. This is a daily repetition of penitence wrought by the law and of faith wrought by the gospel. The Spirit mediates a daily repetition of Christ's death and resurrection in us, not an evolution of our indwelling religious and moral strength by which the meaner tendencies in us are being checked. Luther therefore says that the Spirit, as long as sin is not completely expelled (and this does not take place before the last day), has not been given us in a full measure but only as first fruits.[13] That the Spirit is an eschatological category or concept, which was clearly evident in the young Luther, is now even more clear. The powers of the world to come are by the Spirit active in the midst of the world of sin and death. But inasmuch as sin and death are constant realities, the Spirit is only given us as first fruits.

Justification and sanctification, forgiveness of sin and expulsion of sin are an insolvable unity in the Spirit. They canot be separated, because there is only one Spirit. They can no more be separated than the law and the gospel, or *opus alienum* and *opus proprium,* or the death of Christ and his resurrection. Justification and sanctification are not seen as two different processes for which it is necessary to find some rational and easily understood connection. This is a problem of a later Lutheranism. Luther views justification and sanctification as one inseparable act of God: namely the work of the Spirit, which tears the man out of the kingdom of the devil and leads him into Christ's kingdom and preserves him there. Man by being taken out of the devil's kingdom is also relieved of the power of the law. And by being covered by Christ's alien righteousness no longer may he be guilty in his conscience before the law.

---

13 *W. A.,* XL, 1, 599, 7 (Rörer, 1531); also XV, 435, 24 ff. (Rörer, 1524); XX, 635, 2 ff.; 729, 5 ff.; 750, 17 ff. (Rörer, 1527); XL, 1, 538, 3 ff.; XL, 2, 24, 4 ff.; 81, 1 ff. (Rörer, 1531), XXIX, 1, 356, 9 ff. (*5. theserække mod Antin.,* 1538).

He is in the state of grace. And in this position, even though the final renewal is yet to come, he is already saved by virtue of the forgiveness of sin. The grace of God is always total. This is justification.

But Christ's alien righteousness which covers man's sin is not merely an ideal quantity which in principle is imputed to man. Where such a view is held we are within the system of legalism. There the alien righteousness of Christ is made into a transferable act of the law.

We have previously seen—and this still applies—that Christ fulfills the law for us. This is not done in a manner which makes the law's demand constantly valid because the law is satisfied by merely transferring an act of law fulfillment, but it is done by Christ fulfilling the law by conquering and abolishing it. The law as a conquered tyrant is only permitted to be a tutor to Christ. The tyrant has no longer any power in the conscience. Therefore the alien righteousness of Christ is not of the law but of the gospel. It is not a God-demanded but a God-given righteousness. Therefore it is the only righteousness recognized by God. As a God-given righteousness this alien righteousness is not a mere ideal quantity. God does not give as a niggard. Alien righteousness, as God-given righteousness, is a living reality, the living Christ himself, present by the Spirit. God does not content himself by giving ideas; he gives himself complete and undivided. As long as the righteousness of faith is considered as something less than God himself with all that he is and has, we have not understood what Luther means with the alien righteousness of faith. To believe in Christ does not therefore mean merely to have received his righteousness as a transferable act of the law—such a faith would be the work of the law even though it proclaimed itself ever so much as something wrought by the Spirit—but to believe in Christ means to live through his reality. This life through Christ by the Spirit is a mediated, redeeming reality in us. Faith is an incarnated faith.[14] Faith unites within itself justification and sanctification because both are a

---

[14] *W. A.*, XL, 1, 426, 11; also XVII, 1, 443, 23 ff.; 445, 1 ff. (Rörer, 1525); XXXIX, 1, 321, 12 ff. (*Disp. de veste nuptiale*, 1537); XLVI, 190, 27 ff. (Rörer, 1538).

release from the power of the law. Justification is a deliverance from the power of the law in the conscience as a religious basis for life. Sanctification is a deliverance from the power of the law over our works as an ethical basis for life.[15] The life of faith through the reality of Christ is a reality in us. Therefore this is sanctification. Sanctification is a *real* life outside the law.

Faith always exists only in the kingdom of the gospel or Christ, that kingdom into which the Spirit leads us when he has brought us out of the kingdom of the devil. Faith fulfills the law because by living in the realm of the gospel, that is, living by that which God gives us in Christ as a reality, it has completely overcome the law.

When Christ's alien righteousness is not understood as the living Christ himself but as a transferable fulfillment of the law, it is a sign that one is living within the realm of the law. There justification is understood from the point of view of the law that by Christ's alien righteousness (understood as a transferred fulfillment of the law) it has become possible to satisfy the demands of the law. But such a fulfillment of the law is not understood as a victory over the law. Sanctification thereby becomes a problem. Sanctification cannot directly be based on such a nomistic view of justification. Sanctification must then be understood as a new and partly human fulfillment of the law, a "real righteousness" within the realm of the law. In this way sanctification must become a double problem. On the one hand it must, because it is considered from a nomistic point of view, be constantly viewed as a limitation of justification by faith alone. The sanctification-righteousness must be considered as a constant competitor of justification-righteousness. On the other hand it becomes an unsolved psychological mystery, how sanctification should be thought to proceed naturally from this strictly legalistic justification. Here we are in the center of

---

15 *W. A.*, XXX, 1, 192, 24. Also XVII, 1, 129, 7 (Rörer, 1525); XVIII, 765, 15 ff. (1525); XXXI, 2, 69, 24 ff.; 769, 17 ff. (Lauterbach, 1527-30); XLV, 149, 9 ff. (Rörer, 1537); XXXIX, 1, 321, 12 ff. (*Disp. de veste nuptiale*, 1537); 365, 2 ff.; 372, 20 ff.; 375, 4 ff.; 388, 4 ff.; 398, 11 ff. (*1. disp. ctr. Antinom.*, 1537); XLVI, 124, 17 ff. (Rörer, 1538); XXXIX, 1, 436, 9 ff. (*2. disp. ctr. Antinom.*, 1538); XLIV, 761, 24 ff.; 770, 9 ff. (*Genesiskommentaren*, 1535-45).

the problems of later Lutheranism in which it was necessary to maintain the strictly legal character of justification and thereby the complete separation from all sanctification and simultaneously the connection of sanctification with justification as its fruit. This is an absolutely impossible task.

The alien righteousness in Luther is a righteousness of the gospel and therefore a living one. Christ himself is present by the Spirit. Therefore faith in him means life out of his reality as a gift, life under his merciful dominion. This dominion, however, is an eternal dominion, which will only be completed in the coming eon. Then man shall be fully under the dominion of Christ so that no sin and no death can threaten him or, what is the same thing, he shall then possess the Spirit in full measure. In this world, however, sin and death are still realities. Therefore the dominion of Christ in this world has a double aspect, which it does not have in the consummation. On the one hand it has the forgiveness of sin, because Christ does not reckon sin to man. It is *peccatum regnatum*. On the other hand it is considered as the expulsion of sin because sin which is not reckoned is condemned to death. It cannot continue to live when man has come out of the realm of the law and into the realm of Christ, that kingdom which in the consummation has completely overcome *all* sin and *all* death. Sin belongs to a world that disappears while the fruits of the Spirit belong to the world to come. The flesh shall die and be buried with our old body; the Spirit shall rise again to eternal life together with our new body.

The Spirit is present only in this world as first fruits. But it is truly present as first fruits, as something which has the powers of the harvest within itself.

It is easy to see how justification and sanctification belong together. Both are seen from the point of view of the gospel and not of the law. Both are an expression for the same unbroken act of God in the Spirit. Justification means that God in the Spirit is present with us. He struggles in the midst of the reality of sin and death. This is the forgiveness of sin. Sanctification means that God in the Spirit also in the future remains near us, struggling in the midst of the final destruction of sin and death. Justification is the redemptive act of God seen in the perspective of the present. In the present (this eon) we are always sinners, and the presence of God is always the forgiveness of sin. Sanctification is the same act of God seen in the perspective of the future. In the future (the coming eon) we are entirely outside of the domain of sin and death. The unity of these two perspectives is found in God and his work. That is, the unity between justification and sanctification can be seen only in the light of the gospel and not of the law.

The law is anthropocentric in its outlook. It views man's salvation as a way which must be traveled by man step by step. Here there is no necessary connection possible. For every single step may lead either forward or backward. Justification and sanctification under the perspective of the law become two stages in a human development, and between these two stages there is no necessary connection. The law can only postulate that there *ought* to be a connection: sanctification *ought* to follow justification. The gospel however is theocentric in its view. It views man's salvation as an assimilation in an all-embracing, saving, eschatological totality. This totality is an act of God, the elements of which, creation, redemption, consummation, cannot be separated any more easily than the three persons in the Trinity. These elements are the one, eternal, identical act of God unfolding in that of God's "gratuitous" agape in the history of man. Thus in the historic plan of God creation, redemption, consummation follow one another with *necessity,* but not with a necessity clear and logical to us, but with God's miraculous necessity, and with the inner necessity of his gratuitous agape and his inconceivable faithfulness and righteousness. Luther expresses it this way: for God the last day has already come and the work is finished. In the perspective of the gospel therefore justification and sanctification are insolubly united. Their unity proves the continuity of God's eschatological, saving act.

Where this unity is broken and the relation of sanctification to justification has become a problem, it is certainly proven that justification and sanctification have been taken out of connection with the gospel and placed under the law. They are no longer seen as an expression for a continuous act of God but as two succeeding stages in a human development.

Consequently we see in the older Luther the same tendencies in the understanding of the Spirit's relation to empirical piety as we found in the young Luther. On the one hand there is the critical tendency. All empirical piety is ambiguous. It may in every moment be described either as flesh or Spirit. This critical tendency demarcates Luther's evangelical view from every form of nomistic Christianity, an example of which is the pietistic identification of the new man and converted man (which is anticipated in the moralism of Erasmus and the enthusiasts) and of the medieval doctrine of the effectiveness *ex opere operato* of sacramental grace. In the conflicts with scholasticism, Erasmus, and the enthusiasts this tendency is very pronounced. This is most clearly seen in the two major works, *De servo arbitrio* and the *Commentary on the Epistle to the Galatians.* On the other hand there is the positive tendency. Where the Spirit is—and Christ in the Spirit—there something real takes place. There God is present working toward his eternal goal. There sanctification always follows justification. This second tendency is as important to Luther as the first is. This becomes very clear in the older Luther because of his conflict with the antinomians.

Luther finds in antinomianism, just as in nomism, a denial of the Spirit. Nomism denies the Spirit by replacing, with empirical righteousness wrought under the category of the law and the free will of man (aided by grace, a very necessary aid indeed), the righteousness of the present and living Christ. Antinomianism denies the Spirit by replacing a *doctrine* of the forgiveness of sin because of the satisfying work of Christ for the living Christ truly present by the Spirit. Therefore antinomianism becomes a message about Christ without the Spirit, that is, a message of an idea of Christ instead of Christ himself, a *false* Christ. Where Christ is present he is always the *living One*, the One who has begun his attack on sin. A Christ who is not thought of as the living Christ is a false Christ. Where grace is preached without the expulsion of sin there, contrary to the Bible's clear teaching, *gratia* has been separated from *donum*. And when this has been done the true Christ is not present.[16]

In contrast to antinomianism Luther's realism appears with a special force. But simultaneously with that the gulf between Luther and later Lutheranism becomes very clear. The later, orthodox theology became a compromise between antinomianistic and nomistic tendencies. Such a compromise was natural since antinomianism itself is a form of nomism, antimoralistic nomism. Orthodox theology became in principle antinomianistic in its justification doctrine and nomistic in its sanctification teaching. But the nomistic principle, which contains this compromise, signifies a break with Luther's spiritual realism. In place of Christ present by the Spirit, orthodoxy operates with the pure doctrine of satisfaction by Christ. Christ is the content of this doctrine, he is an idea. No doubt Luther would make the same objection to the abstraction of the orthodox doctrine of justification as he had made to the antinomians: here the Spirit has disappeared, here *gratia* and *donum* have become separated. Therefore the talk about the blood of Christ is *false*. It is not the genuine blood and the true Christ which in this manner can be abstracted from the Spirit.

The orthodox compromise between an antinomianistic doctrine of justification and a nomistic doctrine of sanctification could not be maintained constantly. The antimoralistic and the moralistic tendency fell apart. The latter joined pietism, which gradually squandered the Lutheran teaching of justification. The former went into a long series of antimoralistic reactions against pietism, which rarely stayed clear of antinomianism, and for which the possibility of "ethics" therefore became a constantly unsolved and insoluble *theoretic* problem. Even in our present evangelical theology (and church life) we suffer from a sterile tug-of-war between the two tendencies. This development confirms the early loss of the genuinely Lutheran spiritual realism. Thereby it also under-

---

[16] *W. A.*, L, 599, 25 (1539); 600, 8; also 624, 26–625, 28. XL, 2, 421, 4 ff. (Rörer, 1532); XLV, 150, 3 ff.; 183, 20 ff. (Rörer, 1537); XLVII, 729, 1 ff. (Rörer, 1539); XXXIX, 2, 202, 28 ff. (*Promotionsdisp.*, Heinr. Schmedenstede, 1542); XLIV, 473, 35 ff. (*Genesiskommentaren*, 1535-45).

scores the important central position of the testimony of the Holy Spirit in Luther's theology.

In the previous sections we have seen how the young Luther's critical and positive analysis of empirical piety on the basis of the testimony about the work of the Holy Spirit is evident again in the older Luther. The latter of the two tendencies is even more emphasized than the former because of the polemics with the antinomians. There is, however, in this comparison a point on which we have not as yet touched. In describing the young Luther's view of the relation between the Spirit's work and empirical piety we have emphasized how the life through the reality of Christ mediated and redeemed by the Spirit had a definite *content:* a double motion of faith and love. How does the older Luther look at the question of the content of the new life in Christ as it is given by the Spirit?

It would be too involved to go into a detailed account of the older Luther's view of the content of the new life. It would mean the start of an entirely new work, a complete and logical description of Luther's ethics. Instead, we limit ourselves to the presentation of certain characteristic traits which relate the older Luther's view with the thoughts about faith and love as a logical, interacting faith-relationship caused by the Christ-imparting Spirit of the young Luther.

Both the younger and the older Luther summarize the content of the Christian life in the three theological virtues: faith, hope, and love as the new life wrought by the Spirit. Through these virtues the Spirit sanctifies the *soul* of man according to the *first* table of the law. According to this description faith, hope, and love according to the first table embrace the relation to God above. We have previously characterized this as the motion of faith. Love then is not understood as a love directed to our neighbor but as the unselfish love of God hardened in *odium sui* in accordance with the thoughts from the lectures on Romans. Hope is the perseverance in the hardening process of inner conflict. But this sanctification of the *soul* shows its reality in the sanctification of the body according to the *second* table. That is, faith, hope, and love show themselves as living by the fact that they are alive in the work in favor of the neighbor through the calling and station in life of the individual. If the sanctification of the soul according to the first table does not prove itself active in the sanctification of the body according to the second table, then nothing has been perceived either of Christ or of the Spirit.[17] The sanctification according to the first table means that, in inner conflict under the tyranny of the law, man will be completely deprived of his own strength and forced to rely on Christ. Sanctification according to the second table means that the sinner, who is thus deprived of all strength and forced to rely on Christ, is used by him as a tool in the works of love for the neighbor in the daily grind of one's calling.

The works of the second table are all works which do not directly concern man's immediate relation to God and which are not able to give man any sense of righteousness before God. They are works performed by sinners whom Christ covers with his righteousness while he simultaneously uses them to further *his* work. These works, therefore, have outwardly a very insignificant character. They do not resemble "holy" or "Christian" works—and they are not supposed to. They do not have the pious man as a subject, but the Spirit of God. Therefore their aim is very different from that of making man pious or Christian in appearance. On the other hand they must serve the creation of God outside the narrow sphere of interest of the pious. They are the fruits of the Spirit. For the Spirit is not just another name for piety. The Spirit is God himself in his loving concern for the welfare of his creation. Therefore the Spirit completes the creation of God even in places and in works which have no significance for the piety of the pious. The papists cannot understand that. In their view such outward works as that of taking care of wife and children, obeying the government, etc., are only works of the flesh. They do not serve as an exercise of piety. And these are works which not only non-Christians do, but they do them constantly. And yet these are true spiritual works.

---

17 *W. A.*, XX, 641, 11 ff. (Rörer, 1527); XL, 1, 401, 4 ff. (Rörer, 1531); XLVI, 186, 15 ff. (Rörer, 1538).

That works are fruits of the Spirit cannot be understood by the idea of a supernatural causality. The thought of the fruits of the Spirit in Luther is of an entirely different type from the scholastic thought of "infused" virtues. Luther does not think of the fruits of the Spirit as works of a finer quality than natural works, or that because of that they should have a supernatural causality. Such a view is based on the law according to which works must aid in the relation to God and give man a quality of righteousness. The works which belong to a higher place on the ladder of merit than natural gifts are able to reach demand a supernatural causality, the Spirit which works through the infused grace.

This is not the way Luther looks at it. It is essential to him that the works which he designates as the fruits of the Spirit are not outwardly to be distinguished from the natural works of man. These works are not evaluated from the point of view of the law with a certain importance to him who performs them. That they are the fruits of the Spirit does not mean that they are so good (that is, for the one who performs them) and so important (again to him who performs them) that it is necessary to postulate a supernatural causality to them. It means, however, that simultaneously with the works which are performed in a natural manner and which many non-Christians perform in the same way, they are performed within the sphere where God in the Spirit is truly present with his all-embracing, eschatological, saving work in Christ. In this way these naturally performed works within this sphere become a part of God's own creative and redemptive work and not a part of man's attempt to establish his own righteousness.

Therefore the order of these works is the *calling*. For in contrast to all self-chosen works the calling is the order of God's gracious work in favor of his creation. The different relations in which we are placed as people with a calling do not help us but they serve in God's constant goodness to his creation. However, as Gustaf Wingren often emphasizes in his studies of Luther's view of the calling, it is true that man in his calling is compelled to do God's good work even against his will. This is because the calling, which is not dependent on the whims of the individual, as a divine order compels even evil men to work for the realization of the purpose on which God decided by the establishment of the calling and station in life. Through this calling and station God discharges the work of the secular order in which also nonbelievers and evil men must serve. This order corresponds to the first use of the law by which man outwardly is driven to do the will of God while the heart is evil. But there is a difference between being called and driven against one's own wishes by the first use of the law (by its threats and promises) and being called and driven by the Spirit of God. For when we are driven by the Spirit we act freely and gladly, not by compulsion. The works themselves are not different. Seen from without they are the same as those of the unbelievers. It is the method used which is different.

When man in his calling is driven by the Spirit of God his aim is not, as otherwise is the case, to establish his own righteousness through the calling. But man is by the Spirit's work united with the living Christ and justified in him. Therefore he does not aim to establish his own righteousness. But his will, made free by justification in Christ, has been drawn into the purpose of God. The work of man does not through the Spirit serve a double purpose: the establishment of one's own righteousness and the reluctant serving of the purpose of God's love. Man is made free in the Spirit to serve not his own righteousness but only the love of God toward the neighbor.

Luther describes the whole problem in *De servo arbitrio* by the concept of *cooperatio*. By the Spirit we become God's co-workers, included as instruments in his all-embracing act.[18] It is in this perspective that all Luther's statements about the new life as fruit of the Spirit should be seen. Therefore Luther in his commentary on Galatians calls this life *aliena vita*.

The same realistic concept of the Spirit, which we met in the account of Christ's real presence and in the relation between justification and sanctification is found here to carry the whole burden of thought. The Spirit is not the distant, supernatural causality of

---

[18] *W. A.*, XVIII, 754, 8; 695, 28 ff.; 753, 33 ff.; XIV, 681, 28 ff. (1525); XLIII, 68, 24 ff. (*Genesiskommentaren*, 1535-45).

a growing empirical piety which man himself uses under the law to work himself up toward God. The Spirit is God himself present with his all-embracing, eschatological, saving work in Christ, present as a sphere of life in which our whole existence and all our work are lifted out of the isolation of our own selfish religiosity and placed in the act of God. The Spirit is not a divine power put into the service of man, he is God who draws man into his service. Therefore life lived in the reality of the Spirit always contains a double motion: faith which in inner conflict takes man away from himself and casts him upon the alien righteousness of Christ, and love which also takes man away from himself and takes him through his calling to the distress of his neighbors. In this double motion man is taken out of the realm of the devil and placed in the realm of Christ.

The words "faith" and "love" corresponding to *spiritus precum* and *spiritus gratiae,* in the young Luther signified this double motion. We find the same double motion in the thoughts of the older Luther about sanctification according to the two tables. By the strong accent which the earthly calling has received in the older Luther the double motion becomes even more apparent. And by understanding the calling as a co-operation in God's own creative and redemptive work the realism of this concept is seen even more clearly. The Spirit himself is God, present in his Christ-work embracing us from every side and drawing us into this work with all that we are and have. This realistic view can only be adequately stated in the words of the New Testament. The Spirit is the new life's eon, present in the midst of the old eon as the first fruits of the coming eon. The Spirit is the law of life in the kingdom of the risen and victoriously coming Christ, who is the new eon appearing in the midst of the world of sin and death. The older Luther's statement about the new life as the fruit of the Spirit has no meaning unless it is understood in the realistic manner. This does not mean that an empirical righteousness has sprung up within us which now is able to manifest itself in new works. Rather the new life means that the reality of God is present with us and he uses us constantly according to his own will. We are not concerned with the question of whether or not we have become better. Only when the reality of God thus dominates us do we become truly "better." Only then is sin expelled, and only then are we no longer interested in our own moral beauty, but we are used by God until he in the resurrection makes us new creatures completely.

Luther's thoughts about the new life are very clear if they are understood just as realistically as the testimony of the New Testament about the Spirit. His thoughts are a compact unity. It is the pure gospel's theology in contrast to both medieval and orthodox as well as pietistic compromises between the nomistic and the evangelical tendencies. In Luther the testimony about the Holy Spirit is the Bible's limitless expectation of God who has become alive anew and blasted all the compromises which always arise where the expectation is quenched. Therefore it is substituted with the guarantees of the law—either in one form or another, either by one or another compromise between "grace" and "free will," between gospel and law, between faith and morality.

The Total View of the Trinity

The view of the Spirit's relation to his means, the Word and the sacraments, is treated in the next chapter in which we shall give an account of Luther's testimony of the Spirit in its contrast to that of the enthusiasts. This introductory chapter in which we attempt to establish the continuity of Luther's account of the Spirit, apart from the special sphere in which the struggle between him and the enthusiasts took place, must therefore naturally be concluded with a study of the older Luther's view of the person of the Holy Spirit and with a summary to produce a total picture of each of the thoughts which have been discussed.

In the first part of our work we saw that the Trinity doctrine answered the question about Luther's view of the person of the Holy Spirit and simultaneously made a natural summary of the different aspects of Luther's account of the Spirit. No change in Luther's view has been made on this point. The doctrine of the Trinity has the position and the same function in the older Luther as it had in the young Luther.[19] As for Luther's attitude to the traditional Trinity doctrine it is sufficient to refer to our previous presentation which is also completely valid in the older Luther.

In the discussion of the earlier period of Luther's theology we saw how the general trinitarian view of the Spirit's work and person was concentrated in the expression, *spiritus creator*. And we clarified the content of this expression by referring to the catechetical presentation in *Eine kurtze Form*.

It is therefore natural with respect to this period also to give a summarizing presentation from the point of view of a catechetical presentation. In the catechetical presentations we can be sure that we have the view of Luther in its clearest and most authentic form. These catechetical presentations are first of all original Luther texts. And second, they contain Luther's view in a systematic summary just as he himself wanted the congregation to get it. Because of the popular aim of the catechisms it is of course not possible to use them as an exhaustive presentation of Luther's view of any individual point in his theology. But as the classic presentation of the central part in Luther's view they can always be used as a test of the validity of Luther's interpretation. An interpretation of Luther which is opposed in a decisive way to the teaching of the catechisms cannot be genuine no matter how many "proofs" it may have. Therefore we conclude this section with a presentation of Luther's account of the Holy Spirit in the *Large Catechism*, in which we shall try to present this account as a whole, and through which the continuity in the young Luther's view appears.

In the discussion of the young Luther's Trinity doctrine we learned who the Spirit is. In the doctrine of the Trinity Luther showed that the Spirit, whose work we have learned to know as a mediation by Word and sacrament of the living Christ's presence as our sphere of life, is God himself, not just some power coming from God. It has often been stated that Luther's explanation to the third article of faith, in contrast to the method used in the

---

[19] J. Köstlin, II, pp. 82-94; R. Seeberg, *Lehrbuch der Dogmengeschichte,* IV, 1, 4th ed., pp. 230-236. *W. A.*, XIV, 181, 11-182, 2 (Rörer, 1537); XLVI, 436, 5-438, 12 (Rörer, 1538); XLV, 446, 8-30; L, 197, 1-198, 17; XXVI, 500, 10 ff.; XXXIX, 2, 253, 1-255, 23; 287, 1 ff.; 339, 1 ff.

second article, contains nothing about the person of the Spirit. It has no clear confession of the divinity of the Spirit and his relation to the other persons in the Trinity. It simply gives a description of the office of the Spirit.[20] This, however, is only true in a superficial sense. Already at the start of the explanation is the Holy Spirit designated as God's Spirit. This is in contrast to all other spirits, such as the human spirit, heavenly spirits, and the evil spirit. Herein is contained the confession of the divinity of the Spirit. Where the Spirit is absent man lives under the law and attempts by his own works to be saved. This piety is also the fruit of spirit, but of a spirit which is not of God—the human spirit and the evil spirit. By this the distinction has been sharply drawn between God's Spirit and everything else which calls itself spirit. The confession of the divinity of the Spirit is very clear. Every form of spirit and spirituality which is not the person of God himself, will sooner or later reveal itself as a means to further the piety of the law.

Just as the explanation to the third article of faith clearly proclaims the divinity of the Spirit in contrast to all other spirituality, it also gives the Spirit a distinct position in his relation to the other persons in the divinity. Also in this explanation the Spirit is understood as *spiritus creator*, and his work is thereby one with the continuous act of love of the Triune God in creation, redemption, and sanctification. Redemption and sanctification are simply the completion of the work of creation. By the Fall we got out of direct relation to the Creator and got under the wrath of God, sentenced to an eternal damnation, and given into the power of sin, death, and the devil. In this way the highest form of the creation threatened to get away from God. But by the redemption the Son of God from heaven came and routed our tyrants to become our master and thus to restore the blessing of creation. But this victory would be as a dead treasure, if the Spirit did not bring it to us. Only by the work of the Spirit are we placed in the reality

---

[20] *W. A.*, XXX, 1, 9, 33 (Rörer); 44, 28; 91, 1, 3; also L, 274, 13 ff. (1538); XI, 122, 6 ff. (Rörer, 1523); XLV, 182, 19 ff. (Rörer, 1537); XLV, 732, 22 (Cruciger, 1537); XLVI, 421, 12 ff.; 422, 16 ff. (Rörer, 1538).

of Christ the redeemer. Thus the work which was started in creation and carried on in the redemption only reaches its fulfillment in the work of the Spirit. This means that there is one and only one continuous act of God. It is the divine agape calling us out of nothing and giving us life in Christ. There we also speak of one God in three persons. Here there is no place for either tritheism or modalism. Where these tendencies appear it means that the unity in God's person and therefore also the unity in the downward-directed divine act of agape is broken to make room for man's upward effort toward God.

The Spirit is therefore not understood on a human religious basis. It is not seen in the anthropocentric perspective of the law as the transcendent cause of the higher form of piety needed for our salvation, a form which we are not able to produce. Instead it is seen entirely from the theocentric perspective of the Trinity doctrine. The work of the Spirit is the eternally identical act of the divine agape which goes from creation to the consummation just as this act of God here and now has come into our life and has taken it out of its narrow selfish endeavor and placed us in the all-embracing act of God.

This theocentric perspective becomes very evident in two ways in the *Large Catechism* in the explanation of the third article of faith in the great emphasis on the *church* and on *eschatology*.

Naturally it must not be overlooked that in the very wording of the text of the third article there is a reason why the subjects such as the church and eschatology have been so closely knit together in the discussion of the Spirit's work. The article itself mentions the church right after the Holy Spirit and closes with the resurrection of the body and eternal life. But the decisive fact is not that the church and eschatology are treated in connection with the account of the Holy Spirit, but how this connection is brought about, whether it is of an outward mechanical nature or an expression for an inner, organic connection. This last view is the case in Luther's explanation of the third article of faith.

As the last part of that unbroken act of agape the work of the Spirit is to make the redeeming work of Christ a present reality.

This is done through the Word, which is the means of the Spirit. But the Word is proclaimed by the *church*. In this way the church becomes the mother who gives birth to and nourishes every Christian. As the preaching church, the church is inextricably attached to the Spirit. Where the Spirit is there is also the church. For the church is nothing else than the place where the Spirit through preaching makes the redemptive work of Christ into a present reality.

But the fact that the church is the messenger of the Word, which is the means of the Spirit and, in that sense, the prerequisite for the Spirit's work, does not according to Luther's view mean that the church as an institution is Lord over the Spirit.[21] For it is not only true that the Spirit does not perform his sanctifying work outside the church but that the church does not exist without the Spirit. When, therefore, the church is a prerequisite for the work of the Spirit then it is a prerequisite which the Spirit creates again and again, not a prerequisite which he has to discover. For it is the Spirit himself who creates the church and thereby he makes the prerequisite for his own continued work. The church is the "seed" of the Word. The church therefore rightly seen is not an "institution" at all. The church is the people of God which the Spirit creates.[22]

Because the Spirit's work is not something isolated but is God's all-embracing act of agape present in our reality, therefore the Spirit's work cannot be understood from the point of view of the individual's narrow outlook. In the perspective of the law there exist only the individual and his psychological development toward perfection. In the perspective of the law the work of the Spirit can only be isolated episodes, attached to the individual's psychological development as aids in his struggle to reach upward to perfection and to God. In the perspective of the law it is the psychological

---

[21] *W. A.*, XI, 111, 23 ff. (Rörer, 1523); XV, 545, 7 ff. (Rörer, 1524); XVII, 1, 268, 23 ff. (Rörer, 1525); XXVIII, 50, 16 ff. (Rörer, 1528); XXXIX, 1, 186, 5 ff. (*Disp. de potestate concilii*, 1536); XLV, 575, 27 ff. (Cruciger, 1537), as well as, 618, 17 ff.; 627, 16 ff.; XXXI, 2, 450, 6 (Lauterbach, 1527-30).

[22] *W. A.*, XXX, 1, 190, 4; also L, 624, 27 ff.; 625, 21 ff.; 629, 7 ff. (1539); XI, 53, 25 (Rörer, 1523); XLVI, 402, 16 ff. (Rörer, 1538).

development of the individual which creates the continuity, while the work of the Spirit falls apart into several individual episodes.

It is the very opposite in the perspective of the gospel. There it is the Spirit's work which is the true whole. It is one unbroken act of God stretching from the creation to perfection. In the creation the Spirit is active in redemption, in the church, and in the resurrection. The fragments there, however, are the lives of individuals. The church through the Spirit's creation is something that goes far beyond that of the narrow boundaries of individuals and the individual generation. By joining the church we are not accepting the Spirit's work as an aid in our own efforts toward perfectness so that the work of the Spirit and the church become a fragment in the whole of our existence. It is contrariwise the Spirit which takes us into his work, by which we are made into a "part" of the church in which the Spirit will remain till the last day. The church as a congregation and the church as an institution of salvation are not separated in the *Large Catechism* as two different "church ideas." Because the congregation is the people assembled by the Spirit with Christ as the head, it has no special existence and aim of its own to pursue. Its aim is the aim of the Spirit—to finish the work of sanctification. Therefore, the congregation is, as a congregation, the institution which proclaims the Word and brings men from the kingdom of Satan into the kingdom of Christ. It is the thought of *cooperatio*, which we met in *De servo arbitrio*, and which is found again in the concept of the church in the third article of faith in the *Large Catechism*.

The thought of the church is thus an organic part of Luther's account of the Holy Spirit. The life in the reality of the Spirit is an ecclesiastical existence, because the life of the individual in the realm of the Spirit is taken out of the narrow sphere of bondage to the law and placed in the wider sphere of God's universal act of agape. And that means that the church does not become an episode in the pious life of the individual, but the individual in his whole existence becomes a "part," a "member" of the organism of the church which is the eschatological people of God, the fruit of the eternal work of the Spirit down through the generations to the last day. The idea of the church in its organic connection with the testimony about the Spirit is thus a confirmation of the theocentric perspective of the Trinity doctrine in which this testimony is found.

The thought about the church leads us right into eschatology. For the account of the church in the *Large Catechism* has eschatological color. The church was the people of God who were assembled by the all-embracing, saving, eschatological act of the Spirit. The following parts of the third article of the Creed: the forgiveness of sin, the resurrection of the body, and the eternal life are in organic connection with the previous parts.

The section on forgiveness of sin is not an isolated particle between the other parts, but it forms the organic connecting link between the church and eschatology in a more narrow sense: the resurrection of the body and life everlasting. The forgiveness of sin imparted by the church here and now in the Word and sacrament is the beginning of an unbroken act of God, of which the conclusion is the resurrection and life everlasting. The forgiveness of sin is first seen in its proper light when it is placed in this all-embracing perspective which stretches from the creation to the consummation. The forgiveness in the *Large Catechism* is, therefore, not seen from the narrow horizon of human piety as something which is necessary in order to give the restless and religious soul "peace." This anthropocentric perspective, so natural to Melanchthon, is not present at all in the *Large Catechism*.

The forgiveness of sin is an eschatological reality. The forgiveness of sin is the beginning of God's expulsion of sin which is expected to be finished in the resurrection. The life in the forgiveness of sin is therefore filled with struggle and hope. Life in the forgiveness of sin is marked by a constant struggle against the remaining sin, and in this struggle it gives a constant hope about final victory. This is because the forgiveness of sin, given by the Word and the sacrament, is the work of the Holy Spirit, and as the work of the Spirit it is the admission into the totality of God's all-embracing, saving, eschatological act. The forgiveness of sin and the resurrection of the body are not two "parts" in the formula of the confession, which are joined together in a mechanical way, but they are the insoluble elements belonging together in one and the same unbroken act of God. In the same way justification and sanctification are not two separated psychological processes, between which it is necessary to find some kind of natural psychological explanation. But they are two aspects of the same unbroken act of God: the present and the future aspect of the sin-conquering work of the Spirit.

It may therefore be said that the whole explanation of the third article in the *Large Catechism* is eschatological in content. Both the church and the forgiveness are understood as eschatological realities. This is because they are seen as the reality of the Spirit's work in this eon. Thereby they prove the theocentric perspective of the Trinity doctrine which characterizes all Luther's interpretation of the Spirit.

Therefore, the explanation of the third article in the *Large Catechism* may well serve as a summary of the older Luther's total understanding of the Spirit and his work. Here we have an account of the Spirit which is not influenced by, and not even touched by the polemics against the enthusiasts and yet it summarizes all the main lines in Luther's understanding of the Spirit. Here we meet inner conflict as the place where the Spirit's work may be seen most clearly. Here we find the Spirit's sanctifying work explained as the mediation of Christ's real redeeming presence. Here we find sanctification understood not as a gradually increasing real righteousness but, because of the forgiveness of sin, as the constantly repeated putting to death of self and being raised with Christ, as a liberation from the bondage of one's own efforts to reach perfection, and as an admission into the all-embracing act of agape of God. All the Spirit's work is seen here in the sight of the Trinity. The Spirit is not an independently working, spiritual power which may be used by man striving for perfectness. The Spirit is the third person in God, insolubly one with the Triune God in his all-embracing, saving, eschatological act of love. The person of the Spirit is God himself.

The previous description of the older Luther's understanding of the Holy Spirit and his work has thus become confirmed in the presentation in the *Large Catechism*.

Therefore the continuity between the younger and the older Luther has become substantiated. The complete description of Luther's account of the Holy Spirit with which we concluded the first part of this work is also valid with respect to the older Luther. On one point, however, we have not as yet established this continuity, namely, with respect to the relation between the Spirit and his means, the Word and the sacrament. Therefore we still lack the decisive trait in the picture: the tense unity of the Spirit's reality and sovereignty. But this cannot be described before we have studied Luther's view of the relation between the Spirit and the Word as it is developed in contrast to the spiritualism of the enthusiasts. This is the subject of the next chapter.

Chapter V

THE ACCOUNT OF THE SPIRIT IN THE STRUGGLE WITH THE ENTHUSIASTS

The Fundamental Difference Between Luther and the Enthusiasts

When in the following we are to discuss Luther's polemics against the enthusiasts the main viewpoint is the same as we have used throughout the present work. The purpose of the comparison between Luther and the views with which he disagrees is not to give a complete historical explanation of the advocates of the opposing views but, through this comparison, to clarify Luther's own view. The views compared to those of Luther therefore have no independent value in this connection. It would have been otherwise in a purely historical work. Therefore they are not treated as independent objects of the presentation on the basis of special studies of the sources but exclusively as material of comparison to explain the peculiarity in Luther's thinking.

We must use the same method with respect to the enthusiasts. We do not study the movement of the enthusiasts as an historic phenomenon. We do not mention any special representative unless he is directly mentioned in the quotations. We are not attempting to give a historically "just" picture of the opponents of Luther. Whether Luther himself was "just" in his often rather severe judgment of them, we shall not decide here. We shall only treat the movement of the enthusiasts as a typical tendency which is diametrically opposed to Luther's understanding of Christianity. If the representatives of this tendency have had other tendencies, which might have considerably modified Luther's picture of them is another question. We shall leave that to the historians.

When in the following we discuss "the enthusiasts," we discuss a tendency which Luther definitely noticed as a typical tendency and which he fought. Therefore we also describe it as Luther saw it, that is, on the basis of Luther's descriptions of it, and not on the basis of the writings of the advocates of the tendency. Such a plan, which in an historical work is absolutely wrong, must be used here as the only one justified. It is not the enthusiasts as such who interest us but the tendency Luther saw in the enthusiasts, and which he opposed. This is not only an historical phenomenon, but a typical tendency which may manifest itself at any time, and which in its typical peculiarity is more clearly seen in Luther's polemics than in the writings of its own adherents. The last point is based on the fact that Luther in his polemics really considered the enthusiast movement as a peculiar type of piety different in principle from his own view of Christianity. By this he also strongly emphasized its peculiarity, while the representatives of the enthusiast movement often considered their own piety as consistent and original Lutheranism. It should also be admitted that a preacher does not always understand himself better than the hearer who is superior to the preacher in knowledge. In order to avoid all misunderstanding it must be stated at the outset that the enthusiasts who are treated in the subsequent discussion are enthusiasts according to Luther's view and not enthusiasts *"an sich."* Only in this sense do the enthusiasts have any value for our subject. Only in this manner can they be used to explain Luther's own thought.

Where did Luther find the decisive contrast between himself and the enthusiasts?

In the treatise against the heavenly prophets Luther says that the real error of the enthusiasts is that they turn the order of God upside down. We all agree that God deals with us in two ways, an inward and an outward. Outwardly he deals with us in the gospel and in the sacraments, and inwardly through the Spirit and his gifts. But the real struggle is about the order existing between God's outward and inward dealing with us. God, however, has decided that the outward "parts" must come first and the inward afterwards and dependent upon the outward.[1] This order is changed by the enthusiasts. Not only do they ask for the inward before the outward; but that which God has arranged as something outward, they turn into something inward and vice versa.

What is back of this disagreement about God's "order" of the inward and outward? It might seem as if Luther's reason for this order was closely related to the doctrine of grace by Occam. The relation between the outward sign and the inward grace seems only to be a positive order by God, and as such it should be accepted for what it is without further proof. Sometimes these thoughts have also been associated with Scotistic or Occamistic positivism. However, this interpretation of Luther's statement about God's order and plans does not set forth any real understanding of the contrast between Luther and the enthusiasts. Aside from the greater or lesser possibility that Luther has taken over the expressions about God's order and plan from Scotistic or Occamistic metaphysics, such a formal similarity is not a proof of a real agreement. A closer observation reveals that Luther's thoughts about God's order are not as Occamistic as they seem at first.

The order of which Luther speaks is not only a joint order of an inward grace and an outward sign. Back of it is a higher and more comprehensive order. This has to do with the "order of salvation" using a later Lutheran expression. In *Deuteronomion Mosi cum annotationibus*, 1525, Luther gives a detailed presentation of this order in close agreement with the thought in the treatise against the heavenly prophets. This order begins with *the law* which precedes the gospel and which convicts of sin, thus destroying man and creating the longing for another Word which is able to make alive. This other Word giving life is the gospel. When that is heard the Holy Spirit is granted as a gift. And it is the Spirit who works the

---

[1] *W. A.*, L, 245, 1 (Schmalkald art.); XV, 565, 31 ff. (Rörer, 1524); XVII, 1, 269, 28 ff. (Rörer, 1525); XVIII, 136, 9 ff. (1525); XX, 790, 2 ff. (Rörer, 1527); XXXI, 2, 265, 21 ff.; 654, 5 ff. (Lauterbach, 1527-30); XXXI, 1, 341, 31 ff. (Veit Dietrich, 1530); XL, 1, 142, 1 ff.; 151, 5 ff.; 156, 14 ff.; 330, 2 ff.; 333, 10 ff.; 336, 3 ff. (Rörer, 1531); XXXIII, 279, 26 ff. (Aurifaber, 1531); XL, 2, 410, 11 ff. (Rörer, 1532); XLVI, 426, 13 ff.; 476, 6 ff. (Rörer, 1538).

justifying faith in whom he wants to. That does not mean that the Spirit necessarily accompanies the Word which is heard. The Spirit is not dependent upon the Word, but retains his sovereignty over the Word.[2] Here we note that the polemic against the enthusiasts does not make Luther ignore the thought about the sovereignty of the Spirit and the insufficiency of the outward Word. On the contrary, this thought is strongly emphasized in the midst of the polemics. Thus Luther's opposition to the enthusiasts has not forced him to yield his previous "Augustinian" position. On the other hand it is always in and by the outward Word that the Spirit performs his work, wherever he pleases. That the Spirit works through the Word means that the justifying faith in the Word is not our own work. For this reason it releases and makes the conscience quiet and the heart glad. It is the Spirit himself who overcomes the trembling of inner conflict before the wrath of God and teaches us to pray "Abba, Father!" It is only when man is under the power of the Spirit that he becomes *active* in his relation to God. But it should be noted that this activity is not directed toward God, for before God man can only receive. Instead, the activity is in the direction from God against the world, that is, *ad extra*. The activity within the realm of the Spirit is not man's activity before God but his participation in God's activity in the world. The first step, therefore, in this activity is the continued preaching of the Word by which we ourselves were saved. Thus we ourselves heard the Word from others who had heard it and then preached it to us. The preaching of the Word is the exercise of the regime of Christ. Therefore, the activity into which the Spirit directs us when he makes us preach the gospel means an expansion of the boundaries of the kingdom of Christ. But participation in the government of Christ by the preaching of the gospel invariably makes us take up the *cross*. For the gospel always stirs the hatred of the world. This cross serves as a purification of faith so that it is hardened into hope. Not only the world about us, but our entire old man strug-

---

2 *W. A.*, XIV, 681, 20; also XVIII, 602, 14; 695, 30 (1525); XVII, 1, 125, 10 ff.; 283, 2 (Rörer, 1525); XVI, 597, 8 ff. (Rörer-Bugenhagen, 1526); XX, 790, 2 ff. (Rörer, 1527); XXXIX, 1, 383, 25; 406, 15 (*1. disp. ctr. Antinom.*, 1537); XXXIX, 1, 579, 1 ff. (*3. disp. ctr. Antinom.*, 1538).

gles against this activity of the Spirit in us. The next step, therefore, is the mortification of the old man. This struggle against the
old man is done by the Spirit himself in order to complete his own
purpose. But the activity of the Spirit is not only of an "ecclesiastical" type. It is not only a matter of the preaching of the gospel, it is
concerned about all good works in favor of our neighbor. The
mortification is, therefore, followed by the third step, the good
works by which faith witnesses to the neighbor. These works are
not man's own, but those of the Spirit.

This is the true order in a Christian's life. Of course, these different steps are not to be understood according to a methodical
scheme of different succeeding stages in the development of the
religious man. Where the order of salvation is understood in this
way, the perspective is anthropocentric. The synthesis between the
different elements is here the development of the pious man. To
Luther these steps are the elements of one, single, concrete act of
God. The perspective is theocentric. This causes the elements in
the life of the individual to be constantly joined together because
God continues to work. Thus it is not stated that the work of the
law belongs only to a single episode of man's life (e.g., before and
during the struggle of penitence). Neither does the mortification
belong to a definite period. But the whole *ordo*, the particular steps
of which we have followed, is one, single, concrete act of God. All
the elements of this act are included in that which takes place when
God by the Spirit speaks his Word. This act of God, therefore, has
the direction of all acts of God. It begins in God himself from
whom the Word proceeds and it ends with the neighbor, with the
creation of God, which is sought by his agape. It is the direction
from heaven to earth which characterizes this *ordo*.

Here we notice how Luther puts something into his words about
God's definite "order" which goes far beyond a Scotistic arrangement of the work of inward grace and outward signs. To be certain,
this arrangement may be found in the thinking of Luther. But it
is not an isolated fact based upon an incidental order of God. The
connection of the inward work of the Spirit and the outward sign
and the succession between them are based on the more compre-

hensive order which we have described here as the order of salvation. It is by virtue of this more comprehensive order that the outward sign always must precede the inward work of the Spirit and not just because of an arbitrarily arranged "covenant." Or better stated: the order to which we must submit—as Luther stated it in *De servo arbitrio*: fear, love, and worship—is not only the narrow order of the relation between the outward Word and the inward work of grace, but it is first of all the more comprehensive order of salvation. And this order which we have learned from *Deuteronomion Mosi* and *Wider die himmlischen Propheten*, is nothing else than the total view of the Spirit's work, which we have attempted to set forth in the whole previous development of our work. In Luther's *ordo salutis* we have been able to follow all the individual parts of this total view: the Spirit's office of correction by the law in inner conflict, the overcoming of inner conflict by the Spirit through the Word of the gospel, and the Spirit's free and sovereign dominion in Word and sacrament, by which he gives the faith where and when he pleases. This work of the Spirit is a unity of righteousness and sanctification with a double content of sanctification, that is, the mortification of the old man and the new man's participation of God's activity in the world. No decisive part is lacking here. The main point is the direction of the theocentric perspective which we have met everywhere in our study of Luther's account of the Holy Spirit. It is the direction from heaven to earth, from God to his creation. The method we first established in understanding Luther's polemics against the enthusiasts from a comprehensive total view has thus been proven in the documents of the polemics itself. It is Luther's own method in this polemics not to stop at the externals but to trace the contrast all the way back to the total view. And just as this total view in the polemic against the enthusiasts is described as a theocentric *ordo salutis*, it is in close harmony with the total view of the Spirit and his work, which we have found outside of this polemic.

The *ordo salutis* of the enthusiasts Luther places over against his own total view. Their view has an entirely different structure. It begins with mortification, which is divided into many different steps. This mortification is the prerequisite for both justification and the outpouring of the Spirit. No one can attain to righteousness unless he has first traveled the entire way of mortification. Then only does the Holy Spirit come. The enthusiasts therefore do not receive the Spirit by hearing the Word, which they on the contrary despise as something outward. This is because they constantly find sin in those who live by the Word. They believe, and that is what is behind their theory of mortification, that they must put sin to death before they can receive the Spirit. But that really means that they re-establish the way of works. For mortification becomes a perfect preparation for grace by human effort. With this view of mortification as our own perfect preparation for the coming of the Spirit it follows that Christ is only thought of as an example. Faith in Christ is changed into *imitatio*. The spiritualistic doctrine of the Lord's Supper is closely connected with this nomistic thought of *imitatio*. The remembrance of Christ which really is the remembrance of the gospel about him, that is, the reception of the living Christ himself as a gift, Karlstadt makes into an imitation-exercise. The remembrance of Christ which is a spiritual (but *outward*) remembrance, because it is the gift of the Spirit, is by Karlstadt made into a human devotion, an effort, and therefore it becomes a remembrance of the "flesh" (even though it is very "fervent"). The nomistic element in Karlstadt appears most clearly in the view of the Supper. The suffering of Christ is not to him a present reality which is truly given by the Spirit, but a mere idea which is exhibited to us for contemplation as through a glass and something to see and smell and enjoy as a food, for it is not given to us as our real food, as our personal possession. That which signifies the "order" of the enthusiasts is the fact that they begin with mortification and conclude with the Spirit. The outpouring of the Spirit becomes the result of the finished mortification. The outpouring of the Spirit is not understood as the source of mortification (as the source of all Christian life), but as its effect. Luther correctly describes this piety as a new *larva operum*, as a new assertion of the importance of the free will and the works in relation to God. All this piety is of the law. The direction of this movement is from the earth upward. Through the exercise of mortification man is to work himself upward to the possession of the Spirit. Luther says that the enthusiasts do not teach how the Spirit comes to us but how we may come to the Spirit. This is a striking expression for the difference between the two views of the Spirit. It is from this point of view that we must understand the indifference of the enthusiasts to the outward Word and the sacraments. The outward Word and the sacraments are the bridge or the ladder on which the Spirit comes down to us. But he who intends to work himself up to the Spirit has naturally no interest in a way that leads from heaven downward.

It is this difference between a theocentric-evangelical and an anthropocentric-nomistic total view which Luther states when he says that the enthusiasts turn the right *ordo Christianae vitae* upside down. It is on the basis of this fundamental difference that all points of disagreement between Luther and the enthusiasts must be seen. It is not just a coincidence that Luther opposes the imitation-piety of the enthusiasts as the decisive difference. With keen accuracy Luther has struck at this point as the source of the enthusiasts' declarations about the Spirit. For this enthusiasm made the Spirit the crown of the piety of the law, the reward of the perfect, instead of the source and spring of the gospel, the comfort of the poor. Luther exposes the central tendency of the movement of the enthusiasts when he points to its nomistic order of salvation. This struggle is not concerned with externals, but with the heart of the gospel, whether we as Christians are to accept Christ as a gift or to work ourselves up to him.

On the basis of this fundamental difference we must understand the strong emphasis on the outward sign which characterizes Luther's words about the Spirit in his polemics against the enthusiasts. In the following section we turn to this antispiritualism of Luther.

The Spirit and the External Sign

When the enthusiasts wanted to separate the granting of the Holy Spirit from the external sign, the Word and the sacrament, it was because they placed the Spirit in sharp contrast to all things visible and bodily. It was the Spirit's own essence to belong to the world of the invisible. The Spirit cannot be directly mediated by the outward means. For these means are in their whole nature essentially different from all spiritual realities and, in regard to the spiritual, they can hardly be given more than a symbolic function. In the question of the Supper this spiritualism was bound to become an important problem. To the spiritualistic concept the doctrine of the real presence necessarily got to appear as an improper materializing of the spiritual. In the words "Flesh is of no avail," (John 6:63) they expressed their distrust in every form of piety which emphasized the outward rite. Flesh got to signify an all-inclusive expression for everything outward, visible, and bodily.[3] Against that Luther strongly maintains that the Spirit, where he performs his comforting and life-giving work, always manifests himself in visible and outward signs.

What is back of this different valuation of the outward means?

We first stress the fact that Luther holds there is no metaphysical connection between the Spirit and the outward signs. The older Luther does not know a doctrine of the means of grace by virtue of which the outward sign in itself is given a divine power which, through the sign, inevitably comes into the possession of the receiver. It is true that in speaking of the Word and the sacrament both the older and the younger Luther often use the concept of an instrument. The Word is the tool of the Spirit. Or the Spirit is given in, by, through, and with the Word. The expressions for the relation between the Spirit and his means varies almost without limit.[4] But this great variation in the forms in which Luther de-

---

[3] *W. A.*, XXIII, 193, 28 (1527); also 173, 25 ff.; 261, 8 ff. XXVI, 436, 12 ff. (1528); XX, 759, 6 ff. (Rörer, 1527); XXXI, 2, 51, 8 ff. (Lauterbach, 1527-30); XXXVI, 629, 3 ff. (Rörer, 1532).

[4] *W. A.*, XVIII, 692, 20 (1525); XIV, 663, 24 (1525); XXX, 1, 188, 12; L, 629, 4 (1539); 647, 6. XI, 52, 3 ff. (Rörer, 1523); XV, 480, 3 (Rörer, 1524); XXX, 1, 54, 20 (Rörer, 1528); *per:* XI, 54, 15 ff.; 85, 1 ff. (Rörer, 1523); XVII, 1, 135, 12 ff.; 245, 21 ff. (Rörer, 1525); XL, 1, 593, 4 ff. (Rörer, 1531); XXXIX, 1, 217, 17 ff.; *(Promotionsdisp.,* Palladius and Tileman, 1537); XLVI, 413, 9 ff.; 475, 13 ff. (Rörer, 1538); *cum:* XV, 669, 17 ff. (Rörer, 1524); XL, 1, 571, 10 ff.; 572, 10 ff.; 574, 11 ff. (Rörer, 1531); *adfert, adducit, secum:* XV, 467, 33 ff. (Rörer, 1524); XVII, 1, 405, 15 ff. (Rörer, 1525); XX, 722, 13 ff. (Rörer, 1527); XL, 1, 336, 6 ff. (Rörer, 1531); XLI, 427, 23 (Rörer, 1535); *pons et semita:* XVII, 1, 125 (Rörer, 1525); *vehiculum:* XX, 779, 20 ff. (Rörer, 1527); *janua et fenestra:* XX, 451, 7 (Rörer, 1526).

scribes the connection between Spirit and the Word (sacrament) already clearly indicates that he does not understand the connection as an inner metaphysical function. It is not possible on the basis of the different prepositions and figurative expressions used by Luther to read into them any definite metaphysical doctrine of the means of grace either of the Thomistic or of the Franciscan type. Now the Word is seen as an instrument in the hands of the Spirit by which the merits of Christ are given or the church sanctified, and then it is seen as an instrument in the hand of the Triune God by which the Spirit is given. Thus in the one case the Spirit is *over* the Word, and in the other case the Spirit is *in* the Word. And in the last case "in the Word" sometimes indicates an instrumental relation, the Spirit comes *by* the Word, and sometimes an accompanying relation, the Spirit comes *with* the Word (or the Word brings the Spirit with it). Sometimes illustrations are used which seem to partake both of the concept of instrument and of the idea of accompanying. This is the case when we say that the Word is a vehicle of the Spirit. It is the door or the window through which the Spirit comes to us, or the bridge or path on which he moves.

To draw out of these very variant expressions a definite metaphysical concept of the connections between Spirit and the Word is a hopeless task. The only thing these expressions explain is that Luther never thinks of any metaphysical, rationally understood, inner relation between the Spirit and his means. Luther's view has nothing to do with either the Thomistic or with the Franciscan concept. If by the aid of the "instrumental" expressions the attempt has been made to place Luther near a Thomistic concept, then all the expressions that illustrate the ideas of accompaniment may just as well be used as a proof of kinship with the Franciscan view. That both types of expressions and also a number of other expressions are used by Luther at random in a carefree manner shows that it is not right on the basis of these different expressions to ascribe to him a definite metaphysical concept of the connection between the Spirit and the Word. By the presentation of Luther's total view of the work of the Spirit, we know that he does not consider the Spirit as a power which by the aid of the means of grace is placed at the disposition of man. The Spirit, also when he is considered as *donum*, is viewed by Luther as a personal being. The Spirit is God himself, present in his own person, drawing us into the totality of his saving, eschatological act. Consequently, the Spirit cannot be considered as confined in the means of grace through a metaphysical theory by which the Spirit is placed at our disposition.

It is not correct, as it has been stated, that Luther gradually made closer the connection between the Spirit and the Word and thereby—at least to some extent—reduced his original "Augustinian" assertion of the sovereignty of the Spirit and the insufficiency of the outward Word. It is incorrect to interpret Luther's strong emphasis on the outward Word in that way. On the contrary, we have already seen that the emphasis on the outward signs does not contain a tendency which is against the "Augustinian" position of the sovereignty of the Spirit and the insufficiency of the outward Word; but this emphasis is closely connected with this position. Even in the midst of the most central connection in Luther's polemics with the enthusiasts, and in the insoluble unity with the thoughts about the insufficiency of the outward Word and the sacrament, we have met the principle *ubi et quando visum est Deo,* and this thought did not disappear after 1525, but we found it as late as in the disputations against the antinomians in the years after 1530.[5] Luther found no contradiction between the anti-enthusiastic assertion of the outward Word's *necessity* and pre-destinate emphasis on this necessary Word's *insufficiency.* Wherever these two tendencies, in clear opposition to Luther himself, are considered as opposing one another and competing for the leading position, we reveal that we have not understood Luther's view of the Word of the Holy Spirit. Luther never, not even in his most heated debates with the enthusiasts, viewed the Word and the sacrament as means of grace which contain grace in themselves

---

[5] *W. A.,* XVIII, 602, 11 (1525); 781, 33; XIV, 726, 33 (1525); also XI, 53, 11 ff.; 112, 10 ff. (Rörer, 1523); XV, 565, 35 ff. (Rörer, 1524); XVI, 131, 10 ff. (Rörer, 1524); XVI, 328, 10 ff. (Rörer, 1525); XX, 395, 16 ff. (Rörer, 1527); XXXI, 2, 450, 6 ff. (Lauterbach, 1527-30); XXXIII, 145, 23 ff. (Aurifaber, 1531-32); XLV, 310, 6 ff. (Rörer, 1537); XXXIX, 2, 356, 10 ff. (*Promotionsdisp.,* Petr. Hegemon, 1545).

in such a way that the principle *ubi et quando visum est Deo* should be even slightly attacked or rendered superfluous.

When we compare the idea about indispensability of the external sign with the basic difference between Luther and the enthusiasts which was discussed in the previous section, the fact of the matter becomes very obvious. The thought about the means of grace as a metaphysical unity of the Spirit and the outward sign is an anthropocentric thought. It is certainly a clear contrast to the spiritualism of the enthusiasts, inasmuch as it is strongly centered about the outward signs which are of no real interest to the enthusiasts. But it is a protest against the spiritualism within its own anthropocentric outlook. When the means of grace is understood as being united metaphysically with the Spirit, the Spirit is understood as being a divine power which by the means of grace is placed at the disposition of man in his efforts to reach God. The difference between spiritualism and antispiritualism is then only the understanding of how to get possession of this divine power. The enthusiasts point to *imitatio* and *mortificatio,* the antispiritualists to the effective sacrament. In contrast to the former view, the latter may seem more genuinely evangelical. It emphasizes "grace" much more and God working alone. But in the final analysis the difference is not very great. For where the means of grace itself contains the grace, we can hardly avoid to understand it as *opus operatum.* Where the effectiveness of the means of grace is considered as an exclusion of the principle of *ubi et quando visum est Deo,* there the sacramental piety becomes no less work-righteousness than imitation and mortification. The whole consideration in both cases is seen from the point of view of man's efforts in reaching God. It is only the means which man may choose to use that are different. The total view of Luther, however, was characterized by a completely different perspective. The work of the Spirit was not seen from the point of view of man's way upward to God but from the opposite view of God's way downward to man. The work of the Spirit was not understood as a part of man's pious endeavors but as a part of an unbroken act of God in behalf of man. Therefore it is impossible for Luther to think of the Spirit as a divine power which by an inner metaphysical tie is continued in the outward means of grace. Luther understands the relation between the Spirit and Word in such a way that the perspective continues to be theocentric and that the Spirit's work is seen exclusively as a part of an unbroken act of God. That means that the Spirit's sovereignty over the "means of grace" must be fully retained and Luther did this consistently. At no time did Luther lose sight of the fact that the Spirit, which manifests itself by the outward means of grace, is the sovereign, living God acting personally.

But when Luther does not think of any inner metaphysical connection between the Spirit and the Word (sacrament), but maintains the sovereignty of the Spirit over the external sign (*eusserlich ding*), which in itself is powerless, what does he mean by his strong emphasis on the indispensability of the outward sign? To answer this question we must turn to the well-known concept of *signum* which we found in the young Luther. The Word and the sacraments are signs of the revelation under whose veil God is present. When Luther maintained an insoluble connection between the Spirit and his outward means, it is not right to think of this connection through the concept of an effective means of grace. For this concept belongs to an anthropocentric view. Wherever this concept is used to explain Luther's thoughts about the Spirit and the Word, perhaps even with more or less striking parallels of different forms of scholastic, sacramental doctrine, the understanding is hopelessly bungled and contrasts and problems are read into Luther which are not found there at all. They have simply been brought into the picture by using this wrong category. The concept, which in the theocentric view takes the place of the concept of the effective means of grace, and which does not contain any opposition to the thought of the sovereignty of the Spirit and the insufficiency of the outward Word, is the concept of the sign of revelation.

In the first part of our work we have already studied the *signum* concept and its significance in Luther's theology. We saw there that the *signum* concept expressed a real presence of Christ even in his humanity and thereby our whole existence has been drawn into the work of God by Christ and by this our life received eschatological quality. In the *signum* concept, as we learned to know it at first, we found a double function. On the one hand it was a sign of revelation. The sign as a part of Christ's humanity reveals God in his presence by hiding his majesty under the protecting veil of Christ's humanity. As a sign of revelation the sign prevented all loose speculations about God's majesty which is the false concept of God in pious legalism, and it showed us God as he truly is, God who for us is in Christ. But the same sign was also an instrumental sign, the means by which God made our existence conform to Christ and gave it eschatological quality. The sign always has within itself this double function. When it reveals God to us as he truly is it simultaneously changes our own life. This means that God who is revealed in the sign is the God who in the sign has come right into our own existence. We cannot dispense with either of the two views of the concept of the sign. They may be emphasized with different degrees of strength. While in the young Luther and especially in his doctrine of baptism the instrumental function of the sign is emphasized very strongly, it is the revelation function which in the older Luther gets the strongest emphasis. The *signum* concept here is not only used in the sacrament as a sign of confirmation of God's *promissio* but it becomes a summarizing designation for the outward means which the Spirit uses, both the preaching and the sacrament, yes, even the incarnation itself as it is continued in the Word and the sacrament. As a sign of revelation the sign, as it appears most clearly in the sign of the Supper, is a visible pledge of God's (Christ's) own visible but real presence. The main emphasis is in the fact that where the visible sign is, there God is truly present wrapped up in the garment of the sign. This we must not doubt.[6]

The sign therefore becomes a challenge both to reason which, by way of speculation, and to piety which, by way of works, en-

---

[6] *W. A.*, XI, 54, 7 (Rörer, 1523); XVI, 210, 4 (Rörer, 1525); also 174, 4 ff.; 178, 8 ff.; 179, 5 ff.; 214, 4 ff.; 424, 7 ff.; XX, 529, 11 ff.; 389, 7 ff. (Rörer, 1526); XLII, 184, 14 ff.; 185, 5 ff.; 295, 32 ff.; 668, 32 ff.; XLIII, 32, 21 ff.; XLIV, 685, 18 ff. *(Genesiskommentaren).*

deavor to reach God. These attempts are hopeless because by way of speculation and works you only find God in his unveiled majesty, as the *Deus nudus* of the law. And to meet God in this way means to die. The sign signifies that God is present in another way. God is not there as a God for us where our flighty thoughts or our own chosen works might decide to place him. He is only there where God himself has *chosen* to be in our midst in our own impotent nature. God may truly be found in the very *definite,* concrete, outward signs chosen by God. External signs—in all their poverty and insignificance, in their concrete appearance as an unimportant straw—obstruct all ways of our own to God, and they only leave open God's own concrete, unforeseen, incalculable, and inexplicable way. Where we depart from these outward signs, such as baptism, preaching, the Lord's Supper, it always means that we are beginning to enter the dangerous way of speculation or work toward *Deus nudus.*[7]

The sign-concept as an expression for God's freely determined presence here on earth in "our nature" prevents all dominion of the law in our relation to God. Every endeavor from earth toward heaven is swept aside by that God who from his heaven seeks us here on earth. To Luther the sign-concept is a means by which to express the gospel's way of salvation, that we are not to run after Christ in heaven, but that Christ runs after us here on the earth. It is important here to notice that it is the sign's visibility and outwardness which make its function in behalf of the gospel possible. Luther often uses the description *certum signum*. In contrast to the ideas and speculation which are "flitting" and uncertain the outward signs are solid and immovable. In their outwardness and firmness the signs are also *public* in contrast to the private way of salvation of the piety of the law. When we are under the law each one finds himself on his own step on the ladder toward God. Therefore we cannot really have anything external in common with others. The emphasis of this type of piety will be found in the inward things, in the private life. It becomes "a Christianity for

---

7 *W. A.*, XL, 2, 329, 7 (Rörer, 1532). XLII, 10, 3 ff.; 11, 19 ff.; 625, 7 ff.; 635, 11 ff.; XLIV, 95, 31 ff.; 96, 2 ff.; XVI, 179, 1 ff.; 210, 4 ff.; 212, 6 ff.; 424, 7 ff.

me only." One enters the monastery, another makes a trip to Compostella. They all seek a corner where they are able to develop their own private piety. This is the way the sects get started. But the signs of revelation, which are God's way to us, are public. They seek us all where there is no distinction between us as to our distress and our perdition. Therefore the gospel is not preached in closed circles but *in media civitate*. This public aspect of the signs underscores their firmness. When God comes to us he does not hide himself in a corner where only the especially initiated or those especially fortunate may find him. No, he appears publicly before all. It is *so* public that the representatives of legalistic piety at all times are provoked that they are compelled to mix with such bad people who are gathered for such a public worship. The sign of revelation is a sign of the *church*. While it is a work of the presence of God in the world it is simultaneously a work of the presence of the church before all sects and parties, the sect of the pope as well. The churchly aspect of the sign emphasizes its visibility in contrast to the hidden spirituality of pious sectarianism.

But in order that the sign shall be the true sign of revelation it is not only necessary that it be visible and external, that it be in our world, and that it be accessible for us so that our reason and our piety do not by-pass the sign and on pure spiritual wings flutter up to heaven on their own ways. The sign must be known simply as *sign*. Not every visible or external thing reveals God. If the sign is not visible as a sign differing from the many other visible and external things which are not signs, the result will be that we just "flutter" about among the many visible things selecting, according to our own whims, the "signs" which God never has ordained as his signs. The visible and external sign must be separated from all visible and external things, which are not signs at all. The Word helps to fix the limit of the sign. The sign therefore consists essentially of something outward and visible and of the Word which marks out this outward and visible element. This is the case with respect to the bread and the wine in the Supper. By virtue of his ubiquity Christ is present everywhere. But he is not present everywhere as a sign. As a sign, which indicates God's *gracious* presence, he is only present where by his Word he has separated the definite outward signs of grace, the bread and the wine, from all other food and drink as conveyers of his truly present body and blood.[8] This is also the case with every sign of revelation.[9] The Word itself (understood as an outward thing), the office of preaching (or the Scripture), is also a sign of revelation. That an ordinary human word is God's Word is not something we understand as a matter of course. The human word which designates itself as the Word of God, outwardly seen, is not different from other human words. Therefore it must be said by God himself that it is God's Word. The Word as an outward affair has the same need of the interpreting and demarcating Word as that of the bread and the wine in the Supper and the water in baptism. Not all bread and wine and water are holy, and not all human words are God's Word. The office of preaching is instituted by God to preach the gospel from the Scripture. It is based on the clear command of God in the same manner as baptism and the Supper. This commissioning Word of God demarcates the preaching office as a sign of revelation.

The Augustinian definition of the sacrament, *accedit verbum ad elementum et fit sacramentum,* which Luther valuates so highly, covers the whole concept of the sign of revelation. By virtue of God's own will expressed in the Word, the sign is distinguished from all other visible reality as the place of God's gracious presence among us. The Word here has exactly the same function as in the sacramental doctrine of the young Luther. The Word which institutes the sign has the character of *promissio.* It is because of the promise of God that Christ is present under the bread and the wine, and the Spirit present in the Word of the sermon. It is clearly seen how the Lutheran concept of the sign separates itself from the Roman Catholic concept of the sacrament as a *signum efficax.* Also to Luther the sign is a *signum certum.* But the certainty to him is not a metaphysical arrangement by virtue of which

---

[8] *W. A.,* XXIII, 151, 25 (1527); also XX, 387, 11 ff., 400, 23 ff. (Rörer, 1526); XXX, 1, 223, 28 ff. (1528).

[9] *W. A.,* XLV, 447, 13 ff.; XVI, 211, 2 ff.; 304, 5 ff. (Rörer, 1525); XX, 387, 24 ff.; 400, 25 ff. (Rörer, 1526).

grace always follows with the visible sign. The certainty does not consist in the fact that the Word of consecration produces a metaphysical change in the outward element, or places it in a metaphysical arrangement by which it becomes an effective sacrament. The certainty is in the fact that the Word is accepted as God's personal Word of promise to us about his own personal presence. The sign of revelation does not as the "means of grace" mediate a divine power, but as a sign of promise it mediates God himself.

The sign of revelation therefore reveals God, but it reveals him by enclosing him as a veil. Only hidden behind the veil of the sign of revelation is it possible for God—without ceasing in the fullest sense to be God—to be personally and truly present with us. The sign of revelation is therefore not something in addition to the gospel but it is the gospel itself in the actualized form. In the very fact of the sign of revelation the divine agape is made manifest. In close connection with the thoughts about the signs of revelation the separation between *Deus nudus* and *Deus involutus* is therefore placed between the God of the gospel and the God of the law. Outside of the signs of revelation God is always present only in his naked majesty as the God of the law who puts to death. As the God of the gospel, God is that God who for our sakes humbled himself so that he put on the poor garment of the sign of revelation, that is, our nature. In this descent to our life God associates with us as his dear children. External signs are as a mask or a veil God puts on, or a lattice through which he shows himself, so that behind such a protecting cover he may be in our midst as our helper and not as the judge who puts us to death. However, that also means that God in his gracious presence cannot be demonstrated or singled out. He can only be *believed*.[10]

We are now able to see why the concept "effective means of grace" must contain a contrast to the predestinarian thoughts of Luther about the sovereignty of the Spirit and the outward sign's insufficiency, while the concept of the sign of revelation does not

---

[10] *W. A.*, XXXI, 2, 655, 6 (Rörer, 1530-31); XLV, 522, 7 (Cruciger, 1537); XXXIII, 189, 32 ff. (Aurifaber, 1531-32); XLV, 184, 9 ff. (Rörer, 1537). T. Harnack, pp. 41-56 and 97-113.

contain such a contrast, but on the contrary it is closely bound together with this predestinarian tendency. The effective means of grace "contains" a divine power, while God himself is really distant because "the power" is there to aid us in getting closer to God. This concept does not permit the outward organ's effectiveness being made a problem. It is even more important that it *need* not be a problem, because a divine power is not God himself; it is not *living*, it is not *Lord*, but a *means*, a *cause* over which God has permitted man to dispose. It is very different with respect to the sign of revelation. In the sign of revelation God himself is present covered by the veil of the outward sign. This means that God is present as the living One, the predestinating—as the Lord. This again means: God is present in such a way that man does not get power into his own hand, rather God takes man into his hand. The Spirit is unconditionally a free master over that which takes place in and with the sign of revelation. This fact does not permit itself to be confined and directed by man through any form of metaphysical explanation. God is truly present as the hidden God. He cannot in any way be singled out, but only believed. Where faith does not lay hold on the living One in the Word, there the Word is only word, only an "outward affair." For the outward veil is the protective cover which makes it possible for faith to lay hold on the living God himself, but only through faith. And the Spirit is the unconditional master over faith.

Here we again meet the thoughts of the young Luther's sacramental doctrine. It is true now as it was then that the "hiatus" in Luther's doctrine of the sacraments is something *essential*, if we are not to say *the* essential point. Just as emphatically as Luther maintains the necessity of the outward organs of the Spirit, just as clearly does he maintain their insufficiency. They are necessary as the protective cover of God's majesty. Without this protective cover we should be devoured if we are to meet the consuming fire of the naked God. As the cover of the majesty of God they are in themselves nothing. It is *God* who back of the cover is present as the sovereign, acting One. He alone governs over the "effect" of these organs. Only where he by his Spirit produces faith, which in the outward signs that both cover and reveal God lays hold on the living God himself or rather on which the living God lays hold, only there is the *effect* brought about. The unity of the necessity and insufficiency of the sign is therefore found in the concept of the sign of revelation itself in its contrast to the concept "effective means of grace"!

By the aid of the concept of a sign of revelation we have been able to see the reason for Luther's emphasis on the outward signs over against the pure spirituality of the enthusiasts. Where the outward signs are avoided, there you associate with *Deus nudus,* that is, there you are within the system of the law. Only where we adhere to outward signs is our expectation directed to God of the Gospel. The basic difference between Luther and the enthusiasts, as we have seen, was between the different orders of salvation, the anthropocentric order of the law and the theocentric order of the gospel. We have seen how this emphasis on the outward did not exclude, but rather included the understanding of the Spirit's sovereignty and the insufficiency of the outward sign. When all this has been said we only need to draw the conclusion which was present all the time during the presentation of Luther's doctrine of the signs of revelation. The conclusion is that the signs of revelation belong to Christ and the understanding of them is a Christological problem. Only as Christology does the doctrine about the signs of revelation have a full meaning. The question of the connection between the signs of revelation and Christology will be treated in the next section.

The External Sign and Christ

What was said previously about the signs of revelation may also be said about Christ without any modification. The humanity of Christ is also a concrete, earthly reality through which God reveals himself by veiling himself under it. And the humanity of Christ needs the Word in order to limit it toward all other humanity. The humanity of Christ as the revelation of God can only be retained in the faith which is given by the Spirit. Everywhere the description of the sign of revelation corresponds to Luther's

Christology. Or rather, the description of the sign of revelation is an indispensable part of Luther's Christology. This connection we must study more thoroughly.

Christ as *Deus incarnatus* is the real sign of revelation. Luther at times uses the word *signum* about Christ. In the description of Christ as *Deus incarnatus* we rediscover all the lines of the sign of revelation. The main point in Luther's Christology may be found in Colossians 2:9, "For in him dwelleth all the fulness of the God-head bodily," which may be connected with John 14:9, "He that hath seen me hath seen the Father." The Christology of Luther is completely expressed in these two Scripture passages. The humanity of Christ is God's sign of revelation under whose protective cover God's whole protective majesty is near as God to us. Therefore the way of the humanity of Christ as God's way to us is also the rejection of every way from man to God. The way of speculation and work is blocked by the humanity of Christ. There are countless instances, especially in the sermons of Luther, where (with[11] or without[12] reference to John 14:9) the *Deus nudus* of speculation is placed before the *Deus involutus* of incarnation as the proper ladder of Jacob. Here the humanity of Christ is not as Ritschl liked to interpret Luther—concerning his ethicoreligious personality. As an example this is seen in Luther's tendency to dwell on the child in the cradle (and on the crucified One) when he speaks about the humanity of Christ. The concept of Christ's humanity does not, as in the interpretation of Ritschl, contain any concealed criticism of the orthodox doctrine of the "two natures" of Christ, but it presupposes it. "Christ's humanity," however has no meaning in Luther's thinking before it is correlated with the concept "the divinity of Christ" (understood from the orthodox point of view). It is only by the contrast to the hidden divine majesty that the concept of Christ's humanity receives its real

---

[11] *W. A.*, XVI, 144, 1 ff. (Rörer, 1524); XX, 603, 5 ff.; 605, 9 ff.; 727, 6 ff. (Rörer, 1527); XXVIII, 101, 1-12 (Rörer, 1528); XXXIII, 78, 39 ff.; 79, 27 ff.; 80, 1 ff.; 136, 11 ff. (Aurifaber, 1531-32); XL, 2, 300, 16 ff. (Rörer, 1532); XXXI, 2, 38, 23-39, 5; 561, 17 ff. (Lauterbach, 1527-30); XLV, 512, 25 ff.; 515, 21 ff. (Cruciger, 1537).

[12] *W. A.*, XI, 51, 20 ff. (Rörer, 1523); 52, 1 ff. (id.); XVI, 425, 3 ff. (Rörer, 1525); XXXI, 2, 516, 15-27 (Lauterbach, 1527-30); XL, 1, 75, 9-79, 14 (Rörer, 1531); XXXIII, 81, 22-82, 3 (Aurifaber, 1531-32.

content. *Therefore* Luther prefers the child in the cradle as an illustration of this humanity, an illustration which for Ritschl would have no meaning at all. The child in the cradle does not mean humanity in its highest development of moral and religious ability pointing toward God. It means humanity in its total impotence and humility as a cover for the majesty of God, the humanity, "the flesh" as an expression of God's self-humiliation on his way to us. Luther's concept of Christ's humanity presupposes and includes the confession of his divinity.

This is most clearly seen in the doctrine of the Supper which in Luther can only be understood as a part of his Christology. The substance of the Supper, the Body and Blood of Christ, is the human nature of Christ. *Here,* if any place, it is possible to see what Luther understands by the humanity of Christ. Therefore, it is no doubt correct when, in recent studies, the central importance of Luther's writings about the Supper has been emphasized in the understanding of Luther's Christology.[13] If in Luther's doctrine of the Supper we only see a disturbing element in his evangelical view of salvation brought about by the polemics against the sacraments and by a "return" to the scholastic speculations, it simply shows that on the decisive points Luther has been misunderstood. An exhaustive presentation of the older Luther's doctrine of the Supper is not necessary now. We only give the views in Luther's doctrine of the Supper which show the connection which Luther holds between Christology and the doctrine about the signs of revelation.

It is well known that Luther, in the struggle with Zwingli and his adherents concerning the Supper, taught the ubiquity of Christ. Sometimes this doctrine has been considered as a scholastic play of logic without any real religious value, without notice being taken of the decisive importance it has in the understanding of Luther's concept of Christ. The omnipresence of God is to Luther an expression for his divine majesty. If God is not present everywhere in this very vital sense in which Luther understands this

---

13 Erich Seeberg, *Luthers Theologie, II;* Paul-Wilhelm Gennrich; Franz Hildebrandt; Ernst Wolf, *Das Christuszeugnis bei Luther.*

"attribute" of God, then he is not God at all. In the same sense it is true that Christ cannot be one with God unless he is completely one with God in his whole majesty. For if the humanity of Christ truly is to be the sign of revelation before all other signs, then it is naturally assumed that God's whole majesty is *really* present, hidden by the humanity. The insoluble unity of the person of Christ (in the two "natures") is necessary in order that Christ can be God's revelation at all. That is why Luther was so violently opposed to Zwingli's *alloiosis* doctrine and his probable "Monophysitism." Luther clearly sees that every attempt to separate the divine and the human in the person of Christ (e.g. the denial of Christ's exalted human omnipresence by the doctrine of Christ's heavenly residence *in loco circumscripto*) is not a mere harmless metaphysical speculation, but in the last analysis it means that Christ is not understood as God's revelation but as a representative of man in his highest spiritual power. Thus Christ does not become God's way to man but man's way to God. *The passionate retaining of the divine-human unity of the person of Christ is really nothing else than maintaining the principle never to seek God in his naked majesty without the signs of revelation given by him.* For as soon as we are able to separate from Christ the divine attributes, e.g. the omnipresence, in which he is present in his humanity, we have started the speculations about a God who is separated from *Deus incarnatus,* and a humanity which in itself has a religious power independent of the connection with *Deus incarnatus.* Luther's doctrine about Christ's ubiquity makes the demand of evangelical theology, that everything in God, including his omnipresence, shall be understood from the Christocentric point of view. Otherwise we are within the domain of the destructive speculations about *Deus nudus,* the speculations which on their reverse side have the same corresponding speculations about human nature's own religious power.

It is also seen here that the doctrine about the ubiquity of Christ's human nature is not, as has been stated so often, a speculation. It cannot be strongly enough emphasized that Luther does not busy himself with the ubiquity of Christ apart from his presence for us in the Supper. He does not at all utilize the idea of ubiquity in a speculative sense. In his ubiquity, apart from the presence in the Supper, Christ is therefore one with God's unveiled majesty and is not accessible to us. Luther, on the contrary teaches the ubiquity of Christ in *connection* with his presence in the Supper. In this connection the idea of ubiquity means that Christ who is present in the Supper is no less than God himself in his majesty, but God hidden under cover of the humanity of Christ. He is not a mere human Christ or a memory about a mere human Christ. The doctrine of ubiquity is turned sharply against the Zwinglian separation of the substance of the Supper and the divine Christ in his humanity. Luther holds that if Christ is not truly present in the Supper, but contrariwise remains *in loco circumscripto,* and if he in his real presence is not the Christ, who under the cover of his humanity hides the whole majesty of God— for the doctrine of ubiquity is to teach that—then there is no way for us to God in the Supper. Then we ourselves must find a way to God in the Supper, the way of speculation and work. And it was not entirely wrong that Luther saw in the Zwinglian thoughts about Christ *in loco circumscripto* a mere speculation and in the corresponding thoughts about the remembrance he saw part of a meritorious work.

The doctrine of ubiquity in this connection in which we meet it in Luther's doctrine of the Supper expresses the essential lines in Luther's Christology: that *Deus incarnatus* is the real revelation of God, that the fullness of the godhead dwells in Christ bodily (Col. 2:9). By the emphasis on the thought of ubiquity it is maintained that the Christ which we meet in the Supper is really God's true revelation, not a Christ separated from the majesty of God but a Christ who in his divine-human person is insolubly united with God in his majesty. But simultaneously the antispeculative limitation of the idea of ubiquity expresses the second main point in Luther's Christology: that *Deus incarnatus* is a sign of revelation, that the fullness of God in Christ is present even though hidden under the protective cover of Christ's humanity, and that only through the humble humanity of Christ (John 14:9) is it possible to lay hold on the majesty of God. By distinguishing between the absolute ubiquity outside of the Supper, which is not accessible to us, and Christ's gracious presence for us in the Supper by the Word, every way of speculation and work toward the most high and omnipresent Christ is blocked. He is exalted, and he is omnipresent; for if this were not the case we should not meet the real God, when in the Supper he gives us himself. But he is not accessible to us in his absolute exaltation and omnipresence. We can only lay hold on him in his divinity when he clothes it in his earthly, human, and bodily form. It is no more possible to separate the human and the divine nature of Christ—for it is insolubly united in a divine-human person—than it is to separate the exalted, omnipresent Christ present in the bread and the wine. It is one and the same divine-human person. It is the omnipresent Christ we meet in the bread and the wine. If we take omnipresence away from the Christ we meet in the bread and the wine we make him another and a smaller one than he really is. We make him another instead of God himself and thereby we reduce the value of the gift of the Supper. On the contrary, if we attempt to understand or to meet the omnipresent Christ in some other way than hidden in his humble humanity, in the bread and the wine of the Supper, then we speculate on the *Deus nudus* and we do not meet the divine majesty as our God but as our enemy who puts us to death.

We have here reached the point where we can see the connection between the incarnated Christ's human nature and the concrete signs of revelation: baptism, the Supper, preaching, absolution. These concrete signs of revelation are Christ's physical, earthly humanity in the period between the ascension and his second coming. If the incarnation means that God is secretly present in Christ's *bodily* human nature, so that every way to God outside of the *bodily* present Christ is an emotional fanaticism, then it also means that Christ's ascension and exaltation must be followed by another form of bodily presence unless it means that the revelation after the ascension simply has *ceased,* and that man again must rely on the way of speculation and works. This other form is found in the signs of revelation: the Word, baptism, and the Supper. The confession of the divinity of Christ in his historic existence and in the signs of revelation are parallel in Luther, indeed, they are one confession.[14] If Christ after his ascension cannot be *bodily* present with us with his *usus passionis,* then his whole historic existence is changed to a past, factual event which no more concerns us. We may perhaps possess *factum passionis* in the historic memory itself, but we have only *usus passionis* in Christ's renewing, bodily coming to us in Word and sacrament, by which *factum passionis* is given to us.[15] The external sign *(eusserlich ding)* in the sign of revelation is therefore not "flesh" in the sense of a contrast to the spiritual, but flesh in the sense of the human nature, "our nature," which is united with the eternal Word of God in incarnation. To deny the external sign in the signs of revelation as a lack of spirituality is therefore the same as to deny the incarnation. Both in the incarnation and in the signs of revelation the humanity of Christ is the cover for the majesty of God. In both instances it is necessary that we find God not by our own speculations, but in a hard and offensive contrast to our own thought, by the Word of God, spoken by Christ: "Here ye shall find me!" Here it is very clear that the doctrine about the signs of revelation is a part of Luther's Christology and it can only be understood as a part of a greater connection.

The external sign is a part of the incarnation. The spirituality which fears or which takes a superior and complacent attitude to the outward things reveals itself as a denial of the incarnation, as an attempt to reach God by way of speculation or work outside of the once *bodily* incarnated Christ and his repeated bodily signs of revelation. The false spiritual fear of and the complacent attitude toward bodily and outward things are herewith disclosed as the result of another faith, another view of the way of salvation. Where the incarnated Christ is the way to the Father, there you are always depending upon the bodily and outward signs of revelation. Where one considers himself above the bodily sign, there one has another

---

14 *W. A.,* XXIII, 157, 30 (1527); XX, 727, 20 (Rörer, 1527); also XXXIII, 81, 28 ff. (Aurifaber, 1531-32).

15 *W. A.,* XVIII, 203, 38 (1525); XXVI, 296, 32 (1528); also XVIII, 202, 32 ff.; XXIII, 193, 14 ff. (1527); XVI, 332, 6 ff. (Rörer, 1525); XVII, 1, 166, 7-18 (Rörer, 1525); XX, 778, 1-779, 6 (Rörer, 1527).

way to God than by *Deus incarnatus*. All spiritualism—including the spiritualizing doctrine of Christ, Christ-enthusiasm and Christ-imitation—is a denial of the incarnation. Where the Holy Spirit is identified with, or at least postulated as a special relation of the Spirit to "pure" spirituality in opposition to the outward and bodily view, there *Deus incarnatus* has been secretly substituted for man's own higher nature, and the "spirit" is placed in contrast to the "lower" state of the body. Where the contrast, "inward spirituality-outward corporeality" is of any importance at all— that is, in the sense that outward corporeality compared to inward spirituality is considered insignificant or perhaps even harmful— there it is revealed that we have entered into the metaphysics of idealism where the contrast between man's higher, spiritual nature and lower, bodily nature has constitutional value because *Deus incarnatus* is of no account. For where there is real knowledge of *Deus incarnatus*, there the idealistic contrast between a "higher" spiritual nature and a "lower" bodily nature is forever abolished.

Luther does not hold that there is any special affinity between the Holy Spirit and the "spiritual" in the spiritualistic and metaphysical sense. Luther, of course, knows that the Spirit is invisible and his work hidden. That is because the Spirit is God himself. But this hidden spirituality of God has no greater affinity to that which in spiritualistic metaphysics is understood as the "spiritual," the "inward," the incorporeal, the idea, than to the outward and visible, to the body. The situation is rather the opposite. Because the work of the Spirit is to mediate the reality of the *bodily incarnated* Christ, therefore the Spirit has a special affinity to the outward and the visible, not to the outward and visible in general, but to the outward and visible as the protective cover for the personal presence of God. Thereby we have not said that Luther's idea of spirit should be more "materialistic" and directly antispiritualistic in the sense of despising everything "spiritual." Such a view of Luther is impossible because the incarnation itself abolished the contrast between the "spiritual" and the "bodily," which is why we in metaphysics can play them against one another as competing factors. The *whole* man, "spirit" and "body" is "flesh" in contrast to the

Spirit of God. The *whole* man, "spirit" and "body," under the dominion of the Spirit of God is "spirit."

In view of this connection based on the incarnation as a sign of revelation between the Spirit and the outward and the bodily, we should consider Luther's thoughts (which are generally made heretical) about the body's participation in the blessing of the sacrament. In the writings during the struggle about the Supper, especially *Dass dies Worte* . . . , Luther in accordance with Irenaeus and Hilarius teaches that there is a bodily fruit of celebrating the Supper.[16] These thoughts in Luther are generally minimized, partly by suggesting that they have been taken from the Greek fathers and partly because they occur so seldom in Luther. These thoughts are considered a naturalistic, philosophical speculation foreign to Christianity. In an apologetic manner scholars try to explain away these thoughts as a foreign element in Luther's theology.

With respect to the influence of the Greek fathers it should be noted that except after careful consideration Luther did not generally permit himself to be influenced by the fathers. He had a very sharp eye for the weaknesses of the fathers, and he was not afraid to criticize them when he thought that they got away from the clear light of the gospel. That Luther in a careless moment should have permitted Irenaeus and Hilarius to influence him more than he wished, and that even in the direction opposed to the gospel, is so bizarre an idea when you think of Luther's general position relative to the fathers that it reveals its nature as an "excuse." It is not much better than the other "excuse" that these thoughts occur so seldom in Luther. This assertion is from the first edition of J. Köstlin's work about Luther's theology which was published before the Weimar edition. Köstlin maintains that the thought of the bodily fruit in the Supper is only found once in Luther after the struggle about the Supper. This strange assertion from Köstlin has been accepted without further study even though in the meantime the Weimar edition has provided us with much more material

---

16 *W. A.*, XXIII, 255, 14 (1527); also XXIII, 157, 1 ff.; 181, 12 ff.; 191, 17 ff.; 193, 6 ff.; 203, 26 ff.; 205, 9-25; 229-237; 259, 4 ff.

than that which was accessible when Köstlin wrote his first edition— and which he has not corrected in his second edition. Even G. Ljunggren, in 1931, quotes Köstlin as authority for this false assertion. The thought about bodily fruit of the Supper is found not only in the *Large Catechism* and in the report from the Marburg colloquy but also in the many sermons of the fifteen-thirties.[17] This thought is therefore not so rarely to be found in Luther as Köstlin and Ljunggren attempt to make it. And even if we might be able to find only seven or eight proofs for the thought besides those in the writings about the Supper, these certainly are sufficient. This definitely indicates that the thought is not just a passing one which Luther revoked shortly after the polemic about the Supper.

But even more important than the frequency of the thought is its connection with the total view of Luther. This thought about a bodily fruit from the celebration of the Supper is not an unevangelical diagression at all. Rather is it a pregnant expression for Luther's evangelical concept of the Spirit. We are not speaking of any naturalistic, philosophical speculations at all. Luther does not know of a Communion outside of faith and the Word where the element directly affects our bodily nature. Luther strongly emphasizes that the bodily fruit of the Supper springs from and depends on the "spiritual communion" of faith. The mouth only enjoys its blessing of the Supper, because it is *des hertzens gliedmas* and *umb des hertzen willen*. The mouth and the heart help one another. The mouth enjoys it bodily on behalf of the heart—which cannot receive it bodily—and the heart enjoys it spiritually on behalf of the mouth—which does not understand what it eats. But the enjoyment of the mouth depends on that of the heart. It is the mouth that is *des hertzen gliedmas*, not the opposite. Luther does *not* say that "immortality" is directly mediated from the element to our bodily nature through the mystery of nature. But he says very clearly that it happens *verborgen ym glauben und hoffnunge bis an Jüngsten tag* ("hidden in faith and hope until the Judgment Day").

---

[17] *W. A.*, XXX, 3, 126, 27. XXXVI, 666, 9 ff. (Rörer, 1532); XLV, 202, 5-18 (Rörer, 1537); XLVI, 479, 26-480, 11 (Rörer, 1538); XLVII, 775, 19 ff. (Rörer, 1539).

Luther does not represent any kind of "naturalism" as an equipment of the elements with mystical powers, or of making the bodily divine as such. He never suggests that the body is considered "as something special in itself," which means that he does not want the soul considered "as something special in itself." This is the view in the emphasis of the body's part in the blessing of the Supper. It is precisely the same view about the relation between man's bodily and spiritual natures based on the incarnation which we have previously met in Luther in his polemics against the spiritualism of the enthusiast. This is because Luther does not understand Spirit from the idealistic, metaphysical contrast between man's higher and lower nature, but on the basis of the work of the Triune God in creation, redemption, and sanctification. Therefore the Spirit is not opposed to the bodily but the Spirit (the Spirit of the Father and the Son) certainly seeks the bodily. We have previously seen how Luther, because he is trinitarian in his thinking about creation, understands the Spirit's work also in connection with the work of creation. The Spirit is God in his gracious and blessed preservation of his (bodily!) creation. It is the Old Testament concept of the Spirit of God as the life-giving principle. In the same way the Spirit is active in the redemption, in the new creation. And the new creation in Christ, the bodily incarnated Christ, is not only a spiritual, but a spiritual-bodily creation. For God's unbroken creative-redemptive work covers the whole of man. In view of this unbroken creative-redemptive work of God the contrast between "outward" corporeality and "inward" spirituality so decisive for spiritualizing metaphysics vanishes. Luther's teaching about a bodily fruit in the Supper is not just an incidental addition to his doctrine of the Supper, but simply an underscoring of what there is in the Supper and this would be found in the Supper without referring to Irenaeus and Hilarius. The teaching about a bodily fruit of celebrating the Supper is a protection against the spiritualistic interpretation of the fruit of the Supper, an interpretation which might be very natural because of the strong emphasis on the forgiveness of sin in the words of institution. Because Luther does not know a Christ who is not the *bodily* incarnated God, a purely "spiritual" Christ, therefore he does not know a mode of receiving Christ, which is *only* spiritual without simultaneously being bodily. He does not know of any reception of forgiveness of sin which is not simultaneously a hope about the resurrection of the body. If it is really incarnate Christ we receive, then we receive a *whole* (spiritual-bodily) Christ as whole (spiritual-bodily) human beings. This acceptation is to Luther not a contrast between a "spiritual" (in the sense of non-bodily) enjoyment and a "bodily" (in the sense of material) enjoyment of the Supper, but between a "spiritual" celebration (in the sense of *believing* and therefore always including the bodily) and a celebration of the "flesh" (in the sense of nonbelieving, which also may be the case for the one who has a purely nonmaterial concept of the Supper). Luther's concept of the contrast of the spiritual and the bodily is so different from that of the spiritualists that for Luther a spiritual celebration of the Supper always contains the bodily fruit. In contrast to a modern spiritualistic-Protestant relinquishing of Luther's clear and logical insistence on the thought of a bodily fruit in the celebration of the Supper it is possible to be so radical that we insist (and this is entirely within the realm of Luther's thoughts) *that a celebration of the Supper which does not contain the assurance and hope of a bodily fruit is not a spiritual celebration at all.* A celebration of the Supper which does not include the thought of the bodily fruit, commemorates another Christ than the one who is really present. The real Christ is the Christ who is present in the flesh by the Holy Spirit, and whose flesh therefore also is spiritual flesh which makes everything spiritual with which it comes into contact. What is eaten is changed to body in the one who eats, *but this is very different with the spiritual flesh. It changes the body who eats it to itself, that is, to spirit.*[18]

It is important that this thought is not overlooked. For it distinguishes Luther's thought from all naturalistic-philosophical speculations. Luther does not think of bodily celebration of the Supper in the way that the elements of the Supper contain a super-

---

[18] *W. A.,* XXIII, 203, 26 ff. (1527).

natural substance which the human body takes into itself and by which it gradually is made immortal. That would be a naturalistic-philosophical speculation, and it would belong to the idea of the concept of *gratia infusa*. However, Luther does *not* say that the elements contain a supernatural power which the body takes into itself. *He says precisely the opposite.* The "spiritual flesh" cannot be changed into a new body in us. In place of this, Luther says that the Body and Blood of Jesus are a spiritual Body and Blood which receive into themselves and change everyone who eats and drinks them. And this reception and change is not a hyperphysical process in the body of man, but a saving historico-eschatological act with the entire man and therefore also with his body. It is the entire man which Christ receives into himself in the Communion. We find here the concept of the Spirit which we previously have learned to know in the explanation to the third article in the *Large Catechism*. The Spirit is God himself in insoluble unity with the Father and the Son of the Trinity. Where the work of the Spirit is done, there God is present in the unbroken unity of his saving historico-eschatological act of agape. In this unity man's whole existence has eschatological character. Justification and sanctification are an insoluble unity of which the end is the resurrection of the body. The Spirit is the subject of this unbroken and all-inclusive, eschatological act of God. When the body of Jesus in the Supper is called "spiritual body," then it means that it is the body through which the Spirit works because the incarnation is a part of the same unbroken act of God as the outpouring of the Holy Spirit. God the Father performs this act of God *through* the Spirit *in* Christ, that is, in the body of Christ, in his humanity. Therefore the flesh of Christ is spiritual flesh *(Geistfleisch)*. But this also means that participation in this flesh means participation in the unbroken, saving, historico-eschatological act of God, of which the Spirit is the subject. Therefore Luther can no more speak about the believing celebration of the Supper (for the believing celebration of the Supper means participation in the spiritual flesh [*Geistfleisch*] of Christ) the fruit of which does not also contain the resurrection of the body, than he can speak about a justification which in itself does not also contain sanctification and the hope of resurrection of the body. This unity of the faith in the forgiveness of sin and the hope of the resurrection of the body which we find in Luther's explanation of the third article in the *Large Catechism* is not something other than the thoughts about the bodily fruit in the celebration of the Supper. It is the same line of thought with which he confronts us in both places. If we want to discard the last-mentioned thoughts as naturalistic-philosophical speculations, then we must also discard the first thoughts and change Luther's gospel about the forgiveness of sin to a spiritualistic ideology about the pure "spiritual" salvation of the "soul." But such a spiritualism is not Lutheran.

The older Luther's doctrine about the bodily fruit in the celebration of the Supper is factually identical with the eschatological view of the sacrament which the young Luther held. The idea of our body being nourished by the spiritual body of Christ must be understood eschatologically, not from the naturalistic-philosophical point of view. It is identical with the young Luther's thoughts about the Supper as *viaticum*. Luther does not think of the communion between our mortal body and Christ's spiritual body in such a way that our mortal body receives into itself a substance of immortality which changes it, but rather that the living Christ receives into himself the whole of man and, therefore, also gives this poor mortal body hope about resurrection. In the consideration of these thoughts in Luther it is not right to conceal how little Luther speaks about the nourishment of the mortal body in terms of a philosophy of nature. Nothing is said about its hyperphysical transformation but about its *hope of resurrection*. There is therefore no contrast between Luther's general faith in the resurrection and the idea of a bodily fruit in the Supper. The two thoughts are identical. The bodily fruit of the Supper is the resurrection in the last day, not a transformation of the human nature to immortality before death and outside of death.

Therefore we have in the doctrine of the bodily fruit of the celebration of the Supper the logical and consistent expression of Luther's view of the Spirit's relation to the external and the bodily.

To Luther the Spirit is *God's* Spirit, therefore his essence is under-stood on the basis of the unbroken act of revelation of the Triune God who in creation, redemption, and sanctification embraces all in man, including the physical. Where the Spirit works—and he does that in the Supper—his work also embraces the physical. In the Supper we receive the Body and Blood of Jesus as spiritual flesh. If we do not understand this and if we consider the Spirit's work to be limited to the "spiritual," and if because of this we consider every idea of a bodily effect of the Spirit mediated by the Supper as a naturalistic-philosophical speculation, we reveal that we have not understood Luther's witness about the Spirit. Then we also reveal that it is not the Spirit, whose unbroken work reaches from the first moment of creation to the bodily resurrection on the last day, which we consider at work in the Supper. And we reveal that it is not because of participation in *this* Spirit's work that we designate the Supper as spiritual and strive for a spiritual understanding of the Supper. Where the body is excluded from the work which the Spirit performs in the Supper because the body is not "spiritual" enough, but only "natural," there we reveal that we have not received our concept of "spirit" from the revealing act of the Triune God, but from the spiritualistic, metaphysical, psycho-physical dualism. The "scruples" about Luther's teaching concerning the bodily fruit in the celebration of the Supper come from this metaphysics, and from this alone. It does not come from the confession of the God who created us as *whole* men and who redeems us and sanctifies us as whole men.

Here we see how significant it was that we did not base our description of Luther's understanding of the Spirit on his polemics with the enthuiasts, for we have followed the opposite course by first describing Luther's understanding completely independently of his antispiritualism. It was by this description, especially in the first part of our work, that we learned to observe the trinitarian and theocentric perspective which influences all Luther's ideas of the Spirit. It is *this* perspective which is the reason why the Spirit's work *always* embraces also the bodily. The Spirit, in his work in the Supper, *must* be seen as he who blesses and raises *also* the poor mortal body. We are able to see that the antispiritualistic tendency is neither a polemic reaction produced by the over-spirituality of the opponent nor an unevangelical glossing over by the influence of the Greek fathers' Hellenistic philosophy of nature. It is the unavoidable consequence of the total view of the Spirit and his work which was Luther's contention long before the struggle with the enthusiasts and the sacramentalists began. It was the biblical, trinitarian, theocentric, total view, by which the Spirit is not understood on the basis of man's ideal, incorporeal, "higher" nature, but on the basis of the unbroken, saving, historico-eschatological act of God which, as far as man is concerned, begins with the creation of a man with a body and is completed in the resurrection of the body. It is on the basis of this total view that Luther's antispiritualism must be understood, including that part of it which is designated as the bodily fruit of the Supper. There is no meaning in this scheme except on the basis of this total view, while understood in this way the doctrine becomes indeed very meaningful.

That Luther's doctrine about the bodily celebration of the Supper must not be isolated, but that it must be seen on this comprehensive background, is proven by the connection in which Luther has placed it. In *Dass diese Worte* . . . Luther has connected this doctrine closely with the idea of love to the neighbor. Among the spiritual things which in themselves are material (bodily) but have become spiritual by being placed under the power of the Spirit, Luther places the love to the neighbor and the bodily celebration of the Supper side by side. There is a mere physical aspect of love to the neighbor, Luther says, and it is really of no value. But if this material love to the neighbor is spiritually exercised, that is, under the dominion of the Spirit of God, and believing the Word of God, then because of this it does not become less material but it becomes life and salvation because it is a material work which is guided by the Spirit of God. The body does not know what it does in such a work but is driven by the Spirit of God as an animal may be driven. But the heart which believes the Word knows what the body does. Thus work and the Word belong together insolubly. The work must be done by the body, and the body alone can do it. Without the body and the sense of the body the neighbor will not be helped. However, the "soul" or the heart shall lay hold on the Word; the body cannot do that. Thus soul and body must help one another, the soul by believing the Word and the body by performing the work. It is only in the unity of the faith of the heart and the work of the body that the *whole* man is embraced in the saving act of God (*W. A.*, XXIII, 189, 15).

In a complete parallel to this Luther speaks in the following passage (*W. A.,* XXIII, 191, 17) about the bodily celebration of the Supper. Here the body and the soul also co-operate. The body receives the sacrament with the mouth; the heart cannot do that. But the body does not know what it does when it receives the sacrament but eats it as an animal without reason. The heart believes the Word which makes the Body and Blood of Christ present. Thus the heart in behalf of the body knows what it eats. Only in the unity of the eating by the mouth and the faith of the heart is the whole man embraced in the saving act of God. The mouth cannot be satisfied to receive the sacrament without the faith of the heart. That would be a purely animal way of eating. But the heart cannot be satisfied with believing without the eating of the mouth. Thus it is only in the unity of the eating of the mouth and the faith of the heart that the blessing reaches the whole man.

These two lines of thought are formulated carefully in a parallelism, and it is no accident that Luther has placed them side by side. It is the *same* spiritualistic scorn for the external sign (*eusserlich ding*) which causes man in the interest of his own spirit's pious endeavor to forget the love of his neighbor in this corporeal need and despise the bodily celebration of the Supper. The corporeal work of loving the neighbor in one's vocation is as unspiritual to the spiritualist as a bodily celebration of the Supper with the hope of a material blessing. Conversely it is true that the view of man which is implied in Luther's concept of the Spirit and his work is closely related to the concept of man which finds expression in the idea of the ancient church with respect to the bodily fruit of the

Supper. In the realm of the Spirit man is not walking up toward God on the ladder of speculation or work, but he is on the way from God out toward his neighbor as an instrument of God's creative and sustaining work in favor of the neighbor. In the first case, that is, on the way of speculation and work, man is necessarily more interested in the inward "pure" spirituality than in the "outward." For here the "works" aim to help man upward toward God. The works thereby become pious works, not works of charity toward the neighbor. But pious works are of an inward nature. The inward concentration of the soul on the religious man means more here than outward works which are rather considered to belong to the category of "necessary evil." On the other hand, works of a purely spiritual type, such as mortification in the imitation of Christ, receive primary significance. In the other case, not where man in behalf of himself is walking toward God but in behalf of God is walking toward his neighbor, there works by the body alone have significance. The palpable and bodily distress of my neighbor is not relieved by my "inward" piety. This is the different *ordo salutis* which we said was the difference between Luther and the enthusiasts, and which gives a completely different basic valuation of that which is done by the body. In the genuinely evangelical understanding of salvation it is impossible, because of the position of the neighbor, ever to accept the spiritualistic degradation of the outward and the bodily.

It is only natural that this different evaluation of the body is seen in the understanding of the effect of the Supper. It is impossible for Luther to exclude the body from the blessing of the Supper. Luther's view of the body is determined partly because it is an indispensable instrument of God in the works for our neighbor and partly because eschatology contains the hope of the resurrection of the body. The mortal body, of course, does not know anything. But the "heart" cannot be in the right relation to God without the mortal body, for with the ear of the mortal body we hear the *verbum vocale*, in which the gospel comes to us. With the mouth of the mortal body we eat the spiritual flesh of Christ for the forgiveness of sin. How should it be plausible that the true body of Christ—of the same essence as ours—which was sacrificed in death for us (not even this work could Christ do for us without a body) should not also be a help to the whole man when it is given us as spiritual flesh in the Supper. How is it possible that the mortal body, with whose mouth we at the command of Christ eat his Body and drink his Blood, should be forever excluded from receiving any blessing? Where the body then is placed outside, there we yield to philosophical—if not just naturalistic-philosophical—speculations, and there we introduce in the concept of the Supper of Jesus a metaphysical separation between soul and body. This was never the idea of the Bible. In Luther's view there is a connection between the emphasis of the real presence and the bodily effect of the Supper, a connection which entitles us to discuss thoroughly this last thought in a section captioned "The external sign and Christ." When omnipresent, exalted humanity in its divine majesty is *really* present, hidden in the bread and the wine of the Supper, it is obvious that by this type of presence the "spiritual" ways to the fellowship with Christ are to be blocked. We can only meet Christ in his condescension where he *sich auffs aller tieffest erunter gibt,* where he permits himself to be used in a disgraceful manner at the altar and in our mouth, just as he did once on the cross.[19]

This condescension means that Christ will also take care of our mortal body. He does not consider himself too "spiritual" to do that. Otherwise it really means nothing that Jesus instituted the Supper as a meal and said: "Take this and eat it! This do in remembrance of me!" He might simply have said: "Remember me as often as you eat!" In the words of institution of Jesus the remembrance is not an accompanying part of the meal. The meal is itself the remembrance. *This*—that is, the meal—do in remembrance of me. There is no real meaning in this institution and in these words if the body is excluded from participation in the blessing of the Supper. Only in the spiritual and bodily celebration of the Supper with its spiritual and bodily effect is the full meaning of the real

---

19 *W. A.,* XXIII, 157, 30 ff. (1527).

presence understood. Not before the bodily has been included have we understood the condescension in the Supper.

When so often we have looked for the scriptural proofs of Luther's ideas of the bodily fruit in the celebration of the Supper, we have completely overlooked that this idea of Luther does not need any special scriptural proofs because it is inherent in the very fact of the institution and the real presence itself. On the other hand they who deny the body's participation in the blessing of the Supper, in spite of the fact that Jesus has instituted it as a real meal, are duty bound to present scriptural proofs for so sensational an understanding of the words of institution. By presenting this demand to his opponents in the struggle about the Supper Luther is not only right dogmatically, but also exegetically. The "symbolic" interpretation of the words of institution is an exegesis which demands a special scriptural proof. If such a one could be presented Luther had no doubt yielded to it. But he suspected that his opponents would present other authorities than those of the Scripture.

Luther saw very clearly that where we want to exclude the body from participation in the blessing of the Supper we are already secretly trying to spiritualize the real presence. *For a bodily presence without a bodily effect is no genuine bodily presence.* The Lutheran "is" (as used in the Words of Institution, "This *is* my body") contains the thoughts about the bodily effect of the Supper. Without falsifying Luther's view we could very well continue his thoughts in this sentence: We have not understood the full depth of the spiritual blessing (the forgiveness of sin) as long as the body is not considered. The forgiveness of sin is that by which God brings sinners into his fellowship (Nygren), and he stoops down to us in our whole factual misery. If we then get away from the mortal body (which is not only an instrument for good works in favor of the neighbor but by the members of which we have also caused him much pain), God in his condescension is not permitted to care for the mortal body. This means that on the background of an idealistic, psycho-physical dualism we give the soul the highest place in man, that is, a privileged position with respect to the agape of God. The fellowship may perhaps constantly be with sinners. But because we have looked away from the mortal body, the concept of sin has also been spiritualized, and the fellowship with God is therefore not within the deep category of sin. By thwarting the condescension of God, which cannot stop before it has reached the very depth itself, with a metaphysical dualism which tries to stop God's condescension halfway, that is, at the boundary of the soul before the body, we have already infiltrated the *ordo salutis* of the enthusiasts where the fellowship with God does not take place on the level of sinful man, but on the level of the highest faculties of man. Where we fear to make the body a part of the blessing of God's Spirit, it is not possible to understand the depth of Luther's concept of sin. For if the body has no part in the forgiveness of sin, it has no part in sin. Then sin is only understood as a lack in our own striving toward perfectness and not as the many evil deeds which by the aid of the body we have committed against our neighbor because of our unbelief. Just as the faith of the heart cannot be detached from the works of the body for the neighbor, neither can unbelief of the heart be detached. Therefore, it is not a misrepresentation when Luther's thoughts about the bodily effect of the Supper are connected with the forgiveness of sin. The depth of forgiveness of sin is not understood if we distort it to "soul hygiene." *Only in connection with the restoration of the body is it possible to see the dimensional depth in the forgiveness of sin.* Therefore Luther does not teach a separate bodily blessing of the Supper as it often is mistakenly said of him, but together with the spiritual blessing, the forgiveness of sin, and insolubly united with it, he teaches the bodily effect.

Is there not an intimate connection between this *totus-homo* understanding of the blessing of the Supper and the Lutheran idea of love of the neighbor? Both presuppose the Spirit. It is the *same* Spirit who in faith makes the humble Christ really present to us in the bread and wine of the Supper and who in love takes us out to our neighbor. It is the *same* Spirit, the Spirit of God, who from on high is seeking the creation of God to preserve it and bless it, and therefore it is always united with *eusserlich ding*. It is the same *motion* of the Holy Spirit which is found in the doctrine of bodily blessing of the Supper and in the idea of the material love of the neighbor. In both cases the Spirit is active in the one unbroken act of God who blesses and preserves and who looks to the lost creation to give it new life, new life in Christ. It is the Spirit of God who searches in the depths, not the spirit of man which is striving upward. Therefore the final end of the motion of the Spirit is found in the most outward outwardness possible, out with the mortal body and with our poor neighbor's *temporal* need, that need which can only be relieved by the body. Out in the most outward outwardness where, because of its heavenward flight, the human spirit is too proud to walk where the Spirit of God is present, there is the destination of the Spirit of God. Only in the connection with the Spirit is it possible to notice the mutual relation between the different "outward things." From the point of view of the trinitarian understanding of the Spirit, two outward phenomena—the bodily celebration of the Supper with its bodily blessing and the daily grind in one's earthbound calling—get into close contact with one another. They are both a strong testimony of the fact that the Spirit is working, the true Spirit which is the foremost enemy of all "spiritualism," because he leads man away from his own dear spirit's way upward toward the most high and into the Holy Spirit's difficult way toward the deep things of God.

Over and above this way of the Spirit we find the external sign (*eusserlich ding*). We have seen in this section why this is so. The external sign signifies *the humanity of Christ*. The Spirit's way, which is perfected in the most outward things, is the way of Christ, the way he took from heaven via the cradle to the cross, a way he constantly takes from his heavenly throne via the Communion out to the disgraceful body of worms. The Spirit takes all on *this* way to Christ and in Christ to the neighbor. The milestones of this way are: baptism (with *real* water!), *verbum vocale,* the *bodily* celebration of the Supper, work for the neighbor in the *earthbound* vocation, the resurrection of the *body*. This is all external sign. It is a very different way than the one on whose milestones may be read: the *mortification* of the body, *spiritual* experiences, *inward* perfectness, *imitatio Christi,* the immortality of the *soul.* They are two very different ways. The way to which the external sign belongs —and this is the result of the study in this section—is the way of Christ because the external sign is Christ's own humanity, in which God alone is present for us. The way where the external sign is avoided is the *by-passing* of Christ on the way toward the naked majesty of God, the highest way of the most "perfect humanity." The contrast between these two ways follows us all the way out to apparently peripheral questions such as that of the bodily effect of the Supper.

A Summarizing Description of the Contrast Between Luther's and the Enthusiasts' Understanding of the Spirit

In the first section of this chapter we have sketched the basic contrast between Luther and the enthusiasts. In the second and third sections we have traced this contrast into the most concrete question which separated Luther from the enthusiasts, the question about the relation between the Spirit and the outward things. We shall now summarize what we have seen and make a concluding characterization of Luther's testimony about the Spirit in his polemic with the enthusiasts.

In all Luther's difference with the enthusiasts we are concerned with only one thing: the exclusive understanding of the Spirit as the Spirit of God. Over against this is the idea of the enthusiasts about spirit and spirituality, which is orientated from the point of view of a spiritualistic, metaphysical dualism between the body and the soul, between the visible and the invisible, between matter and thought.

To Luther the Spirit is not "something spiritual." The Spirit is the Triune God himself in his real presence as our sphere of life. Everything pertaining to the Spirit is brought into the unbroken, creative-redemptive work of the Triune God, and therefore it is spiritual. This work has its center in Christ, *Deus incarnatus.* Under the veil of his humanity God is secretly present as the gracious, life-giving, and redeeming God. God has by the Word pointed to the humanity of Christ as the place where he is graciously near in our midst. Outside this place indicated by him he is only near in his consuming majesty. The water of baptism, the bread and the wine in the Supper, *verbum vocale,* the office of preaching—these also belong to the humanity of Christ. As signs of revelation they are all a part of the one sign of revelation: Christ's humanity. They are all the one place where God is present in his grace.

But God is present in a *hidden* form in Christ's humanity. Under the veil and condescension of the humanity of Christ God cannot be proven or be experienced. It is the Word which tells us that he is present. Outside of the Word, which in itself is a sign, we have no guarantee that God is present, concealed by the cover of Christ's humanity. This means that God's gracious presence in Christ's humanity corresponds to man's faith. It is faith which by claiming the Word to be true asserts that God as God is truly present in the sign of revelation. But faith is not a human possibility. Faith is the gift of the Spirit. Faith is created when God who is hidden in the Word and in the sign of revelation becomes experience, power, reality in us so that our whole life becomes centered in his presence. From this center proceed both faith and love, prayer and work, and they return to this center. This is the Spirit's work. This work is done by the Spirit in sovereign freedom.

Here we are able to see how the outward, "certain" signs of revelation and the free, inward work of the Spirit belong together. In the treatise against the heavenly prophets Luther says that God treats us in two ways: in an outward manner by the spoken Word of the gospel and the corporeal signs, baptism and the Supper, and in an inward manner by the Holy Spirit and faith as well as by other gifts. The inward and outward work correspond to the Spirit and Christ. The connection between the outward signs and the inward work of the Spirit is based on the Trinity.

The Spirit which Luther here describes, is the one who proceeds from the Father and the Son. His only work is to lead us to the Father through the Son. This can be done in no other way than by the *outward* signs. For in them and in them alone we find the humanity of Christ behind whose protective veil the Father has come to meet us. It is that Christ, clothed in these signs, and he alone, whom the Spirit makes a living power in us.

We are here reminded of the passion with which Luther emphasizes the real presence and the insoluble unity of the two natures of Christ culminating in the thought of the ubiquity of the human nature of Christ. This constant insistence of the "is" in Christology and in the doctrine of the Supper expresses Luther's confession of the incarnation. God has come to us in Christ. But that also means: *only* in Christ. All other ways to God are eternally blocked. The sign of revelation therefore does not contain any problem at all. The two natures in Christ *are* one divine-human person. Even the smallest separation of the two natures makes room for a speculative search for God outside the humanity of Christ. And where there is an access for speculation there is also an access for works since *ratio* and *lex* belong together.

The divine-human person of Christ *is* one with the bread and the wine in the Supper. This allows no room for any insecurity at all. For if we solve the omnipresence of Christ on the basis of the presence in the visible sign proclaimed by his work, and if we attempt with great eagerness and passion to find a way outside of the Christ who is in the bread and the wine to the Christ who is in heaven, then we only find a Christ who in his naked majesty is the stern judge, a Christ who is identical with *Deus nudus,* who consumes. Therefore, do not make the real presence a problem! There, in the bread and the wine, to which we are directed by the word of Christ, there he is in his humanity. There the bread and the wine are his humanity. "This is my body" shall be understood grammatically without any interpretations just as the words sound. The bread and the wine are—literally!—the human body of Jesus. Every time the ubiquity of Christ or the real presence has been made a problem, it means that the way of God to us has been made a problem. By making God's way to us a problem all our own blocked ways to God have all at once been opened. Where the divine-human unity of Christ and the real presence in the Supper have become a problem (and the other signs of revelation!)

there speculation and work-righteousness are at work immediately. There the reign of the law has been reintroduced. Where we have ways to God outside the bodily incarnated Christ, there we are on the way to *Deus nudus* who is the stern God of the law.

Where the signs of revelation have been made a problem, there the incarnation is made a problem. Where the incarnation is made a problem, there God's way to us has been made a problem, and there the gospel becomes a problem and we reintroduce the law (and reason) as a way to God. Therefore Luther boldly cries his "is." Therefore he speaks about the signs of revelation as sure signs. All this part of Luther's view which might well be called his "incarnationalism" has been assigned the function of keeping the way open for the expectation of the Spirit's work. Where it is *certain* that God has obligated himself to these definite signs, which are the humanity of Christ, it is also *certain* that all other ways, and all such ways are in some form identical with the way of the law, are blocked. Only one way is left open—the way of the Spirit. For God, who is hidden in the humanity of Christ, can only be grasped by faith which the Spirit alone gives. However, where we make the signs of revelation a problem and thereby keep other ways (which in these different forms are the ways of the law) to God open, there the expectation of the Spirit is forced back. For where the way of the law to God is kept open, there the Spirit is not the only possibility, it is not even the nearest possibility. And where the Spirit is not the only possibility there he is not expected.

Luther's incarnationalism is a direct expression of his expectation of the Spirit. It is this part of Luther's incarnationalism which is expressed in the request that the outward signs shall precede the work of the Spirit. The thought which we found in the young Luther we meet again in the old Luther. It is stated thus in *Wider die himmlischen Propheten* in speaking of the Word as the double manner in which God deals with us, outwardly by the signs of revelation and inwardly by the Spirit and faith: "*Aber das alles, der massen und der ordenung, das die eusserlichen stucke sollen und mussen* vorgehen. *Und die ynnerlichen* hernach *und durch die eusserlichen kommen,*" and in the same way it was stated in the Smalcald Articles: "God grants His Spirit or grace to no one, except through or with the preceding outward Word." That the outward signs precede the inner work means that they prepare the way for the Spirit by creating the expectation for him. This is the unfailing certainty of the signs which create this expectation. Here and in no other place is the humanity of Christ, here and only here is the Spirit of God the Father and the Son at work to lead us to the Father in Christ.

Here we can also understand that the passion with which Luther struggles, in the doctrine of ubiquity and the real presence as well as in his whole doctrine of Christ and the signs of revelation, against every attempt to make a problem of the "is" of revelation has nothing to do with an objectivity which excludes the free work of the Spirit. It is true that, with the same tenacity with respect to the doctrine of the real presence, Luther has maintained the thought of *manducatio indignorum*. This thought is also a direct continuation of the thought of the real presence and cannot be abolished without spiritualizing the latter. But this "objectivity" does not mean, as it at times has been stated, that Luther in reality gets close to the Roman doctrine of *ex opere operato*. On the contrary, we have seen that the more *confidently* Luther maintained the firmness of the sign of revelation, the more confidently he also narrowed all possibilities of ways to God down to only one: the expectation of the Spirit. Yes, only the expectation of the Spirit! That means, the expectation of God himself personally. The sign of revelation is not an effective means of grace but it is the place where God is present in a *hidden* manner, and therefore he can only be grasped by faith which the Spirit freely and sovereignly gives.

The Holy Spirit is God and thereby he is the sovereign Lord of the Word. He is not confined in the Word. Just as it is certain that God is in Christ and that Christ is in the Word and the sacrament, just as certain is it that the Spirit is sovereign Lord over faith which is the only faculty which can grasp Christ hidden in the Word and sacrament and God hidden in Christ. Between God's outward work in the Word and sacrament and the inward work in the Spirit and faith, there is a hiatus. Over this hiatus Luther has with all possible clearness (even in the midst of the polemics directed against the enthusiasts' separation of Spirit and Word) written the words: *ubi et quando vult.* It is these words which orthodoxy with its verbal inspiration theory and with its doctrine of the Word's *efficacia* has forgotten. But when these words have been forgotten the *decisive* point is by-passed.

It is the message of these words and this hiatus about the sovereignty of the Spirit over the Word which alone prove that it is only in *faith* (and this faith is nothing else but a gift) that a man can lay hold on the gracious presence in Christ's humanity in the Word and the sacrament. Where we attribute to Luther the idea of an *efficacia* of the Word which is an inherent quality in the Word itself, and where we interpret Luther "objectively" and bring him close to the doctrine of *ex opere operato,* there we cannot avoid falsifying the concept of faith in the direction of an act of free will. When orthodoxy emphasizes the indwelling effect of the Word so strongly that every failure of the Word to work must be ascribed to the opposition of free man, the result is that faith is being understood as a *free* acceptance of the Word, no matter how much we underscore that it is derived from the power dwelling in the Word and not from the free will of man, that the "effect" proceeds. Where we speak of real faith it is always a faith over which the Spirit is sovereign Lord. Luther knew what he did when between *auditus verbi* and *donatio spiritus sancti* he placed his *"non quidem omnibus, qui audiunt, sed quibus Deus voluerit. Spiritus enim spirat ubi vult."*

In this connection we must recall Luther's thought about the Spirit's double work as *Deus nudus* in the spiritual use of the law and as *Deus involutus* in the signs of revelation. We have once seen that it was one and the same Spirit who worked in two ways and that it was in one and the same work with one and the same purpose in both cases. The unity in these two methods of work, the unity of the spiritual use of the law and the gospel, of God's *opus alienum* and his *opus proprium* rests in God only, not in man. God alone decides the time of the law and that of the gospel. Every word can be either law or gospel. For it is the method of the

Spirit's presence which makes the difference. In this sense the Spirit is sovereign Lord over faith and the Word. The Spirit decides where the Word becomes law and where it becomes gospel. The Spirit alone is leading the way in *ordo salutis* which proceeds from the spiritual use of the law to the gospel, from the consuming *opus alienum* of God to his life-giving *opus proprium*.

This does not mean that we are left in an arbitrary situation. Nothing is less arbitrary and nothing is more safe than the Spirit's free and sovereign dominion over the Word. And it may be added: nothing is more uncertain on which to build, or more arbitrary than the theory of the inherent *efficacia* of the Word. For with this theory the whole responsibility of the ineffectiveness of the Word is in every case placed upon the free will of man. Nothing could be more arbitrary and insecure. When Luther was so certain that the Word does not return void it was not because he ascribed to it any inherent efficacy for that would have made him insecure. It was because he knew that the Spirit—and not his own free will—was Lord over the Word. There were both certainty and security in this.

The emphasis on the Spirit's sovereignty over the Word protects the theocentric perspective which pervades Luther's whole discussion about the Spirit. In the very moment we forget, as in orthodoxy, to teach the sovereignty of the Spirit, the theocentric perspective disappears, and the anthropocentric takes its place. Luther's strong emphasis on the firmness of the sign of revelation is then changed to an objectivism by which the Spirit is attached to the means of grace and then they both join the service of the religious man. Such an objectivism may well look like a reaction to the subjectivism of the enthusiasts. But it is not a real victory over it. For it is a reaction against the subjectivism which is found within its anthropocentric horizon. Luther, however, overcomes the enthusiasts because he unveils the basic difference in the different orders of salvation. The *ordo salutis* of the enthusiasts is the anthropocentric order of salvation of pious legalism. It can be overcome in no other way than by a complete break with the anthropocentric perspective. And the objective reaction to subjectivism does not want that. It only reacts against the spiritualism of the enthusiasts within the same basic anthropocentric view. Therefore it is also characteristic for Luther that he views the strongly objective and sacramental Roman piety and theology and the subjective spiritualism of the enthusiasts as two variants of one and the same essence.

The anthropocentric, pious man cannot use the Spirit for himself if we maintain the sovereignty of the Spirit. This means that man has been seized by the Spirit and placed in the service of the Spirit. This means in a purely concrete sense that the Spirit as *donum*, the Spirit veiled in the words of the gospel, the Spirit as the source of faith, can only be given to the man whom the same Spirit first put to death by his naked majesty in the words of the law, thereby preparing him for grace. Only by taking man this way, the way of Christ-conformity, of death and resurrection, can the Spirit deprive man of his sovereignty, tear him out of his narrow and self-centered aspiration for a private salvation, and place him in God's all-embracing work as his instrument. The work of the Spirit in the spiritual use of the law is not an episode which belongs to a period of contrition after which man, having successfully concluded the period, may again start to work on his own private salvation. Rather is the work of the Spirit God's continuous work in us in order to tear us out of our selfish life, especially in the matter of our salvation, in order to get us into his work and into the service of our fellow man. There is a continuous connection between God's destruction of our selfishness and his use of us for his own purposes. In the work of our vocation these two sides go hand in hand. The Spirit's sovereignty here means that we do not ourselves decide when the Word is law and when it is gospel, when it leads us into inner conflict and again when it leads us out of it. We do not "possess" this gospel and this effective Word. But the *Spirit possesses it*. We are dependent on the outward signs of revelation, on the words and the sacraments. There and there only is the humanity of Christ. There and there only is God hidden in the humanity of Christ. There and there only is the Spirit working to draw us to the Father in Christ. But, it is the *Spirit*, the free sovereign God, who draws us to the Father in Christ. He does not do that by enclosing himself in the signs of revelation so that we can make ourselves his masters and use him as a means in our selfish aspiration to obtain salvation for ourselves. If it were done in this way he would not get us to Christ. For we ourselves would be permitted to be masters and use both Christ and the Spirit in behalf of our narrow purpose. As long as a man serves himself and even uses Christ and the finished work of redemption for his own selfish purposes, such a man has not been brought to Christ. On the contrary he tries to bring Christ to himself. There is an infinite qualitative difference between a Christ-fellowship brought about by man conquering Christ for himself, and the Christ fellowship which is brought about when that man has been overcome and brought to Christ. Only the latter fellowship of Christ is that of faith. For all true faith is always conformity to Christ, a walking *away from oneself to the alien righteousness of Christ*. Man is first truly led to Christ by faith when he is led away from himself, that is, when he is deprived of working for his own cause. This is, especially for the religious person, a very difficult struggle. It means that the Spirit freely and sovereignly determines when the law must crush us and deprive us of everything in inner conflict, and when the gospel shall restore us and give us life in Christ. This is a free and sovereign decision of the Spirit, *ubi et quando vult*—according to *his* purpose and according to the way *he* in every moment wants to use us, not for our own purpose, and not according to the purpose we may like to use him. *Only under this free and sovereign rule of the Spirit is it possible to take us out of our own circling about ourselves.*

In this free reign of the Spirit there is only one rule. We must not seek God in his naked majesty. It is true that we must by the spiritual use of the law be placed before God in his naked majesty in order that we may be crushed and thus prepared for grace. But this *opus alienum* of God we can and must not seek ourselves. For by seeking it we try to make it an *opus proprium*. The Spirit performs this *opus alienum* in order that he may perform his *opus proprium*. If by seeking God without Christ, without the signs of revelation, we ourselves thus isolate God's *opus alienum*, then we detach *opus alienum* from *opus proprium* so that the law, in place of driving us to the gospel, drives us to perdition. God himself sees to it, when and if he wants it, that we are confronted with him in his naked majesty. However, *only* in the gospel and in the signs of revelation shall we ourselves without ceasing hold fast to *Deus revelatus*. By this we expect God, whenever he permits us to see his naked majesty in the law and thereby puts us to death, to lead us on to the gospel and to the restoration in Christ. By laying hold of the signs of revelation we prove and we expect the *unity* of the spiritual use of the law and the gospel, of *opus alienum* and *opus proprium*. We expect this unity of the Spirit which is sovereign master over Word and signs of revelation, and he is master as the one who pursues his one aim: to lead us through death to life, through our own collapse to Christ, and *in* him to the Father, and from him to our neighbor.

By this summary of Luther's thoughts about the Spirit and the visible signs we have constantly been able to see how the two apparently contradictory tendencies (the emphasis on the firmness and reliability of the sign of revelation and the Spirit's free sovereignty *over* this "certain" sign) are both directed against the enthusiasts' "anthropocentric" *ordo salutis*! It is only a superficial consideration which in these two tendencies attempts to find a vacillation between two points of view, an objective (against the enthusiasts) and a subjective (against the Roman Church). We are not speaking about two tendencies at all, but about one. When Luther so forcefully emphasizes the necessity of the outward signs of revelation over against the inward spirituality of the enthusiasts, it is because in this inward spirituality he sees an attempt to get to God outside of *Deus incarnatus*, that is, without the humanity of Christ—by way of the law, by way of works. When he does not simultaneously emphasize the necessity of the outward signs so objectively in a rational doctrine of the means of grace, rather, with the emphasis on the outward signs' necessity, underscores the Spirit's free sovereignty over them, then he does it with the same purpose in mind. For an objective doctrine of the means of grace changes grace, Christ, the Spirit, to means in the hand of the religious man; which means that grace, Christ, and the Spirit may finally be arranged in the anthropocentric perspective, that grace, Christ, and the Spirit are placed under the superior viewpoint of the law. Such an objectivity there becomes enthusiasm in another way. In both cases man and his pious aspiration are the central point. In the one case he uses his own inward experiences, in the other the "effective" means of grace to reach his own goal: his private salvation. There is no natural way toward the neighbor in any of these cases for man is traveling the pious way of the law away from his neighbor toward his own perfection—with greater or lesser assistance from God. Luther's struggle against the scholastic concept of grace and the spiritualism of the enthusiasts is therefore really not a war on two fronts but a struggle on one front, the struggle against the religion of the law.

The emphasis on the outward signs' necessity and the Spirit's free sovereignty over the signs is one single tendency: the theocentric tendency, the tendency of the gospel. This double emphasis can in reality only be understood from the trinitarian point of view. It is an unbroken act of God which takes place when God leads us to the outward signs of Christ's humanity and when he does not permit us to be masters there, but gives us over to the free lordship of the Spirit. Only in this way are we taken out of our own false sovereignty and drawn into the act of God.

During these different emphases Luther is constantly thinking of the direction of the divine act of revelation which is from heaven to earth. This is very much opposed to the motion of the false spiritualism: from earth toward heaven. It is this contrast which is constantly dominant between Luther and the enthusiasts. When the outward signs' necessity is emphasized before inward spirituality it is the motion of incarnation, from the heavenly majesty of God down to the earthly, humble state of the signs of revelation, which Luther defends against the motion of the enthusiasts from the zenith of spiritual experiences up toward *Deus nudus*. When the sovereignty of the Spirit over the outward signs is emphasized before every objectivism it is again the same motion from above and downward which is maintained. In this case it is the motion of the Spirit crushing everything that aspires upward and using everything that has been crushed as his instrument in the divine agape motion, from the majesty of God down toward the distress in the world. This is in opposition to an objective sacramentalism which attempts to use the means of grace in the service of spiritual aspiration upward.

In each case therefore, both when we maintain the necessity of the outward signs and when we proclaim the Spirit's free sovereignty over them, we find they are in opposition to each other: the witness of the Spirit of God who bows down to seek man among lowly things in order to take him through Christ to the father and then out to his neighbor opposed by the witness of the Spirit of man which abhors lowly things in order that it may swing itself to heaven.

We notice that this decisive contrast appears with special vigor in three different instances in Luther's struggle against the enthusiasts. It is first of all seen in the understanding of the *blessing of the Supper*. The false spirituality always betrays itself by its fear of admitting a bodily effect of the Supper. For it is the false spiritual characteristic's tendency to avoid what might come under the concept, "the lower nature"—all that might retard "a higher nature" in its heavenly flight. Such a restriction, of course, is the poor, mortal body. On the other hand it is true that Luther's understanding of what the Spirit is hardly appears in sharp contrast to all spiritualism in any other place than in the concept of the Body and the Blood of Christ in the Supper. He calls it *Geistfleisch*, or spiritual flesh, which by the celebration of the Supper contains the whole man, body and soul, and gives it life. This is the "heart" here and now, the life of hope, of faith now, the body, and the resurrection in the last day. Here it is seen that to Luther Spirit is not contrasted with the body but that the Spirit of God has not reached its goal with man before man's body is included in the Spirit's plans. Here it is also seen that the Spirit of God is not, as the false spirituality, a timeless abstraction behind the actual world, but that the Spirit of God is an eschatological reality who works as a constant dynamic in the factual world until his goal is reached in the resurrection in the last day.

In the understanding of spiritual life we discover this same contrast between the Spirit of God which seeks lowly man in order to lead him to the Father through Christ and from him to the neighbor, and the false spiritualism which escapes the lowly to by-pass Christ in order to aspire to the "naked" God. To Luther spiritual life is that life in which the heart in faith receives Christ as his righteousness while the body as the instrument of God performs the works of love for the neighbor in the daily grind of our earthly life. Here it is true that the Spirit has not reached its goal for man before his body is included in the plans of the Spirit. The work of the body is here the daily grind of life's vocation in sharp contrast to the celestial, "spiritual" atmosphere. Here by the work of the body the Spirit produces the right fruits, and not in the falsely spiritual, religious solipsism. No one has understood anything of what Luther considers spiritual life so long as one views daily work in the earthly vocations only as a necessary ethicosocial appendix which one may discard at will! The *real* and *central* in Luther's understanding of the gospel appears in the doctrine about man's vocation.

Finally, we also find this same contrast even in a third variation. God's Spirit, which seeks us in the world of sin to lead us in Christ to the Father and from him out to the neighbor, is at work in the church and not in the sect. The church is the people of God. According to Luther, God is present in their midst in his signs of revelation. The Spirit sanctifies them by his work. They are a holy nation, a people of God, a church. But the work of the Spirit takes place in the outward, *public* signs of revelation. It is by these signs that the Spirit performs his sanctifying work. In a certain sense this work is hidden—and thereby also the church itself—because the Spirit sanctifies by the *Word* and by the *faith*. The new life of the Spirit is hidden till the day of resurrection. But in another sense this sanctifying work of the Spirit in the church is visible—and therefore also the church itself—for the work is performed by the public and visible signs of revelation. The enthusiasts, as always, turn things upside down. They want their new life to be a *visible* holiness. Therefore they are not interested in the visible and public signs of revelation. They can have no fellowship with the many who gather about the visible and public signs of revelation, but who have (perhaps) an inferior piety than their own. Therefore they withdraw into closed circles with their visible holiness. But it is the same tendency we meet in the two other cases. The enthusiasts avoid everything inferior and visible and therefore also churchly fellowship with the public signs of revelation. They do this that they may aspire to greater and greater holiness and to a closer and closer presence of God together with their like-minded in spiritual piety.

With this summarizing characteristic of Luther's witness about the Spirit in opposition to the enthusiasts we have come to the end of our study. Luther's ideas about the Spirit have not been changed through the polemics with the enthusiasts. It is the same total view of the young Luther which is here unfolded again. Luther's polemic with the enthusiasts has not forced him into new positions, rather his position has forced him into the polemic against the enthusiasts. The summarizing characteristic of Luther's witness about the Spirit with which we finished the first part of our study is therefore valid for all Luther's writings. Also in the struggle with the enthusiasts we have this peculiar dynamic in the tension between the reality and sovereignty of the Spirit, which we described by referring to the name, *spiritus creator*. The Spirit to Luther is the present Spirit, near as the Creator himself in the midst of our death and our lost condition. In the young Luther the witness about the Holy Spirit found its clearest expression in the description of the distress in inner conflict, by which the Spirit did its creative work through its unutterable groanings. In the struggle with the enthusiasts Luther's trouble becomes clear in his doctrine about the substance of the Supper as spiritual flesh, which not only nourishes the soul but also the mortal body to eternal life out of the despair of inner conflict and the disgrace of the mortal body. The realism of Luther's concept of the Spirit is shown in these two places of the Spirit's work. The Spirit is *near* in the lowly and insignificant. But it is the *Spirit* which is near. When the Spirit overcomes man in the world of sin, man is displaced as the helmsman. The Spirit is master and draws man—with soul and body—into his own purpose where man does not work himself up toward high things, but where, by the conformity in inner conflict with the suffering Christ, wrought by the Spirit as the *Deus nudus* in the words of the law, he takes refuge in the alien righteousness of Christ. This is wrought by the Spirit but enveloped in the Word of the gospel and the signs of the sacraments. The conformity with the risen Christ in loving work for the neighbor is wrought by the Spirit through the Word and by the work of the human body in the earthly vocation, and tried by the cross. This closes the circle and leads man again into inner conflict and justifies and sanctifies him from day to day until this sanctifying work is finished in the resurrection on the last day.

Spiritus Creator

The present and sovereign, reigning Spirit, the Spirit of Jesus Christ and God the Father—this is *spiritus creator*.

With this witness Luther is in strong opposition to most of what has been said about the Spirit in the long history of theology. We have tried to make this contrast clear in the relation to the *caritas* idealism of scholasticism, to the spiritualism of the time of the Reformation, to Lutheran orthodoxy and pietism, and to modern Protestantism and its Luther research. At times this contrast has been so strongly felt that, as a Lutheran theologian, I have found myself asking the question: Is it then Luther who is the heretic? Has he withdrawn from the universal view which seems to embrace them all: medieval scholasticism, orthodoxy, and pietism, with their strong aftereffects even in present theology? Only one answer can be given by evangelical theology: the Holy Scriptures alone may decide this question.

We have not undertaken here an independent study of the relation between Luther's pneumatology and the Scriptures. In such a study we would have departed from the scope of the book decided upon in the introduction. There we limited ourselves to the purely phenomenological analysis of Luther's own thought in its peculiarity. But at the close of this study the question must be raised.

For it is only by the answer to this question that the phenomenological investigation approaches the field of real theology.

And answering this question is an absolute necessity both for Roman Catholic and evangelical theology. Luther's strong, even offensive realism in the witness of the Spirit is a constant question both for Catholic and evangelical theology. Luther's realism gives a clear idea of Catholic thinking as a synthesis of metaphysics and the Bible, and it thus raises the inevitable question: is this synthesis the real meaning of the Bible, or is it the veiling of this meaning? To make Luther heretical does not do away with the question. For the question is raised by the very existence of the Bible. Luther maintained that he raised his criticism against the Roman teaching because he was forced to do so by the Bible. Was it or is it the Bible which compelled Roman theology to reject Luther? Or is not the Bible asking the question, the Bible with its realism even stronger, even more challenging in its contrast to the imposing, balanced synthesis of revelation and philosophy, of the Spirit of God and the spirit of man, of agape and eros, of incarnationalism and supernaturalism? Does Lutheran theology still have a task before the Roman Church? If it has not as yet locked itself up in confessional self-sufficiency then it must keep this an open question. Its questioning of Roman theology will always concern itself with the *Spirit*, because it is the sovereignty of the Spirit which breaks the synthesis, the synthesis which is the real essence of Roman theology.

But Luther's realism in the understanding of the Spirit is just as much a question to evangelical theology. For, as a confessional theology, Lutheran orthodoxy did not retain this realism. It was lost in orthodoxy, pietism, and rationalism. If there is any point in Luther's theology where the gulf becomes visible between him and orthodoxy which wanted to carry on his ideas, it is in his witness of the Spirit. This point is not a peripheral affair, but is the very heart of Luther's understanding of the gospel. As far as Lutheran theology is concerned, the present study means that the question of Luther and Lutheran heritage is raised anew in a concrete manner. Is Lutheranism truly "Lutheran"? The question can also be raised with respect to our confessional writings. The Danish Church is fortunate in that it is not confessionally tied to any form of Lutheran orthodoxy. Our two confessional documents of the Reformation allow the point of our study a genuinely Lutheran interpretation (compare Augsburg Confession, Articles I and V). Is the development which led to pietism and rationalism by way of orthodoxy with its inspiration theory more than a formal faithfulness to the intention of the original confessional writings? If these original confessional writings are seen in their relation to Luther's own view and, together with this, as a reference to what the Scriptures say, then it must be stated that, in its teaching about the Spirit, Lutheranism has not generally been Lutheran. With this fact in mind the question is again raised whether it is Luther or orthodoxy, pietism or rationalism which have best understood the Scriptures' witness about the Spirit. By constantly confronting the original Luther (as much as it is possible to draw him forth) with the so-called Lutheran heritage, a phenomenological study of Luther must prevent Lutheran theology from becoming a sterile confessionalism which only lives by the use of the heritage in an orthodox ideology. Truly evangelical theology can never become confessionalism. Confessionalism always means the death of evangelical theology. For where theology has become confessionalistic, there the heritage has become "authority" in place of Scripture. Truly evangelical theology has only one authority: the witness of the Scripture. And the tradition of the Reformation (together with all the other traditions, not least from that of the ancient church) has only this task: to keep alive the critical question of Scripture and our doctrine's relation to it.

Our work with Luther's witness about the Holy Spirit has raised this question. We have not answered it. We have been content to indicate that Luther agrees with the strong pneumatological realism of Holy Writ when he opposes the many attempts in the history of theology to subdue this realism and to fuse it with the idealism of philosophy and piety. But to give an extensive answer to this question is the task of evangelical dogmatics. For the present our task has been solved by the fact that this question is raised by contrasting our own confessional Lutheran heritage, which in so many ways is saturated with scholasticism, orthodoxy, pietism, and rationalism, with Luther's own free and living witness of the Holy Spirit in his direct contact with the Scriptures' own realism. Can we do anything with this witness? Can we get a discussion started about it? Or shall it be put aside as a part of history, as some beautiful but very much out-of-date history? Can it wake us up to hear the Scriptures anew or does it merely leave us indifferent?

BIBLIOGRAPHY

Barth, Karl. *Die Theology und die Kirche.* Munich, 1928.

———. *Die Kirchliche Dogmatik.* I, 1, Munich, 1932. I, 2, Zollikon, 1938.

———. & Heinrich. *Zur Lehre vom Heiligen Geist.* Munich, 1930.

Bartmann, Bernhard. *Grundriss der Dogmatik.* Freiburg, 1928.

Billing, Einar. *1517-1521.* I, Uppsala, 1917.

Bohlin, Torsten. *Gudstro och Kristustro hos Luther.* Stockholm, 1927.

Bornkamm, Heinrich. *"Äusserer und innerer Mensch bei Luther und den Spiritualisten,"* in *Imago Dei* the G. Krüger *Festschrift.* Giessen, 1932.

Bring, Ragnar. *Dualismen hos Luther.* Lund, 1929.

———. *"Ordet, samvetet och den inre människan,"* in *Ordet och tron. Till Einar Billing på hans sextioårsdag.* Stockholm, 1931.

———. *Förhållandet mellan tro och gärningar inom luthersk theologi.* Lund, 1933.

———. *"Gesetz und Evangelium und der dritte Gebrauch des Gesetzes in der lutherischen Theologie,"* in *Zur Theologie Luthers. Aus der Arbeit der Luther-Agricola Gesellschaft in Finland,* I. Helsinki, 1943.

Brunner, Emil. *Erlebnis, Erkenntnis und Glaube.* Tübingen, 1921.

———. *Die Mystik und das Wort.* Tübingen, 1924.

Bühler, Paul. *Die Anfechtung bei Luther.* Zürich, 1942.

Diem, Harald. *Luthers Lehre von den zwei Reichen.* Munich, 1938.

Elert, Werner. *Morphologie des Luthertums,* I. Munich, 1931.

Ellwein, Eduard. *Vom neuen Leben.* Munich, 1932.

Engeström, Sigfrid von. *"Tro och erfarenhet,"* in *Ordet och tron. Till Einar Billing på hans sextioårsdag.* Stockholm, 1931.

———. *Luthers trosbegrepp.* Uppsala, 1933.

Fridrichsen, Anton. *Omkring Jesu gudsriketanke; Svensk teologisk kvartalsskrift.* Lund, 1932.

———. *Kyrka och sakrament i Nya testamentet; Svensk teologisk kvartalsskrift.* Lund, 1936.

Gennrich, Paul-Wilhelm. *Die Christologie Luthers im Abendmahlsstreit, 1524-1529.* Göttingen, 1929.

Grass, Hans. *Die Abendmahlslehre bei Luther und Calvin.* Gütersloh, 1940.

Haar, Johann. *Initium creaturae Dei.* Gütersloh, 1939.

Hamel, Adolf. *Der junge Luther und Augustin.* I, Gütersloh, 1934. II, Gütersloh, 1935.

Harnack, Theodosius. *Luthers Theologie, I, Neue Ausgabe.* Munich, 1927.

Hase, Karl. *Hutterus redivivus, oversat af A. L. C. Listow.* Copenhagen, 1841.

Hermann, Rudolf. *Luthers These "Gerecht und Sünder zugleich."* Gütersloh, 1930.

Hildebrandt, Franz. *EST. Das lutherische Prinzip.* Göttingen, 1931.

Bibliography

Hirsch, Emanuel. *Leitfaden zur christlichen Lehre.* Tübingen, 1938.

Holl, Karl. *Gesammelte Aufsätze zur Kirchengeschichte, I, Luther*[4-5]. Tübingen, 1927.

Iwand, Hans Joachim. *Rechtfertigungslehre und Christusglaube.* Leipzig, 1930.

Josefson, Ruben. *Ödmjukhet och tro.* Stockholm, 1943.

————. *Luthers lära om dopet.* Stockholm, 1943.

Jørgensen, Alfred Th. *Luthers Kamp mod den romersk-katholske Semipelagianisme.* Copenhagen, 1908.

Köstlin, Julius. *Luthers Theologie in ihrer geschichtlichen Entwicklung und ihrem inneren Zusammenhange.* I-II, Stuttgart, 1st ed. 1863, 2nd ed. 1883. I-II, 2nd ed. Stuttgart, 1901.

Lerfeldt, Sv. *Forsoningen i Luthers Teologi; Dansk Teologisk Tidsskrift VI, H. 1-4.* Copenhagen, 1943.

Lindroth, Hjalmar. *Katolsk och evangelisk kristendomssyn.* Uppsala, 1933.

Ljunggren, Gustaf. *Synd och skuld i Luthers teologi.* Stockholm, 1928.

————. *"Luthers nattvardslära,"* in *Ordet och tron. Till Einar Billing på hans sextioårsdag.* Stockholm, 1931.

Loewenich, Walther von. *Luthers Theologia crucis.* Munich, 1933.

Meinhold, Peter. *Die Genesisvorlesung Luthers und ihre Herausgeber.* Stuttgart, 1936.

Müller, Hans Michael. *Erfahrung und Glaube bei Luther.* Leipzig, 1929.

Normann, Sigurd. *Viljefrihet og forutbestemmelse i den lutherske reformasjon inntil 1525.* Oslo, 1933.

Nygren, Anders. *Den kristna kärlekstanken genom tiderna, II.* Stockholm, 1936.

Nøjgaard, Niels. *Om Begrebet Synd hos Luther.* Copenhagen, 1929.

Olsson, Herbert. *Grundproblemet i Luthers socialetik.* Lund, 1934.

Otto, Rudolf. *Die Anschauung vom heiligen Geiste bei Luther.* Göttingen, 1898.

Pinomaa, Lennart. *Der Zorn Gottes in der Theologie Luthers.* Helsinki, 1938.

Ritschl, Otto. *Dogmengeschichte des Protestantismus, II, 1.* Leipzig, 1912.

Runestam, Arvid. *Den kristliga friheten hos Luther och Melanchton.* Stockholm, 1917.

Scheel, Otto. *Dokumente zu Luthers Entwicklung.* 2nd ed. Tübingen, 1929.

Schempp, Paul. *Luthers Stellung zur Heiligen Schrift.* Munich, 1929.

Schmid, Heinrich. *Die Dogmatik der evangelisch-lutherischen Kirche.* 4th ed. Frankfurt am Main-Erlangen, 1858.

Schott, Erdmann. *Fleisch und Geist nach Luthers Lehres unter besonderer Berücksichtigung des Begriffes "totus homo."* Leipzig, 1928.

————. *Luthers Anthropologie und seine Lehre von der manducatio oralis in wechselseitiger Beleuchtung; Zeitschrift für systematische Theologie, IX.* Gütersloh, 1932.

Seeberg, Erich. *Der Gegensatz zwischen Zwingli, Schwenckfeld und Luther; Reinhold-Seeberg-Festschrift, I.* Leipzig, 1929.

————. *Luthers Theologie, Motive und Ideen; I. Die Gottesanschauung.*

Göttingen, 1929. *II. Christus Wirklichkeit und Urbild.* Stuttgart, 1937.

————. *Studien zu Luthers Genesisvorlesung.* Gütersloh, 1932.

————. *Grundzüge der Theologie Luthers.* Stuttgart, 1940.

Seeberg, Reinhold. *Lehrbuch der Dogmengeschichte, IV, 1.* 4th ed. Leipzig, 1933.

————. *Lehrbuch der Dogmengeschichte, III.* 3rd ed. Leipzig, 1913.

Skydsgaard, Kristen Ejner. *Metafysik og Tro.* Copenhagen, 1937.

Sommerlath, Ernst. *"Luthers Lehre von der Realpräsenz im Abendmahl,"* in *Das Erbe Martin Luthers; Ihmels-Festschrift.* Leipzig, 1928.

Stange, Carl. *Studien zur Theologie Luthers.* Gütersloh, 1928.

Thieme, Karl. *Die sittliche Triebkraft des Glaubens.* Leipzig, 1895.

Vogelsang, Erich. *Die Anfänge von Luthers Christologie nach der ersten Psalmenvorlesung.* Berlin-Leipzig, 1929.

————. *Der angefochtene Christus bei Luther.* Berlin-Leipzig, 1932.

————. *Luther und die Mystik; Lutherjahrbuch, XIX.* Weimar, 1937.

————. *Die unio mystica bei Luther; Archiv für Reformationsgeschichte, XXXV.* Leipzig, 1938.

Walter, Johannes von. *Mystik und Rechtfertigung beim jungen Luther, I, 1.* Gütersloh, 1937.

————. *Die Theologie Luthers.* Gütersloh, 1940.

Weber, Hans Emil. *Reformation, Orthodoxie und Rationalismus, I, 1.* Gütersloh, 1937.

Wingren, Gustaf. *Luthers lära om kallelsen.* Lund, 1942.

Wolf, Ernst. *Staupitz und Luther.* Leipzig, 1927.

————. *" 'Natürliches Gesetz' und 'Gesetz Christi' bei Luther,"* in *Evangelische Theologie, 1935, H. 8.* Munich, 1935.

————. *"Die Christusverkündigung bei Luther,"* in *Jesus Christus im Zeugnis der Heiligen Schrift und der Kirche.* Munich, 1936.

Wolff, Otto. *Die Haupttypen der neueren Lutherforschung.* Stuttgart, 1938.

Type used in this book
Body, 11 on 13 Baskerville
Display, Baskerville Bold